D0428956

Tropical Gangsters

OTHER BOOKS BY ROBERT KLITGAARD

Controlling Corruption
Elitism and Meritocracy in Developing Countries
Data Analysis for Development
Choosing Elites

TROPICAL GANGSTERS

ROBERT KLITGAARD

BasicBooks
A Division of HarperCollins*Publishers*

Library of Congress Cataloging-in-Publication Data
Klitgaard, Robert E.
  Tropical gangsters/Robert Klitgaard.
    p.   cm.
  Includes bibliographical references (p.   ).
  ISBN 0–465–08758–2 : $21.95
  1. Equatorial Guinea—Economic policy.   2. Economic as-
sistance—Equatorial Guinea.   I. Title.
HC960.K55   1990   90–80243
338.96718—dc20   CIP

For Mom and Dad,
who taught by example how to love.

CONTENTS

vii

PREFACE

"**Y**OU say you have spent two and a half years with one tribe," the great French anthropologist Marcel Mauss once remarked to a colleague. "Poor man, it will take you twenty years to write it up."[1]

Sometimes I have feared that Mauss was right: sometimes the "writing up" has seemed endless. Fortunately, however, the present book does not have the aim of "representing a culture," the intimidating task Mauss set for himself and his students. Instead, it tries to tell a story and capture a mood, a story and a mood that I think have importance beyond the borders of the tiny country where I spent my two and a half years.

The story concerns a poor country trying to reform its economy. Today a movement toward the free market is sweeping the globe. Despite all the drama in China and the Soviet Union and especially Eastern Europe, it is Africa that has been at the forefront of change. More than thirty African countries have undertaken major economic reforms in the past half-dozen years, one of them being Equatorial Guinea. Its story, Africa's story, has implications beyond the continent.

Equatorial Guinea is one of the most backward countries in the world. But an extreme case may help us see more clearly what is happening in more typical instances. As in most other countries carrying out free market reforms, Equatorial Guinea's leaders have not always known quite how to make the new strategy work—or, in some cases, whether they should really try. This ignorance and reluctance, though extreme, are in many ways prototypical, and they raise general questions. How does one go about assessing an economy's strengths and weaknesses? How does one go about developing the institutions needed to make free markets work? And how can one help a recalcitrant, inefficient, sometimes corrupt government move forward? These questions are at the heart of my story; and they are relevant to much of the world.

Another part of my story concerns the role of international aid. In Africa, the key perpetrators of change have been the World Bank and the International Monetary Fund. In the past decade their leverage has grown mightily, to the point where they are accused of neo-imperialism. My story involves a World Bank project that hopes to transform a ruined economy, a project with about one seventh of the country's gross national product under its control. It was a project I administered, working with a team of three Equatoguinean ministers. The country wouldn't get this money unless it agreed to a host of policy changes and would not get more unless our team developed a detailed economic strategy. New questions arise. What are the creative possibilities and the inherent limitations of such outside assistance? What are the tensions between aid and dependency, between benevolence and autonomy? And how would you have gone about the task—how would you have acted—if you were me?

The story I tell raises all of these difficult questions. The mood I try to convey is harder to summarize, and *mood* may itself be the wrong word.

Africa can be a brutal and paranoid place, and it is the world's economic basket case. But it also has smiles and guitar solos and an awesome ability to persevere. One can be overwhelmed by Africa's problems at one hour and be enthralled by the cultures and natural beauty in another. Africans themselves are, I believe, caught in these radical swings in emotion and perception. Intimacy can soon be followed by intimidation, careful thought by thoughtless rage, discipline by dissipation. Outsiders may perceive in all of this nothing more than African inconstancy and confusion, even deceit. But I feel it and felt it differently. The environment of today's Africa—broadly interpreted to include not only nature but knowledge and tradition and lacks thereof—puts one constantly at the edge, heightens every sense and every moral dilemma, renders one perennially unsure of what comes next. Can we call this a mood?

It is in this context that economic and political changes are taking place in Africa. Distrust, delay, exaggeration, ignorance, exuberance: all enter in unanticipated ways. They complicate the usual questions of reform—the what-to-do and the administrative how. And so the story and the mood interact. The details of their interplay are no doubt everywhere unique, and yet—though I am acutely aware of the limitations of the account presented here—I hope that sharing one particular instance of economic reform may provoke by comparison and contrast an improved understanding of others.

The reader will, I hope, discern throughout this account my sense of privilege in having been able to live and work in Equatorial Guinea. My friends and colleagues there—many of whom could not for reasons of space or story line be included in the book—enriched my life, and my debts to them are immense. Since these debts are of friendship as much as of instruction, I must hope that they were partly discharged in the course of incurring them, for certainly this book alone is insufficient repayment.

The characters and events that appear here are all true, though I have changed most names and a few details to mitigate possible embarrassment. The character I call Saturnino has a particularly sensitive story, and I shared with him the parts of the penultimate draft that told it. He agreed to its inclusion on grounds that "it will help the country." But later he asked that details of his own identity be further disguised—though he admitted that, even so, insiders would know who he was. I have followed his wishes.

Saturnino is the only Equatoguinean who read earlier drafts of this account—mostly because language and logistics made sharing difficult. But other friends and colleagues have kindly read and criticized various stages of the writing up. Foremost among them is Phoebe Hoss of Basic Books, whose extraordinary pains with the manuscript led to major improvements, though perhaps not as many as she hoped. Martin Kessler of Basic Books saw in scraps I showed him the potential for a book, encouraged me, and helped improve the final product. I am also grateful for the advice and encouragement of Will Adamopoulos, Mahenou Agha, Cathy Bartz, Tora K. Bikson, Marilyn Cvitanic, Roger M. DiJulio, Laurence A. Dougharty, Joseph Giampa, Gus Haggstrom, James Hammitt, Cord Jakobeit, Mildred S. Klitgaard, Robert M. Klitgaard, Marc Lindenberg, Anne Marchot, Richard E. Neustadt, H. Lindsey Parris, Jean Parris, John Rolph, Michael Schiffer, Lisa Simonson, Geralyn White, and Maureen A. White. Most of the first draft was written with Geralyn White in mind and heart.

I finished the book during a wonderful year as a Visiting Scholar at the RAND Corporation. Special thanks go to Charles Wolf, Jr., for making it happen; and to James Hosek, Phyllis Pierson, Darlene Wilson, and Patricia Williams for their support.

Santa Monica, California
5 January 1990

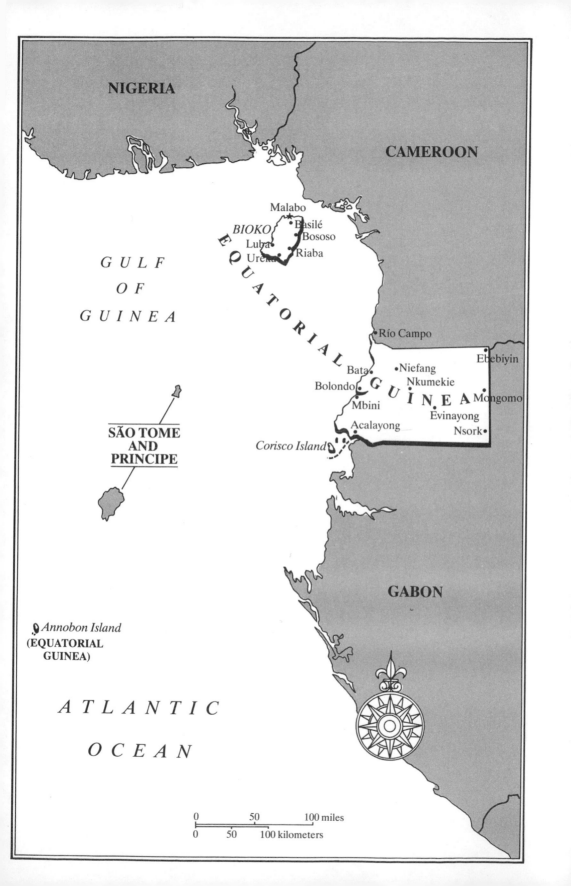

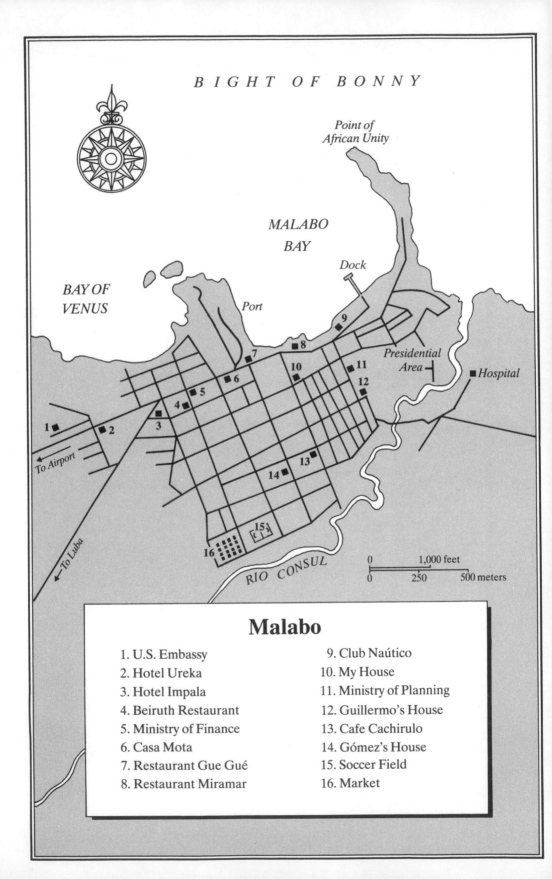

Malabo

1. U.S. Embassy
2. Hotel Ureka
3. Hotel Impala
4. Beiruth Restaurant
5. Ministry of Finance
6. Casa Mota
7. Restaurant Gue Gué
8. Restaurant Miramar
9. Club Naútico
10. My House
11. Ministry of Planning
12. Guillermo's House
13. Cafe Cachirulo
14. Gómez's House
15. Soccer Field
16. Market

1

Giving and Receiving

IT is a little past noon on the third of August 1987. Under the heavy gray clouds of the rainy season, Equatorial Guinea is celebrating the eighth anniversary of the *golpe de libertad*, the "coup of liberty" that got rid of the terrible dictator Macías and brought his nephew into power. I am sitting at the southwest corner of the second floor of my dilapidated colonial house, waiting for the parade to begin. All three shutters are raised so, sitting on one of the rattan chairs, I can feel the breeze and look right out at the view: an intersection, the palm trees across the way, the town rising gently toward the dark green hills, and the mighty volcano in the background.

Across the street is a tawdry lot with random piles of trash. A dead tree stands at one corner, and a big palm at the other. Two families live in a little house of white concrete. At attic height the wall has fallen apart, and you can look in under the dilapidated tin roof to see two-by-fours propped at irregular intervals to support the beams. Behind the house are banana trees, and above them two large trees with small leaves. Almost a rural waste.

But as you look left down the street, you realize you are in the middle of Malabo, the tiny capital of this tiny African backwater. The snappy white concrete structure next to the lot is Guinextebank. Handsome arches and a covered sidewalk. Bright green shutters on the second floor, massive black grillwork over the windows on the first. This is one of the nicest

1

buildings in Malabo, redone in the colonial style since the *golpe de libertad.* The renovation works.

Unfortunately, the bank doesn't. Unpaid loans to Spanish businessmen and government officials have left Guinextebank broke. Honest people cannot retrieve their savings or take money from their checking accounts. Taxes cannot be paid. Consequently, business limps and government crawls. Now a French affiliate is open and for a predatory fee will change your travelers' checks or open an account for you that actually works. Too bad if you want foreign exchange, though. The new currency, the Central African franc, is pegged at fifty to one to the French franc and is supposed to be freely convertible. But when I sought some French francs for a European trip, the bank said they simply did not have enough foreign exchange in stock to help me.

Looking farther left down the street, you see more of the tattered but still appealing arches and structures of the old colonial town. There is a building in faded yellow, also with arches and covered sidewalk; then a white building with one wall in faded orange and a balcony area in pink with part of a pillar painted blue. Then the office of Air Inter Guinea Ecuatorial, which is white cement on the first floor and a dingy salmon stucco on the second. After three more buildings with the arches and the shutters, your eyes arrive at the edge of Malabo's plaza. All the roofs are of grooved tin sheets that slant gently like the covers of a book you've left open on the desk. An old book: the roofs range in color from the original tile-like orange to rusty salmon, to rust and dim tin, to just plain rust the color of mangy old fur. Mostly the last.

The street itself is of aged asphalt with repair patches. The sidewalk's cement has grooved little squares and from here looks like a long waffle iron. From metal telephone poles hang unhealthy-looking wires. Two scraggly fifteen-foot palm trees in white trashcan planters have been brought in for the occasion with the (unsuccessful) idea of a festive touch. The gloomy sky lends the scene the tone of an antique amateur photograph.

Below me, people are starting to gather. Men in suits are shaking hands. Children are dressed up and sitting with their parents against the walls. A few stray dogs scurry by with their noses surveying the ground: big times on the olfactory front. Across the street a group of twenty women in identical African dress practice a song. A bunch of employees from the Ministry of Information and Tourism stand in front of Guinextebank. They wield two big signs on white cloth whose stenciled letters offer support to the President. A van crawls by with a loudspeaker. It blares out the proper order of the various ministries in the procession. First the employees of the presidency, then of the Ministry of the Public Function, then the Ministry of Mines and Hydrocarbons, and so forth—more or less in order of how geographically close their home buildings are to the presidential compound. The van's announcement goes on and on, reminding me how many government agencies there are in this tiny land. Equatorial Guinea may have more ministries than college graduates.

Suddenly a man appears at my side, a man who has entered the house without ringing. He is wearing a black velvet suit jacket, a green striped shirt with a green tie, and dark olive pants so long he has rolled them up like Tom Sawyer's blue jeans. He says good afternoon, he is from the police. I introduce myself, and we shake hands. He says his name is Benjamín. He speaks in nervous catches. The shutters should be closed "b-b-because the President's coming." Okay, no problem. One of the shutters is, however, broken through and is thus in effect wide open. So he tells me to keep away from that one. Benjamín is quite courteous, even deferential. I can watch the parade through the shutters, just don't stand in the open window. Unasked, I bring Benjamín a glass of ice water. He sits down contentedly in one of the rattan chairs.

Two huge motorcycles roar down the street. They are followed by trotting soldiers in combat fatigues and berets. Then comes the President's big black Mercedes. This is flanked and followed by twenty suit-clad Moroccan presidential guards. They have to run to keep up but the car isn't traveling at a smooth pace, so they must suddenly halt, then sprint. The antennas of their walkie-talkies wave back and forth like track batons. Through a hole in the car's roof, the President stands rigidly, bedecked in sashes and a green army uniform as stiff as papier-maché. His white-gloved right hand waves mechanically. Though the singers across the street are chanting and spectators are clapping rhythmically, there's not a lot of noise. No cheering. Not many people on the street.

The President and his joggers reach the plaza. He gets out. Lots of saluting and milling about. He is greeted by the ministers, including the three I work with—Don Bonifacio, the Minister of Finance; Don Diego, the Minister of Planning; and Don Camilo, the Minister of Industry, Commerce, and Enterprise Promotion. Everything here is done on a first-name basis, as long as you put that respectful Don first. The country's phone book, about fifty pages for the entire nation, alphabetizes by first names. Look for me under Roberto.

Now below me and to the right, the bureaucrats and secretaries are starting to line up behind their white cloth banners. Looking back to the right on the other street of the intersection, I can see the soldiers getting ready. Dress right, dress. The sidewalks are filling up with spectators. The parade is about to begin.

A military band leads things off: white suit jackets and blue pants with red stripes, funny hats, playing thumping old military music. As in most of the developing world, the national anthem sounds like nothing so much as the mediocre compositions of the colonizers. The uniforms have the same aspect: an instantly recognizable variant of Western garb but awkward, old-fashioned, second-rate.

Next comes the army, six platoons of forty men in camouflaged fatigues, rifles on their left shoulders. Then the sailors in white. Some other brand of troops or police are dressed in tan, and they are followed by some guys in light blue with caps like the one Claude Rains wore in *Casablanca*. All go marching by, rifles and bayonets aloft.

Then it's the turn of the bureaucrats, ministry by ministry, with public enterprises tossed inbetween. Within each group, the chief functionaries are up front, then junior officials, then the secretaries: virtually all of the first two groups are men; all of the latter, women. The order reflects both hierarchy and Equatorial Guinea's sexually segregated labor force. The exception is that the banners in front of each delegation are carried by women. This makes cultural sense. In rural areas women carry the food and firewood. Here as elsewhere in Africa, bearing is women's work.

The stencils on the banners aren't quite uniform, but there is evidence of a common mind. At least five signs bear the unusual expression *inquebrantable adhesión*, or "unbreakable adhesion"—namely, to the President and his program of economic reform. Another sign "condemns energetically the machinations tending to perturb peace, order, and democratic institutions."

"Democratic"? Earlier this year the President declared a one-party, as opposed to the former no-party, state; his party is called the Democratic Party. Multiparty elections? No, not that kind of democratic. But something creative was announced in today's issue of the government's mimeographed newsletter. Law number 4 of 1987, dated 6 July, begins by praising the country's peaceful politics ensured by the formation of the Democratic Party and says that not everyone has to become a party member:

> On the other hand, it is evident that said political ambience in general favors peace, tranquillity, order and the citizenry's security for the promotion of everyone in Equatorial Guinea, and does not just benefit party members but also those whose names for one reason or another were not in fact found

registered in the book of the General Register of Party Members; consequently, it is logical and natural that these latter people also should be billed in favor of the Democratic Party of Equatorial Guinea.*

So from now on, mandatory contributions to the party will be withheld from paychecks. Businesses will also have to ante up. How much? To be announced.

This is African creativity: a poll tax, without the polls.

A couple more signs in the parade decry "machinations," as uncommon a word in popular Spanish as in popular English. These machinations, says one sign, have been perpetrated by "the broken-down ambitious and the eternally discontented." I like that. My pleasure is diminished slightly by another sign referring to the eternally discontented; then two more signs talk about that unbreakable adhesion. Well, I guess these things do have to be organized.

The ministries have passed, and now come the *barrios* of Malabo and the villages of the island. This is lots more fun. Each group has about forty folks. Many of the women are dancing and singing. One town features a group of guitarists; another has drummers; a third has girls and women in grass skirts. The music is African—no more second-rate European marching songs—and I can see smiles now. It's party time.

Several towns on the eastern part of the island showcase dancers in outrageous costumes. Imagine a big set of horns that loop up and around again and again. Now cover them with colored paper and put all over them automobile mirrors, gold-foil flowers, green-foil leaves, pompoms, metallic wreaths, more mirrors, and colored streamers. That's just the headdress. Now cover the guy completely from scalp to ankle in cloth that looks like leopard skin. Attach seven rearview mirrors to his nape. Put a pillow in his buttress. Tie a colored apron on him and turn it around so that it covers his backside. And now have him pirouette wildly through the streets. (These dancers move well, in part because they are wearing tennis shoes. Like Bruce Lee karate films, Madonna cassettes, and Dallas Cowboy T-shirts, tennis shoes from Taiwan and Korea have penetrated the remotest places on the planet.)

I once went to a festival in one of these villages and after the performance talked with one of the becostumed dancers. I asked him what the getup meant and where it originated. He said they'd had it for ages, but neither he nor the village elders I asked knew where it came from or what

*Here and throughout the book, translations from the Spanish are mine.

it represented. Later an old book on Spanish Guinea provided the answer. The outfit dates back to the last century when it was brought by black laborers imported from, of all places, Cuba. The costume represents the devil. The rearview mirrors are obviously of recent vintage: the eyes in the back of Lucifer's head?

I like the signs carried by the towns. One village that marches to a samba-like beat carries a poster thanking the President for the coup that "liberated us from slavery." The district of Bioko Sur gratefully acknowledges in huge stenciled letters the coup's promotion of "Justice, Tranquillity, and Cultural Development." As if as an afterthought, at the very bottom of the sign smaller and clumsier letters add "As Well As Economic Development in General."

There follow contingents of traders from other African countries. The women from Benin are smartly dressed in wild and different African prints. Cameroonian women wear standardized prints with matching bandanas in their hair. Nigeria: Hey, look at this! A dozen guys in shorts with painted chests and faces, wearing bands of reeds on their biceps, dancing and waving palm fronds to a polyrhythmic beat. (No men in the contingents from Benin and Cameroon; the Nigerian women, much less animated, bring up the rear.)

Next comes the private sector. Trucks full of agricultural workers bearing signs. In a slow-moving van from the local hardware store, I count twenty-two people, and five more large men are hanging out the doors. The chassis is a hand's breadth off the ground. A dump truck goes by with ladders, sawhorses, and shovels jumbled like a pile of pick-up sticks; on top of the pile, a small generator looks like a big dusty paperweight. Some sportsmen pass. About eight of my young tennis-playing colleagues march together. They are in tennis togs and bounce balls on their rackets. "Hey, Javier, let's see the backhand!" The policeman asks me not to yell.

Things are winding down. A few more business firms pass by, but there is no more music. Spectators are wandering off. Finally Benjamín bids me a courtly *adiós*. Across the street to the west of my house, the folks on the second floor turn on their loud, buzzy stereo. We have electricity all day today, instead of the usual few hours: this luxury is part of the celebration. This is good news and bad news: my neighbors' musical collection consists of three pieces of African rock, not inherently bad but now thump-thump-thumping for the twentieth time this week and perhaps the first of another twenty times today. I wonder if they'd accept a gift of a couple of Brahms tapes.

No chance, not today. It's time to celebrate African style.

I had first learned of Equatorial Guinea early in 1985 from an economist at the World Bank. Heinz knew I was interested in a field assignment in a very underdeveloped area of Africa.

"As a matter of fact, we have a project coming up that might be suitable for a person with your skills," he said. "But it is in *Equatorial Guinea.*"

Heinz paused, as if three seconds of silence were mandatory after pronouncing that name.

"We would never assign anyone to Equatorial Guinea who had not visited first," he went on. "Not even people who have spent their lives in Africa. A very difficult country. Equatorial Guinea is the worst of the worst."

Though I had never heard of the place, Heinz's attitude didn't faze me. In the end, I spent two years in Equatorial Guinea, having been there a year at the time of the parade. I wanted to work in Africa. I had been teaching economic development at Harvard and had been a consultant in sixteen countries around the world, mostly in Latin America and Asia. I had become convinced that Africa is where the toughest challenges are—and also where the action is, because, like Equatorial Guinea, many African countries are undertaking radical economic reforms.

Africa has been at the vanguard of a worldwide movement away from state-controlled economies and toward the free market. For years the prevailing wisdom concerning economic development advocated an interventionist state. Government should be the mobilizers and managers of resources. In contrast, the new movement says that the private sector is the key to economic growth, and downplays the state's role as mobilizer and manager.

Africa's reforms are taking place in the context of poverty and disarray. Consider a few statistics.[1] Already the poorest region of the world in 1970, Africa has grown still poorer. (By Africa I mean black Africa, excluding the Republic of South Africa.) The total income of the 450 million citizens of sub-Saharan Africa is today about equal to that of Belgium, which has a population of only 10 million. From 1980 to 1987 alone, real income per person dropped 20 percent. Over the same period, real per-capita investment fell by half, and Africa's terms of trade with the rest of the world deteriorated by almost one third. The value of exports dropped by almost half. Africa's international debt is not large in global terms: it came to about $134 billion in 1988, a little more than Brazil's, or about 10 percent of all debt owed by developing countries. But compared with Africa's means, the debt burden is immense. Debt servicing—that is, simply the interest owed annually—averaged 47 percent of export earnings in 1988.

These miserable economic data have social counterparts. Only about one black African youngster in five will go to secondary school, and only about one in a hundred will get any higher education. The life expectancy in black Africa is about fifty years, compared with seventy-six years in the industrialized countries. One African child in five dies before reaching the age of five from diseases that could be prevented by improved diet, immunization, and health precautions. At the same time, the African population is growing faster than any population has grown ever in human history.

Africa's underdevelopment also has political dimensions. A generation ago, the new African nations made proud promises of democracy and freedom of expression. In most countries, these promises have drowned in dictatorship and censorship. One-party states like Equatorial Guinea's are now the norm. In most of Africa, corruption is widespread, and sexual and tribal discrimination flourish. In words applicable to much of the continent, President Obiang writes of the need to

> overcome first the savage aspects of our aboriginal ethic, ill suited for breaking the isolation of the tribes and organizing them in large states or broader societies ruled by common laws. Because of these tribal customs, political organization, instead of developing toward a more open and universalist human integration, has tended to consolidate personal power, identifying it with the leader's own horde, ethnic group, clan, or tribe.[2]

Faced with these grave and worsening problems, most African countries are experimenting with radical economic reforms that can be compared to Eastern Europe's. (Few, however, are emulating Eastern Europe's move toward democracy.) Why the sudden upheaval in economic strategy? Bluntly put, most African countries have gone broke. Private banks will no longer lend to them, so they need the financing of the International Monetary Fund and the World Bank. The IMF and the Bank are the preachers of free-market economic reforms. To get their blessing, the Africans are converting.

The influence of the Fund and the Bank has grown tremendously over the past decade. The two institutions work closely together—their headquarters are on adjacent streets in Washington. Both are multilateral organizations set up near the end of the Second World War to help the shattered global economy. Today both concentrate on the developing countries, to whom they offer low-interest loans with strings attached. But the two institutions tend to differ in their economic concerns. Although the lines have been blurring, the IMF tends to worry about economic stability in the short run—say, over a year or two—while the World Bank struggles with economic growth in the medium run—say, three to five years. The IMF tends to focus on money supplies and budget balances, whereas the Bank homes in on public investment and pricing policies. Both the Fund and the Bank emphasize exports as the key to growth, as opposed to the old strategy of import substitution, which promoted industries producing goods for domestic consumption. And both institutions stress the move toward free markets.

For a developing country, an agreement with the IMF has become something like a Good Housekeeping Seal of Approval. Unless the IMF says your economic strategy is sound, many aid donors and commercial lenders will not ante up. The World Bank's role is less dramatic, but having a structural adjustment program with the Bank is frequently a facilitator if not a prerequisite for aid from other sources.

An agreement with the IMF and a structural adjustment program with the Bank typically contain common elements. The country devalues its currency, cuts government spending, frees up domestic and international trade, and turns public enterprises over to private management or joint ventures. In the parlance of the World Bank,

> The objective of structural adjustment programs is to restore rapid economic growth while simultaneously supporting internal and external financial stability. As such, these programs have macroeconomic and microeconomic aspects. The major macro objectives are to improve the external balance and domestic fiscal balance. An adjustment program thus commonly includes a combination of (1) fiscal and monetary policies to bring about overall demand reduction and (2) trade policies (mainly the exchange rate and import/export taxes and subsidies) to alter the relative incentives between tradable and nontradable goods. On the micro side, the major objective is to improve efficiency in the use of resources by removing price distortions, opening up more competition, and dismantling administrative controls (deregulation). Such programs include those for government expenditures and the management of public enterprises, including reductions in the government's presence in areas where private enterprise can operate more efficiently.[3]

Structural adjustment means less government, freer trade, and more private enterprise. But the change can be painful. It is often accompanied by a recession. Public spending on schooling and health collapses, while prices rise for food and housing and transport. Foreigners begin to play a greater role in the economy. And the shift is ideologically traumatic: free-market reforms overthrow the gamut of socialist and nationalist policies of independent Africa's founding fathers, men like Ghana's Kwame Nkrumah, Guinea's Sékou Touré, Tanzania's Julius Nyerere.

Since so many poor countries are bankrupt and up to their eyes in debt, they virtually have to do what the IMF and the Bank say. Consequently, the Fund and the Bank often play the role of outside heavies. They insist on reform, design it, monitor its implementation. No wonder such foreign aid is controversial: to many, it smacks of neo-imperialism. And there is controversy over the adequacy of the IMF–World Bank recipe. Not only politicians but also academicians and even Bank staff have qualms.

"I just don't have confidence in the formulas we prescribe, those standard remedies," an old friend, who had worked at the World Bank for years on various African nations, told me in 1985. "It's fine to praise export-led growth, but the evidence is that it doesn't work for a lot of countries. The Bank has terrible morale now, as you have noticed. One reason is that many of us doubt what we are doing."

Especially in Africa. People keep saying that Africa is *different*. Here the standard solutions seem even more problematic. Africa seems always to break the rules, foul up the templates, ruin the recipes. Why is development in Africa so difficult? Why has foreign aid so often failed? How can the new move toward the free market be made to work? These were the questions that lured me. I wanted to find out firsthand; and Equatorial Guinea was said to be a laboratory of underdevelopment.

My job was as the administrator-economist of a large project funded by the World Bank. Working with a team of three government ministers, I would help design a strategy for economic reform. Our team would also decide how to spend $13 million to rehabilitate the country's crumbled infrastructure and to get the economy moving. What the project would become was largely what our team would make of it.

Officially, I was employed by the government of Equatorial Guinea and was not the representative of the World Bank or any other foreign agency. This was good: I wanted the Guineans to perceive me as someone on their side. But the situation was complex. Equatorial Guinea was paying me with funds loaned by the World Bank. I was a foreigner. And so, even though I was working inside the Equatoguinean government, I worried that I might be perceived an instrument of outside interference in the country's internal affairs. Nowadays international aid is infringing on the sovereignty and sensitivities of countries like Equatorial Guinea in new and poorly fathomed ways. Would my own desire to help and to learn contain the same contradictions?

Most societies share certain fundamental moral principles. Two such, I think, are the principles of beneficence and autonomy. Being *beneficent* means doing or producing good, specifically performing acts of kindness and charity. The word comes from the Latin word for favor. *Autonomy* comes from the Greek word for independence and means the quality or state of being self-governing. Sometimes the benefactor's role—his pre-scription—reduces the recipient's autonomy—as can occur, for example, in a medical setting. The physician wants to help, and the patient wants to be helped. But sometimes help becomes prescription, is required. The doctor may end up making and enforcing the decisions—in the process violating the patient's autonomy.

In the case of conditions imposed by multinational agencies, the conflict between beneficence and autonomy is pervasive and severe. To the proud people of newly free nations, conditionality recalls colonialism. What jus-tifies such dictating to sovereign states?

First of all, the IMF and the World Bank do not exactly dictate. A country has to ask for loans from the Fund or the Bank. Some countries have not—Cuba, for example. It is in a strict sense voluntary that a nation submit to some impingements on its autonomy—as private companies sometimes do when they are in financial trouble and allow bankers to sit on their boards or venture capitalists to help manage the company. Or, as patients sometimes do with physicians.

On the other hand, do bankrupt countries have a real choice?

Leverage can restrict sovereignty. Benevolence can undermine auton-omy. Fundamental dilemmas like these often drive people to extremes. We seem to need to find bad guys, someone to blame, and to put ourselves on the other side. We seem to seek simple truths.

"Look," says one extreme position, "these countries want to borrow money and the only way they will be credit-worthy is if they follow this advice. We've seen our recipes work elsewhere. And by imposing these conditions, by using our leverage, we are doing good. Not least, we are saving the people of these countries a little bit from their corrupt and inefficient governments.

"The governments of places like Equatorial Guinea are composed of predatory figures who cloak themselves in concepts of 'African socialism' and 'poorest of the poor' but spend their time with their hands in the till. Those beating the drum of sovereignty loudest are often, in the words of Kid Creole and the Coconuts, the truest tropical gangsters."

But consider another extreme interpretation.

"So-called 'foreign aid' and 'help in economic reform' are nothing more than neo-imperialism, the transgression of sovereignty, and the imposition

11

of the dictates of international capitalism. The standard advice does violence to our country's realities. It also foments domestic monopolies as allies to the international monopolies, who wish again to tell the old colonies what to do.

"The real tropical gangsters are the capitalists, both domestic and foreign, and the aid agencies who promote them. Perhaps even the expatriate so-called experts qualify—such as you."

Which side is right? Or are both? In most poor countries, as the first argument says, governments tend not to work well. But the second argument has a point, too. So-called free markets do not work well in most poor countries either. Nor does the machinery of international credit and foreign aid. Given Africa's poverty, ignorance, disease, and dictators, we should not be surprised to find rampant opportunism, deceit, and distrust; and these in turn foster flaccid and corrupt institutions—public, private, and international. The harsh conditions of underdevelopment encourage tropical gangsters of every variety—government, business, and international aid giver.

So there is no solace in extreme views. One cannot simply say, "Leave it to the market" or, "The World Bank knows best," just as one cannot say, "The government in its wisdom should run everything." In underdeveloped countries, the action is between the extremes of state domination and laissez-faire, between aid and dependency.

In these difficult circumstances, how can the outside world help without hurting, apply leverage without trampling sovereignty? Dilemmas of how to give and how to receive seem particularly stark in Africa, with so much need and so much leverage and so little understood about either. But this tension between benevolence and autonomy is also a fundamental human problem that in myriad ways and circumstances each of us encounters. How can we work for change while respecting what exists? How can we exercise analytical skills and make critical judgments while still affirming the imperfect people and situations we encounter? And how can we extend our limits in order to receive from the people to whom we are trying to give? These questions haunted me each day in Equatorial Guinea—especially on that festive holiday in August, 1987, as I watched the parade celebrating liberty with a policeman at my side.

John Steinbeck once wrote a loving essay about his friend Ed Ricketts, the unorthodox scientist and local legend who was the model for the character of Doc in *Cannery Row*. Steinbeck was trying to understand "the great talent that was in Ed Ricketts, that made him so loved and needed and makes him so missed now that he is dead." Steinbeck concluded that

Ed had a secret for helping without creating dependency—a secret that the givers of international aid, and the receivers of it, might well take to heart. It lay in

> his ability to receive, to receive anything from anyone, to receive gratefully and thankfully and to make the gift seem very fine. Because of this everyone felt good in giving to Ed—a present, a thought, anything.
>
> Perhaps the most overrated virtue on our list of shoddy virtues is that of giving. Giving builds up the ego of the giver, makes him superior and higher and larger then the receiver. Nearly always, giving is a selfish pleasure, and in many cases it is a downright destructive and evil thing. One has only to remember some of our wolfish financiers who spend two-thirds of their lives clawing fortunes out of the guts of society and the latter third pushing it back. It is not enough to suppose that their philanthropy is a kind of frightened restitution, or that their natures change when they have enough. Such a nature never has enough and natures do not change that readily. I think the impulse is the same in both cases. For giving can bring the same sense of superiority as getting does, and philanthropy may be another kind of spiritual avarice.
>
> It is so easy to give, so exquisitely rewarding. Receiving, on the other hand, if it be well done, requires a fine balance of self-knowledge and kindness. It requires humility and tact and great understanding of relationships. In receiving you cannot appear, even to yourself, better or stronger or wiser than the giver, although you must be wiser to do it well.[4]

2

A Passage to Guinea

JUST before my first journey to Equatorial Guinea in 1985, I was visiting Panama on an economic consulting mission for the U. S. Agency for International Development. One evening there was a dinner in the mission's honor at the Union Club, set amidst Miami-style high rises at the southern cusp of the bay bordering Panama City. The host was the local AID director. Also present were assorted sideburned AID officials, some Panamanian economists and businessmen, and bow-tie-clad mulatto waiters.

Beside me sat the deputy director, whose most recent post had been in western Africa. "I'd go back, and so would the family," he said with a smile and a look into my eyes to judge my surprise. "It's a hard place, but we lived well there, and we enjoyed our work."

I mentioned that immediately after this visit to Panama I would be heading to Africa on a three-week consulting assignment.

"Where?" he asked.

"Equatorial Guinea," I replied.

"Equatorial Guinea! You must be kidding! Why on earth would you want to go there?"

At least he's heard of the place, I thought. I hadn't till three months before.

His exclamation galvanized the director, a domineering man in his forties who was fond of guayabera shirts with the top two buttons open, cigars, and strong views.

"Who's going to Equatorial Guinea?" he bellowed from the other end of the table.

I said I was.

He shook his head. "I used to be in charge of AID for that hole. When I was head of the Cameroon office, I also had responsibility for Equatorial Guinea. It's the armpit of the world! On a scale of one to ten, even an African scale, it's a zero.

"What are you?" he added. "A masochist?"

Several weeks later, I was on my way from Madrid to Malabo. The flight was delayed, and we boarded at one in the morning and left about two. Next to me sat a man from Equatorial Guinea named Florencio. He was dressed to do business: fastidious three-piece suit, crisp collar, small-patterned tie tightly knotted. A gold tooth gleamed in his smile. His skin was a luxurious, burnished black.

Florencio said he was returning from Geneva, Athens, and other parts of Europe, where he had been negotiating petroleum exploration contracts for his government. When asked, I told him I was part of a World Bank team whose three-week mission was to work with the Equatoguinean government to design a project to rehabilitate its economy.

"We need everything," Florencio said, in Spanish distinguished by the lisp of the Castilian accent. "We are in very bad condition now. We need people who can help to get us started." Later he said, "Many of the experts who come to assist us are not really experts. They know something in theory, but they do not know how to make it work in a place like our country."

In the heat of the aircraft, I rolled up my sleeves and slipped off my shoes. Florencio did no such thing. Though eventually he took off his pinstriped jacket, his vest remained buttoned, and his necktie's tight triangle was unloosened, undisturbed.

We had to deplane for refueling in the Canary Islands. Our flight then proceeded around the western hump of Africa, and we didn't get to Nigeria until late morning. After a delay in Lagos, we were off on the last leg, lasting one hour, to Malabo, the capital of Equatorial Guinea, located on the volcanic island of Bioko.

The flight itself progressively demonstrated the underdevelopment of the world we were entering. The leg to the Canaries was professionally staffed. There were crisp descriptions of the use of oxygen masks and life preservers, a nice greeting via intercom from the pilot ("You will see the city of Seville on the left-hand side of the plane"), an impressive meal, and a wide array of beverages. The flight crew appeared just to have received the attention of licensed beauty professionals. On the Lagos leg, standards began to deteriorate. Now, on the Malabo run, I felt I was taking part in a parody.

The "meal" offered stale sandwiches containing minuscule quantities of flavorless cheese and dry meat. You had the choice of a beer or a cola. The cabin attendants ignored the cabin, staying at the back of the plane, smoking up a storm, eating mammoth submarine sandwiches, quaffing beers, and enjoying jokes. No words were pronounced about seat belts or life rafts or slides that would materialize if the highly unlikely occurred. The captain, too, ignored us. And no more tight coiffures: the hairdos of this group of stewardesses were distinctly unkempt.

The sea over which we flew was mostly hidden by clouds. We descended toward Malabo. We could see the water now, and it had an odd texture, like the peel of an orange. There was the island ahead—a volcano topped with a cloud bank, dark green trees everywhere, a town. Then the airport. And we were down. Immediately the cabin began to heat up. Florencio still had his tie at full attention. And I was at full attention, too, looking out the window at the grasses alongside the runway, then the banana trees, then the thick wall of lofty trees with leaves of the almost black-green color the skin of an avocado sometimes achieves.

Getting off the plane was to enter a bath of vapor. The humid wall of air made me take a deep breath. People were running around the old shed that functioned as the terminal. Inside was the passport check. Two heavily perspiring Spaniards pushed by me in a "line" that resembled a rugby scrimmage. Health documents were examined in a separate queue.

"Where is your cholera certificate?" the health officer asked me.

I said I was told a cholera shot was not required.

He raised his eyebrows high. "You had better get an inoculation tomorrow," he said sternly. "We have a cholera epidemic here now. It is bad here now."

My eyebrows followed his.

The luggage finally came, in long open carts. My surfboard, marked "FRAGILE" in several languages, had been placed at the bottom of a mountainous load, covered by five or six layers of suitcases and boxes. But, thanks to a padded travel bag, it survived, and eventually I got my other things and proceeded to customs. The surfboard evoked great interest. After much examination and questioning, the customs officers decided that this strange object should be inspected by their chief. I was shunted to a fanless office packed with people and dust. After inspecting the surfboard

thoroughly, the customs chief finally let it pass. With my luggag
emerged onto a dirt parking lot.

I was now in Equatorial Guinea.

I took a deep breath and looked around. In the foreground wer
disheveled bunch of four-wheel drive vehicles. In the distance were fo
hills and then hills and then the rugged jungle-covered cliffs leading up
the ten thousand-foot volcanic peak. That was it. No taxis, no buses, a
most of all, no welcoming party or sign that anyone knew that R. Klitgaa
was, after two nights airborne, in town.

Fortunately, Malabo had only two hotels. Maybe one of them had
reservation for me. Maybe that was where the rest of the team would b
I hitched a ride to town on a dilapidated pickup truck.

The road was freshly asphalted and bordered by thick foliage. I couldn
get over the colors. Only a few days before, I had been traveling by trai
along the Panama Canal, surrounded by double-canopy rain forest. Th
forest was light green, even yellowed in places, as it was Panama's dr
season. In contrast, the island's greens were lush. Its volcanic soil, said t
be the world's richest for the growing of cocoa, was also heaven for grasses
bushes, and dense, tall, wonderful trees. Cocoa historically has been th
foundation of Equatorial Guinea's economy, accounting for about half th
country's exports; when properly harvested, it is the best-quality cocoa ir
the world. As the flat land around Malabo is the finest cocoa land in the
country, I was driving by the chocolate lovers' equivalent of Château
Margaux.

In places along the road where the ground had been cut, you could see
topsoil six feet deep. The soil was not the red dirt of much of continental
Africa but the thick black topsoil of a volcanic island.

We arrived in the town of Malabo. Neither hotel had heard of me. I had
been informed before my departure that the hotel capacity of the capital
city would be severely tried by our team's arrival. Since another mission
of expatriate experts was also in country, a total of fourteen foreigners had
to be found rooms. This had proved too much for tiny Malabo. In the
"lobby" of the second hotel, I encountered another World Bank mission
member, also just arrived and unmet at the airport—a mannered, friendly,
slow-speaking lawyer named Tomás. Together we discovered the two
leaders of our mission, Heinz and Eric, in their ramshackle suite on the
second floor, with folding chairs, a refrigerator, and a small range. Electricity was provided by the hotel's generator, which was blasting away outside
their window.

Heinz and Eric apologized for not meeting us. Emergencies had gotten

in the way, they explained. Alas, they lamented in response to a question from Tomás, they didn't know where we would be staying. Though the news made Tomás worry, I was giddily indifferent, punch-drunk from two nights in the air, jet lag, and this new, humid environment.

Heinz left for a while, to return with good news. He had found a spot for us to sleep at the German technical assistance compound just outside town. Tomás and I went there and were given rooms in a small house, with air-conditioning fed by a generator. True, due to mechanical breakdowns, there was no water. But our cordial hostess smiled a lot and offered us access to the beer and mineral water in her refrigerator.

We went back into town and looked around. Despite all the horror stories I'd heard about local conditions, Malabo made a good first impression. Most buildings were two-story Spanish colonial structures of no small charm—although colors that used to be white and yellow and light green had faded to off-white and battle-scarred tan and moldy green. The water stains on the walls were like mascara after tears. Malabo's little harbor was spectacular. Ridged by steep cliffs a hundred feet high crowned with a majestic row of palms, the half-mile or so of harbor contained one big dock and one small one, and the sea in the distance looked clean and deep.

Before departing, I had received a State Department briefing note on the country—a standard four-pager like those prepared for every country in the world to help Americans know what to expect. The State Department advised visitors to Equatorial Guinea to bring their own food and water, and pointed out that neither hotel had food or water, and that restaurants existed "only periodically."

Now, however, we found two full-time restaurants. The best was the Beiruth, set up by a Lebanese, with a patio of tattered pink cement and roaming chickens and large umbrellas bearing the logo of the French beer Kronenbourg. A covered plant-lined dining area and bar had overhead fans and a record player that alternated between African electric guitar, Lebanese laments, and an old album by Abba. We had a late lunch. The place was full, and almost every face was white.

Tomás had been to Equatorial Guinea once before. "This country is the worst place in Africa, along with Guinea Bissau," he said. He sipped a beer brought in from neighboring Cameroon by large dugout boat. "Nothing works here, nobody cares."

A swarthy Venezuelan turned French West African banker sat at our table. He wore a blue striped shirt and the sort of Hermès silk tie you see at airport duty-free shops. He liked Tomás's theme.

"Nothing works here," he nodded. "People in government do nothing. They are completely corrupt. They know nothing."

I had another beer. It was cold and tasty, and I could not feel cholera coming on. The Abba song they were playing was one of my favorites. The meal was Western: a sort of stew, a sort of salad, and bread. It went down well. I didn't like the negativism of the conversation or the heavy expatriate feel of the Beiruth, but my companions assured me that patronizing the little African bars and eateries that had begun popping up in town these past few months meant risking death.

I returned to the German house and reveled in the air-conditioning. I studied the briefing papers Heinz had given me at the hotel. They described where I was and what I was doing here. Both were good to know. There was a World Bank economic report and several analytical memos about the state of this little nation. By World Bank standards, the data and the analysis were meager indeed. The reports apologized for this, saying that almost nothing is known with confidence about Equatorial Guinea. In statistical reference books with information about all the countries of the world, there are asterisks for Equatorial Guinea in most categories, asterisks meaning "not known."

It is a tiny country, and it is poor. Occupying four islands and a mainland slot between Cameroon and Gabon on the west coast of central Africa, Equatorial Guinea's population is somewhere between 300,000 and 400,000, about one fourth of whom live on the island of Bioko. The economy was in terrible shape. The average income was a little over a hundred dollars, according to one international agency, or a little over three hundred dollars according to another. About four fifths of the population depend on subsistence agriculture, most of them deep in the country's rich jungles and highland forests. The life expectancy is about forty-five years, and about 90 percent of the people contract malaria every year.

The economic report guessed that real income per person had declined in the past twenty years more than in any country in the world.

Statistical information has long been suspect in Equatorial Guinea; but for what they are worth, data published by the Spaniards before independence in 1968 indicate that the colony was then the wealthiest country in the area. One of the books I purchased in Madrid said that Spanish Guinea's per-capita exports in 1960 were $135—perhaps $500 in 1985 dollars—compared with $105 in Gabon, $48 in Ghana, and $12 in Nigeria. The colony exported cocoa, coffee, timber, some foodstuffs, and palm oil. Fishing tonnage exceeded that of Gabon, which had three times the population. Even though "the gulf of Guinea has the sad privilege of counting itself among the unhealthiest zones in the world," as the Spanish book put it, the numbers of hospital beds and doctors per person were higher than in neighboring countries. Ninety percent of school-age children were said to have been in school, and the literacy rate was a remarkably high 60 percent.

The reason for the horrible decline was the havoc wrought by the dictator Francisco Macías Nguema. Africanists who calibrate such things rate Macías as worse than Uganda's Idi Amin, worse than the Central African Republic's Emperor Bokassa. Macías took over at independence in 1968. After a coup attempt in 1969, he grew increasingly maniacal. First there were political murders, then generalized repression; by the mid-1970s, Macías was carrying out large-scale executions of real and imagined opposition, the latter category including many of the people with any formal education. An estimated one quarter to one third of the population were murdered or went into exile.

With Macías's political sins had come economic decline. Some forty thousand Nigerians, who labored on the cocoa plantations on the island, left the country in 1976 and 1977, after increasingly brutal treatment. Cocoa production dropped from thirty thousand tons in the last years of Spanish rule to about five thousand tons in the late 1970s. Coffee and timber exports fell to less than a tenth of their former levels. In 1979, Macías was overthrown in a military coup, tried, found guilty of crimes ranging from genocide to corruption, and executed. The perpetrator of the coup was the defense minister, Obiang Nguema Mbasogo, who was also Macías's nephew. Obiang had been the president of Equatorial Guinea ever since.

The World Bank report noted signs of progress under Obiang's regime. The country had re-established basic institutions such as a public budget. It had opened up to foreign trade and investment. Most important, President Obiang had promulgated a big economic reform package in January 1985. The country devalued its currency by a factor of seven and then entered into a Central African currency union backed by France and including the neighboring nations of Cameroon, Gabon, Central African Republic, Congo, and Chad. The government also removed virtually all price controls, radically changed the tariff system, and began selling off some state-owned enterprises.

But the economy had not responded. The cocoa industry was in decline. Banks were nearly bankrupt. Macroeconomic management was poor, resulting in credit ceilings that were not heeded and budgets that did not bind. Health conditions remained terrible and, in the case of malaria, may even have grown worse. Schools had officially reopened, but conditions were terrible. A visiting mission from UNESCO visited seventeen schools on the island of Bioko. Not one had a blackboard, pencils, or textbooks. Teachers simply stood and talked, and students recited.

Moreover, though the killings had ceased, Equatorial Guinea was still a military dictatorship. Many Equatoguineans remained exiles in Gabon, Cameroon, and Spain—in part, perhaps, because President Obiang and many top officials were from Macías's home town and had served in his ruthless regime.

The World Bank wanted to ease Equatorial Guinea's entry into the new monetary system. It was contemplating a soft loan worth over $10 million—more than $30 per capita or, in a calculation possibly more relevant in government circles, more than $500,000 per cabinet minister—to finance the country's "rehabilitation." According to the ambitious terms of reference for my own assignment, which I was now reading for the first time, my job was to figure out how to link this "emergency, fast-disbursing" program with the nation's "medium-term development strategy." And, as no medium-term development strategy existed for Equatorial Guinea, to advise how one might be generated. Moreover, I was to think about how the proposed project should be administered—which ministries, people, procedures, and so forth. This was especially interesting to me, as I might be the person brought in to help with the administering.

All this was to be accomplished in three weeks. I got up to get a beer.

Starting the Search for Surf

Everywhere but the United States, the first of May is Labor Day and a holiday, so I talked Tomás into taking a tour of the island. This would enable us to get a better feel for the country—and allow me, not incidentally, to look for surf.

Where on the island would the waves be rolling? Neither the State Department's four-pager nor the World Bank's briefing papers contained information about local surfing conditions. I did not know the words for "offshore" or "awesome" in Spanish, or the two local languages, Fang and Bubi. I was unable to locate a Bioko Surfing Association. I studied a map in an old geography book. If waves existed, I reasoned, they would not be on the northern part of the island where the capital city lies and which is only twenty-six miles southwest of the continent. Surf would be in the south. I was intrigued by the only town on the remote southern coast. It is called Ureka, as in "Eureka!" According to the colonial geography book,

Ureka counts over thirty-three feet of rain a year, making it one of the wettest places on the planet. I wanted to go to Ureka, cry out "I have found it," become the veritable Archimedes of local wave riding. If there was no surf, I could ride the storm drains.

I went to the market and was directed to a place where Land Rovers full of people and goods left for various places around the island. It turned out that no roads led to Ureka, only a ten-hour walk from a distant point called Moka. But there was also Luba, facing out into the Atlantic from the island's southwest. How about surfing Luba? I forgot Archimedes and began to imagine an eight-foot point break near Luba, heretofore unridden by Bubi, Fang, or Spanish colonist, now discovered from the back of an aging Land Rover by yours truly.

I chanced upon two government officials who were taking an official vehicle just above Luba to do some work on the Prime Minister's cocoa farm. They said they would give me a lift as long as I didn't need to come back right away.

"We have to visit the Prime Minister's farm, as he is coming later to address his farmers. If you wait for us by the police post late this afternoon, we will take you back with us."

We picked up Tomás and the surfboard. He sat up front with the two Guineans. I stood in the back of the truck with my arms on top of the cab.

The scenery was breathtaking. A few villages came and went—and we saw only one car during the hour-long drive on the narrow, paved, but potted road—but the attraction was the vegetation. There were layers of jungle. Cocoa trees, with cool shade beneath them. Mid-sized tropical trees, often with vines, including palms. Above them all was the soaring ceiba tree, which is on the national flag. The ceiba looks like a ten-story oak tree, and it gives off a cottonlike fiber which, our driver said, "could be made into wonderful clothing if one could develop the technology to do so." The big trees were widely spaced, so that light easily beamed into the lower canopies—in contrast with the Amazon jungle, where a dense triple canopy means that lower levels are in darkness. Here the jungle was airy and bright. The greens were luscious, and the wind in my face made me smile.

Close to Luba, we finally saw the sea. I searched the horizon for eight-foot tubes. But Luba Bay looked like Walden Pond. It was hard to believe, looking at the calm ripples that lapped the black shoreline, that we were at the edge of thousands of miles of unbroken and—some place—violent ocean.

But Luba was a treat. The picturesque colonial town is set at the edge of a splendid bay, with the deep green cone of Bioko's other volcano rising behind it. Just above town, a bright white church spire stands proudly amidst a magnificent cluster of trees. A decrepit dock is home for a few small boats and a larger one designed to search for oil.

We found a little beach. The Land Rover took off to do the Prime Minister's chores, and Tomás and I went for a swim. I got out the surfboard. A few little boys were playing by some dugout canoes. They came over, and I showed them how to paddle it around. Then Tomás and I went on a walk along the road leaving Luba, lined with palm trees on one side and dense bushes on the other, toward an old lighthouse on the bluff west of town. We ascended a narrow path through the jungle. An old man we met along the way showed us plants that looked like tiny ferns and whose leaves, when brushed, closed up like a fist. He led us to the lighthouse and an ornate and apparently abandoned cocoa plantation house nearby. The house was wonderful: three stories, each with a surrounding walkway, elaborate metalwork, beautiful old tiles. We climbed to the top of the house. Below were the plantation's abandoned sheds and workers' housing and a huge drying shed for the cocoa beans. To the west lay the limitless Atlantic. And back to the east, set against the blue of the bay and the green velvet of the island, were the white buildings of Luba, looking from this distance new and clean and full of promise.

We walked back to town, fetched the surfboard from the boys, and found the old Hotel Jones (pronounced "HOE-nase"), where we had been told we could get a meal. Did we ever get one—ice-cold Kronenbourg beer, fresh-roasted fish, and a delicious salad. From our simple table, one of three in the establishment, we enjoyed a view, through flowers and pink foot-long catkins, of a stream where children were playing and swimming. The proprietor, a German with watery red eyes, sat down with us. His shortwave was set on a French station. He told us stories about his former big jobs, his former big house, and his former pair of Mercedeses. The Hotel Jones was one of those strange spots where an émigré escapes from the world—in this case, with a pretty, young wife from Madagascar and a batch of tales about a glorious past—and creates, in a forsaken but beautiful place, a piece of paradise.

Later we wandered around the little town. Apparently since independence, there had been little or no maintenance of roads, docks, or buildings. But the town retains a colonial charm in its dilapidation, reflecting the hardiness of the Spanish conception and the sturdiness of concrete construction.

We waited by the road for the Land Rover, and after a while were rewarded. We clambered into our friends' vehicle and joined a convoy. Up front was another Land Rover, then came the Prime Minister's Peugeot with the emergency lights flashing, and then us. The pace was breakneck. Our vehicle, more suited for thirty miles an hour, was doing nearly double that, and in the back, the surfboard and I bounced through the early evening, back to the darkness of Malabo.

Leverage in Action

The next morning we paid a visit to the Minister of Finance's office. I was told Don Manuel was the key man for me to meet, as he was probably the person I would be working with if I returned.

In most countries, the Ministry of Finance is among the poshest of buildings, being outshone only by the Central Bank. But this one belied the rule. We reached the Finance Minister's office by walking up an outdoor stairway that went up the side and around the back of the heavy concrete building. From there we looked down on a ramshackle set of lodgings constructed of tin and stray lumber. Junk, banana trees, children, and chickens littered the ground.

Inside the walls were light green and blue, the doors tall and green, and green shutters leaned from the top of the windows out into the street. The windows had no glass; they were open to catch the wind, which had taken the day off. There were no fans or air-conditioning. It was hot as a greenhouse. Within minutes my shirt looked as though it had just been laundered but someone had forgotten the dryer.

We went to the office of the minister's secretary. Eric, the World Bank loan officer, gave her his card. He asked whether we might see the minister. The secretary was a woman in her early thirties, whose self-importance exceeded her measurable but not overwhelming sex appeal and may or may not have exceeded her powers as gatekeeper to the minister. She looked at Eric with a stern face. She looked some more. Then she slowly looked back at his business card, eyed Tomás and me, and glared back at Eric. She said nothing. Eventually Eric repeated his request to see the minister. I thought his voice creaked a little as he added, "And if we can't see him now, we can come back later." The secretary looked again at Eric's card. Finally she spoke, using the familiar form of "you" which is seldom heard in formal Equatorial Guinean conversations and is ordinarily employed when talking to children or servants.

"Get yourself into the waiting room and I'll let you know," she said. The tone of her voice could be better rendered as: "Move your ass into the waiting room and if I feel like it, I'll clue you in later."

We moved, and waited for cluing. As we went down the hall, I noticed above the offices 5-by-14-inch cards printed in bold black with "Iltmo. Sr. Secretario General" and "Excmo. Sr. Ministro." "Most Illustrious Mr. General Secretary" was the proper form of address, and the "Most Excellent Mr. Minister" was also called "Your Excellency." One was allowed to use the less cumbersome title of "Don" with the excellency's first name, as with Knights of the British Empire. Formal dress was mandatory for audiences with high officials. These courtly customs were reminiscent of the Spanish empire, perhaps even of Miguel de Cervantes. In contrast, the secretary's manner reminded one of a housekeeper shooing unruly neighbor boys off the driveway.

We sat for a while and sweated. Eventually Eric returned to the secretary's office to ask about the appointment. She told him to come back later. No explanation.

We changed money, visited the United Nations office, and interviewed the director of the central bank. Then we returned to the Ministry of Finance.

We entered the secretary's office and faced her down again. She eyeballed Eric—Eric, the loan officer for this country from the big, bad World Bank—as though he were a delinquent. Eric asked when we might see the minister. It was not clear he would get an answer. During the third long pause, I intervened. On the wall behind her were two portraits of the President: one of him in a military uniform, two huge medals on his chest, furrowed brow; the other featuring a dark civilian suit, and a brow less furrowed. Which of them, I asked with my friendliest smile, did she like best?

"I like the second one," she said. "It was taken two years after the first, after he was more consolidated and more sure of himself in power."

Our conversation quickly moved to her home part of the country in Río Muni, the beaches of Río Muni, the animals of Río Muni, when it rains in Río Muni. Her name, she said, was Esmeralda. She said she would inquire whether the minister would see us. We would kindly go to the waiting room.

We returned to the old leatherette couches with the bottom cushions covered in cloth. Through the open windows came increasingly loud street noise. Construction or destruction, right across the way. There were also the chirps and cries of birds.

The waiting room was slightly cooler than the Sahara. We sat and perspired. I loosened the necktie that was de rigueur for meetings with excellencies. I thought of Florencio on the plane. I thought of a senior World Bank educator who the day before had been sent home because, although he wore a necktie, he didn't have a coat to don at the time the Minister of Education was to receive him. I thought of a swimming pool.

Suddenly Esmeralda appeared and beckoned us to the minister's office.

Don Manuel was sitting with the secretary general, the ministry's chief administrative officer, who was poised to take notes. Esmeralda was not present; she was back on guard duty. The minister looked about thirty-five. His cheeks were bare, but an unusual beard began below the line of his chin. His face was round, and he mopped it often with his handkerchief. He wore a gray suit, checked like graph paper, with a checked shirt and a tan tie with small dots. No rings, a simple watch. His face was impassive, but he looked tough. Throughout the interview his left eyebrow remained menacingly arched, and his mustache had the effect of Fu Manchu.

Eric began talking and then talked some more. He poured forth a stream of prefatory remarks, logistical details, and facts about our mission. Don Manuel listened without much interest. Which showed good taste, I thought.

The machines on the street were getting louder. The minister snapped his fingers at the secretary general to close the windows. Eric handed him a paper. The minister looked at it and spoke in a low voice.

"I think we must reconsider the title of the document. This is not a loan for the Agriculture Ministry, as it says here. It is a loan for the Finance Ministry."

Clearly, it was the wrong paper. Eric blushed, and Tomás began to rummage in his ample satchel, his brow as furrowed as the President's first photo. I looked around the office of the Minister of Finance. The floor was of plain yellow tile, the chairs and sofa of what looked like light green Naugahyde. There was a humble beige formica-like table. The walls, of white stucco, were bare except for a photo of the President. There was a fan, pointed at the minister, who nonetheless was mopping away.

The right paper was found. It began to rain outside. The minister asked questions like, "Do the other co-financiers have copies?" Tomás often interrupted Eric with small points and additions. The secretary general had stopped taking notes.

Before we left, the minister agreed to see me to talk about medium-term development strategies, and told the secretary general to arrange it. As we departed, I was thinking about how the meeting might have been run differently. Give the minister all the names and dates and numbers on a page or two. Present a briefing with three or four points. Talk about ten minutes, not forty-five. Have the right papers organized and ready in advance. Let the minister talk a lot more. As it was, the minister was barraged with details, and must have felt, as I did when we left, that not much had happened.

Eric gave me a list of seven people to interview. Over the next days I tried. I saw one of the seven. The concept of "appointment," for which there is the good Spanish word *cita* and which exists in other Hispanic countries, has not yet found a home in Equatorial Guinea. "When may I see the minister?" is a little like asking, "When will the next solar eclipse occur?" No one really knows, except that it will be a remarkable event when it happens.

One day at lunch, I saw the senior World Bank educator, who was on a separate mission concerning a possible education project. He was fuming.

"I'm ready to go home now and give them no money at all," he said. "I have now waited five times to see the Minister of Education. Each time I had an appointment. But he has not seen me yet. Today I waited for one hour before leaving. I think he is doing it on purpose."

What was the purpose? He couldn't think one up, and neither could I. The World Bank seemed on friendly terms with the government, and there were no major storms on the educational horizon. Maybe it was an overdose of foreign-aid types. No tourists came here and only a few business people, but there was a host of aid missions. One report pegged the gross national product in 1984 at about sixty-seven million dollars. Foreign aid and loans were estimated to be about thirty million dollars. I had never been in a country where foreign assistance made up such a large part of the national income.

The country's dependency was manifest. The International Monetary Fund's agreement with the government stipulated that the only capital investments allowed in the government budget were "counterparts" to existing foreign aid projects. Nothing but what the aid givers wanted to do, could the government do.

So maybe the ministers were busy seeing people like us. Or maybe they were annoyed deep down at aid with so many strings and nooses attached, and avoided seeing us.

That afternoon I explored Malabo's market. What a ramshackle affair—several acres of homemade stalls arrayed along narrow internal roads and paths. The stalls' rusty tin roofs were low, constantly endangering my forehead. The market was noisy and dirty and included clothing stalls, shops something like tiny five-and-tens, food stands, liquor (a big area, set in a concrete semicircle in the back of the market), and services such as tailoring and selling drinks.

One can learn a lot from markets in a developing country. Unobtrusive indicators of economic welfare abound. What kinds of shoes do the women wear—none, plastic sandals, plastic shoes, leather shoes? How nice are the shoes? (The answer for Equatorial Guinea is mostly plastic sandals.) Is the market built on dirt or concrete? (Dirt.) Are there lots of goods or few? (Few, but more than before the *cefa.*) Is there fresh meat? (No—except sometimes you can find a boa, some field rats or porcupines, or a monkey.) In terms of square footage in the market, what is the ratio of liquor and beer to wholesome foods? (Getting near one to one, which is very high.)

While investigating these questions, I unexpectedly found myself in a discussion of truth and relativism.

I was having a shirt made from a raucous African cloth. The seamster liked the idea, as did his amused colleagues. He took one of my shirts as a model and began copying it on his little sewing machine. Meanwhile, I was the subject of ardent attention from his neighbors, including a nearby barkeep and her customers. I joined the crew sitting at their little table and had a beer. They asked me where I was from. When I said the United States, one of the men joked, "We'd better watch out what we say. You may be tape-recording us."

An odd thought in such a setting, but these turned out not to be typical marketgoers. They were teachers at the local school of public administration. We talked about their country and mine, which beers were the best, the fortunes of the local football team. Somehow the conversation turned philosophical. A slight man with a mustache was the glibbest, and he was full of the grandiloquent generalizations of a Latin intellectual. It was he who brought up truth and relativism.

"One cannot affirm—in fact one can emphatically refute—the popular idea that there is one truth that is valid for all. I am instead a relativist. What is true for me is true for me. I will not say it is so for him, or her, or you."

Wasn't it instead a continuum, I asked, from physics at one extreme to subjective tastes at the other? Physics was true for him, the barkeep, and me, whether we liked it or not. At the other extreme, some tastes could be called relative. Perhaps administrative techniques and economics fell somewhere inbetween. In these subjects nothing could be said to be true for all conditions; but on the other hand, complete relativism was also wrong. One could make some good guesses, and we could learn from each other's experiences.

But what really got him was when I gently suggested why extreme relativism is so popular among intellectuals in developing countries. They have been doubly deceived—first, by colonial powers that sold them on a certain view of religion and state as absolutely true; then, by their own governments after independence, by one or another ideology or cult figure. They have been tricked; above all, they do not want to be tricked again. No wonder a primary attribute of the intelligentsia in such countries is suspiciousness. When they receive a new idea, they don't ponder it, play with it, or investigate its applications and utility. They wonder instead why this idea is presented to them by this person at this time. Such suspiciousness can become an excuse for intellectual laziness. It is a way of avoiding the hard work inbetween the poles of absolutism and the doctrine that all truth is relative.

And so we passed an engaging several hours in beery discussion, till at dusk I went home, feeling that I had several new friends.

Saturday night brought, of all things, a rock concert. This unusual event was scheduled for one of Malabo's two defunct theaters, which was used for such events as the installation of government officials. Malabo—indeed, the whole country—had no cinemas, no bookstores, no magazine stands. Entertainment was scarce, and Saturday's main attraction was Maele, the premier rock star of Equatorial Guinea. It sounded like fun, and Salvador, a Guinean who administered the World Bank's technical assistance project in the country, and I decided to go.

We met at the Teatro Marfil at the seven-thirty concert time, paid five hundred *cefas* each (about $1.25), and went inside. The crowd was up for the occasion. I was amazed at the attire. If you imagined how people might have dressed for a sock hop in the late 1950s, you'd be on the right track. Neat, dressed up, even some pleated skirts. Certainly nothing African about the scene, and nothing like a rock concert in the funky, punky West.

The show started an hour and a half late. A couple of locals who had spent time in Nigeria were on first, with their band. Pretending they'd forgotten how to speak Spanish, they greeted the crowd in English, which was translated by the emcee. They boomed out some early 1960s three-chord rock 'n roll. Then Maele was introduced. The crowd cheered. But he wasn't going to sing. He was just the organizer of the concert. The crowd expressed their disapproval. The emcee returned and tried to quiet them with jokes. But he got catcalls: "Music, now! Let's go!"

The emcee himself turned out to be the next attraction. He didn't have it together. The three female accompanists sang in three keys, none of which was his. The lead guitar was out of tune. After one song, the guy behind me yelled, "I want my five hundred back." After two songs, the crowd was whistling and wailing. Salvador and I waded through the crowd and went off for dinner, laughing. I'm not sure the poor emcee-turned-singer escaped so easily.

Another unusual event occurred that day. The World Bank educator told me at dinner that his patience had finally paid off. He had met with the Minister of Education.

Exploring Bioko

I visited Florencio in his office in the Ministry of Mines and Hydrocarbons. He seemed genuinely glad to see his former travel companion. We agreed to get together. I called later to arrange it, and he asked me instead to go Sunday on a trip around the island.

Florencio, his friend Jaime—the head of the country's ports—and a driver picked me up early at the Beiruth. We headed off in their four-wheeler toward the east side of the island. The day was sunny but not too hot yet, and we talked about ports and the days of the Spanish (not bad) and the days of Macías (very bad) and the beauty of the green and the ocean.

I mentioned that I had been reading a bit about Fang folklore. In the tales of the Fang, who hail from the mainland but also dominate the capital on the island, the key figure is the turtle. Called *kulu* or simply *ku* in Fang, this creature has some of the traits of the fox: wiliness, wit, and ability to evade trouble. And he has more. He is as wise as an owl. He can blend into the jungle or the sea—the continent has both land turtles, rather small, and sea tortoises—and can in an instant be invisible to his pursuers. He is diplomatic. When wronged, he will say nothing but later will extract his revenge. I asked Jaime and Florencio about the *ku*.

They regaled me with stories. When one would tell the story, he would laugh and whoop at key moments, and the other would respond with "Yes, that's it, can't you see it?" and a cry of laughter. The driver simply laughed nonstop.

One of their tales concerned the divorce between the tiger and the tigress. (Equatorial Guinea does not have tigers, of course; the Spanish word is used generically for any large jungle cat.) At issue is who will get possession of their child. The tiger thinks he should; the tigress thinks she should. The other animals are consulted. One by one, Jaime described each animal and what it says and how. Each one, up to and including the elephant, says the tiger should get the child. This is part of the animals' tradition of male dominance. Before making a final decision, the animals decide that they should ask the *ku.*

They call the *ku.* He listens carefully to the tiger and the tigress. He asks all the animals to come back the next day at lunchtime, when he will give them his opinion.

The time arrives. All the animals gather. The *ku* walks toward them and, about fifty feet short of the assemblage, enters a large puddle and begins to bathe. Suddenly he begins to weep and moan, apparently overcome by grief.

The animals come over and listen. Jaime did a great job with the splashing and crying and wailing, and the driver, Florencio, and I all laughed loudly. The animals try to console the *ku.*

"What has happened, my friend?" asks the elephant. "What causes you such sorrow?"

"My father-in-law has died," groans the *ku,* and all the animals agree that this is a terrible thing.

"How did that happen, friend Ku?" one asks.

"My father-in-law died while giving birth," the *ku* says.

There is a pause. Finally the tiger speaks.

"Look here, what is this nonsense?" he says in a disgusted voice. "This is the one whom you wish to give a verdict on my case, and he says such idiocies. Why, everyone knows that a man cannot die in childbirth. Only a woman can. Only a woman has that kind of relationship with her child. It is different from a man's."

"Aha!" cries the *ku,* no longer sad. "You yourself have said it. The woman has a special relationship with the child—only she has given it birth. Therefore, I rule that the custody should be with the tigress."

The tiger scratches his head and ambles off, and the other animals decide that the *ku* is right.

We arrived at a village where we stopped and bought some oranges and fragrantly delicious bananas. We ate them as we drove on and swapped more folktales. Then we arrived at one of the most dramatic vistas I have ever seen.

The bridge dates from Macías's days, the early 1970s, and for this country must have been an engineering feat. About five hundred feet long, it stands about two hundred feet above the bottom of a deep, steep canyon, with huge trees and vines and lush bushes everywhere. To the southeast the canyon stretches down and down, all the way to the beautiful ocean below. Looking up the canyon, we gasped at the steep gorge covered in profuse vegetation, misty in the distance like a Chinese painting. A breeze wafted down the canyon, and we walked the bridge and admired the serenity of the scene: a giant slice into the mountain, covered three times over with trees and plants of deepest green, with clouds piled up in the distance over a clear blue sea.

We drove on and began to ascend, turning west. A plantation of oil palms stood abandoned. We found many cocoyam plants, in Spanish called *malanga*. I had never seen them, and we stopped in one little settlement and asked a local farmer to dig one up for us. He uprooted the plant and dug with his fingers for the lavender-colored tuber. He offered us honey, which we ate after brushing away the dead bees and chewing the honeycomb, then spitting out the cellulose.

The villages were humble, but I did not see the destitution that I have found in, say, rural Bolivia or Pakistan. Florencio explained that you could always find food in the jungle, and water was no problem. Hunger in the style of Ethiopia did not exist. The villagers' clothing was Western, though ragged; there was no sign of African costume or distinctive cloths. The huts were also Western in appearance, only smaller and dirtier: they were rudimentary rectangular houses made of wood planks with tin roofs and shutters: no beehive huts or adobe structures.

Turning up a side road, we climbed a narrow track overhung with trees. We finally arrived at a Bubi village called Moeri. On a level clearing in the fertile jungle were about forty houses, tiny but fairly new looking; and at its center a light green lawn surrounded a church. Behind the village the volcano was a wall of darker green, and the clouds at its summit formed a dramatic wreath of white and gray. It was not sunny, but there was no fog; the air was cool and refreshing; and if you looked down the mountain, you could take in the billows and slopes of the forests below, all the way to the sea.

We met Florencio's brother, who taught school in Moeri, and his family. People in the village were going to church. Florencio rounded up big bundles of plantains for the back of the four-wheeler. I wandered toward the lawn, and a song began to emerge from the congregation. The voices were loud and in unison and sounded like children's voices, sweet and strained. It was a Biblical, almost a Baptist-sounding, song. I looked at the church rising up from the grass, bathed in dim light, with the mountain behind, and the wonderful clouds, and thought the music very beautiful.

Florencio bought more than plantains. He also purchased a porcupine and something called an *antílope.* The latter is no antelope as we know it, but a tiny, repulsive creature that has horns, looks like a rabbit in the face, and otherwise resembles a large rodent. Fortunately, both animals were dead. They were placed on the pile of plantains just behind the back seat on which Jaime and I sat.

We descended to Luba. I bought my colleagues a beer at the Hotel Jones and said hello to the family there. We then went to the house of Musto, the head of the Luba port. He offered us a beer. He introduced Teodora, his wife, who was preparing lunch. She was a bulky woman, about forty-five, graced with a remarkable smile. On the wall were several pictures of their wedding, and you could see that same weight but also that same smile, and somehow immediately perceive why Musto loved her.

Musto was an unusual name. Also on the wall was an old drawing of a man with a turban, apparently a Pakistani or an Indian. Musto had a similar mustache but otherwise looked black. Musto said yes, that was his father, and yes, his real name was Mustafa.

He told us of his father's arrival here long ago and marriage to a Bubi woman high up in the mountains above Luba, and of his own upbringing and eventual marriage to Teodora. Musto knew that his father's homeland was Hyderabad, Sind, in what is now Pakistan, but he knew nothing about the place: so when I told him stories about Hyderabad, which I had visited, he was delighted.

Teodora brought out huge land snails, which tasted like dirt. Eventually we all sat down to a repast of porcupine meat, *malanga,* and rice. They laughed at my feigned (or was it?) nervousness about eating the porcupine.

"Don't worry," said Jaime. "It's much cleaner than a pig, which eats all manner of things. This just eats the nicest things, like cocoa and *malanga* and grass."

Well, it was good, I had to say. Not gamey or oily. It is also the only dish I've seen that comes with its own toothpicks.

Teodora told of her activities as the coordinator of women's issues for the southern region of Bioko. She spoke at length, with logic and passion. She had not only started a preschool but had also, with the local doctor and a local priest, initiated twice-weekly classes on nutrition, with mimeographed materials she had prepared herself.

Recently Teodora had returned from her first overseas trip, to a conference on women, in Mozambique. She spoke of her frustration in Mozambique with delegates who wanted to sound off about how bad women had it, but did not want to discuss practical ways to help women. Teodora was a doer. She showed me pictures of her daughter, eighteen years old, now studying in Spain, who wanted (Teodora did not approve) to be an English teacher.

"I realized that I had got to where I was, to be the person I was, because of the love and help my parents had given me, and I have seen in my daughter a curiosity and intelligence that her teachers praise. I know that Musto and I can do much for our own children, but I think we should reach out further. There are many other children here who do not have that background of love and care, and many women who want to learn how to take care of their children. I want to help *them.*"

So would you, after listening to Teodora. While she was talking—and she talked a lot, with feeling—Musto listened carefully, always watching her. His attentiveness said a great deal, and I liked what it said.

And so, on the road back from Luba to Malabo, I felt I had made four new friends. Jaime, with his stories about the *ku* and his gleeful laugh. Musto, with his wise eye and open mind. The redoubtable Teodora. And Florencio: no longer wearing the vest and necktie of the airplane, but now on terms of the familiar *tú* with me, a man who knew how to be quiet but also how to laugh. Florencio had gone upcountry and come back with a load of plantains, his porcupine, and an *antílope.* He said his wife would be thrilled.

Maintaining Health

The health situation was appalling.

It was hard to believe, but scores of children were dying in an epidemic of measles. One day I was having coffee at the Beiruth bar and the usual waitress wasn't there. I asked after her. The answer was that her son had died the day before from complications following measles.

Cholera had been rampant. I visited the Health Ministry and interviewed a French physician about the epidemic. She showed me the time profiles of cholera cases and deaths over the past half-year. Two big outbreaks had occurred. She had traced both to instances where the water system of Malabo had not been not treated with chlorine. The reasons were unclear. Some people said the city had not imported enough chlorine. Others said the Guineans had the chlorine but didn't use it, which pushed the mystery one step back.

I occasionally used a typewriter at the United Nations office. The secretary at the next desk—an expatriate—had two children. One was suffering from a version of elephantiasis. The other had malaria.

One of our World Bank team, a fifty-year-old German of robust appearance, came down with malaria. His fever hit 104°F and stayed there, and after a few days he was evacuated to Germany. He had not been taking pills for malaria; his doctor had advised him against it because of a kidney problem. We learned daily of other cases of malaria among expatriates—even people who had been taking pills; and the disease pervaded the local community, many of whom could not afford the imported medicines.

I had talked with Eric and Heinz about health. I thought the proposed rehabilitation project should include money for pharmaceuticals and medical supplies. At first they had rejected the idea: the project's goal was to invigorate the economy, not to provide social services. They kept using the World Bank's expression "the productive sectors." I kept talking about the importance of human capital. What "sector" was more productive than people? They, too, were shocked by the health situation and eventually agreed to include in the project's tentative budget a few hundred thousand dollars for the health sector.

"But we don't have anyone on our team to look at health," Heinz said. "So if you want it in the project, you'll have to do the background work yourself."

This meant both getting some idea of what imports were needed and also figuring out how to make sure the imports went where they were supposed to go—without rip-offs, waste, and fraud. For there were stories of corruption in the health sector. I met a mechanic who worked on a transportation project run by the American cooperative league, CLUSA. His wife worked in health.

"You know why the kids are dying of measles now, don't you?" he asked bitterly. "Because the drugs that are bought or donated are stolen by government officers and sold in Cameroon or Gabon. My wife can tell you all about it."

I went to the Ministry of Health. Surprisingly, the minister was there and received me. He had recently taken over; his predecessor had been sacked after the measles epidemic broke out and had been sent to Cameroon as ambassador. Some punishment.

I told the minister about the proposed rehabilitation project and asked what imports were most important for his ministry. He said that everything was needed in a country like this. One could highlight the hospitals, ambulances, and pharmaceuticals. The country could not even afford to import enough beds for the hospital or drugs to treat malaria or colitis.

Toward the end of the interview, I mentioned what I said would be a delicate question. If the World Bank were to meet some import needs in the pharmaceutical area, how could one be sure that the drugs would get to the people who really needed them?

He dodged what had happened in the past, saying that he was new to the ministry. But he said he was determined that under his administration there would be no corruption involving pharmaceuticals.

The minister immediately set up a committee of doctors to prepare a list of essential imports. I took Heinz and Eric along to a meeting to receive the committee's report. It was a long list, everything but the proverbial kitchen sink. There were no prices, no priorities. We talked about working the list over. They invited us to see the hospital, and so the next day, with another member of the World Bank team named Harmon, I went.

Set on a hilltop across a green gorge on the east side of town, the main hospital building looked from a distance like a fort that had years ago undergone bombardment and never been repaired. Harmon and I toured it with the hospital's director and a Cuban physician.

The wards were wide but very old, without fans, bare walled and yellow, with crucifixes at the end, apparently put up by the half-dozen nuns who worked in this unholy place. The hospital beds were a disgrace. Thin layers of old foam sat on springs that sagged half a foot in the middle, and some of the springs were missing. The absence of plastic mattress covers, explained the director, meant that cholera could be conveyed via the mattresses. The hospital had no ambulance. The X-ray machine did not work because a resistor was out. A dentist's machine had not functioned for two years because a connecting socket had not been replaced. Surgical equipment was absent. The operating room light with twelve special bulbs was out of order. Why? No bulbs. In its stead, a sixty-watt reading lamp was employed during surgery.

The human costs of these failures were enormous. Harmon and I later investigated the hospital's procurement and repair systems. We visited the "shops" of two electricians who "serviced" the hospital. We learned that these systems barely existed.

Harmon was a delight. He was seventy-four years old. He had solved transportation problems and set up maintenance and spare-parts schemes all over the world. He spoke slowly and strongly, with the force of a man who knows what he knows and doesn't know. At the hospital, when we were shown machinery that was out of order, Harmon insisted on seeing the defective part. He copied down numbers and makers. He asked dozens of good questions about details: "How do you know this is the piece that's bad and not something feeding into it? Where is the repair manual? Who has responsibility for this piece of equipment?" Harmon made an impression, not only on the Equatoguineans but on the World Bank team. *Maintenance* and *rehabilitation of existing equipment* became themes of the proposed project.

Lighter Notes

Like other poor and desperate parts of the world, Equatorial Guinea is not a monochrome study in unhappiness. Where you find poverty, disease, and corruption, you may also find beauty and joy and idealism—in the same places and the same people. Poverty has something to give those of us who have not received it—above all, the lesson of adaptability.

Humor was an indigenous specialty. Every day something would make me laugh out loud, if only at myself in my strange surroundings. My lodging situation was solved, but not via hotel. I got into a house the United Nations used for its short-term consultants. For the first two nights, there were no sheets, no water, no electricity. Since the house was well away from town and transport was nonexistent, I had lots of long walks. The sheet problem was solved when another tenant left; and from the third day, the United Nations generator supplied electricity and cold water during certain hours.

The remaining person in the house was a girlish Uruguayan librarian, blonde and brown-eyed, her high voice continually cracking with astonishment. The cry of alarm "Oooeee!" was her favorite expression. A rainstorm scared her. Insects scared her. Virtually every tropical disease known to man was about to attack her person. Her wardrobe consisted of long African shifts. She sang in the morning. The second day I mentioned that it was nice to wake up to her melodies. Her reaction validated the theory of positive reinforcement. Two mornings later, in a voice upped 50 percent in decibel level since my unthinking compliment, she burst forth with a half-hour—or more (I left for work)—of Sinatra-style but Spanish love songs, Villa-Lobos, and opera. When passing near my room, she twice punctuated the fact that she was making music—once by ceasing her singing and whistling a robust refrain, and later, while belting out a tango, by snapping her fingers and stomping her feet.

There were other sorts of music as well. One night after dinner, when Heinz, Harmon, and I were walking through the warm breeze, Heinz said,

"You want to hear some music? Come on, the next street over they're always playing."

It was about ten o'clock, and that night the city's electricity would be on till midnight. From open windows on the second floor of a building halfway down the block came the full-power sound of African rock. Heinz led us into the building, and we knocked on the appropriate door. We were admitted. We walked through a small sitting room, pulled back a large portière, and entered a huge room pulsating with electric guitars and snare drums. On the walls hung framed posters of Michael Jackson, several African singers, and a white rocker simply labeled "Dave," along with some overblown shots of Maele. Over on the left stood Maele himself, guitar in hand. Next to him were the two Guineans-turned-Nigerians from the rock concert. Three girls were singing backup. There were two more guitarists, a bass, and a guy banging away on a hollow piece of wood. Around the sides of the room dancers and spectators were vibrating in enjoyment. The amplifiers and speakers were the most advanced pieces of technology I had encountered in Equatorial Guinea.

At the end of the song, we were greeted all around. Lots of hand shaking. We said we'd like to listen; they said we were more than welcome. We listened. One of the Nigerians, Dayday, asked whether we played. Pretty soon I was banging away at Dayday's electric guitar, and they were learning "Barbara Ann," "Runaround Sue," and "Spider and the Fly." Harmon did a little work on the drums, to the delight of the other Nigerian, a six-foot-three Michael Jackson devotee complete with jumpsuit and ringlets but without the glove.

We laughed as much as we sang. Our hosts asked us to come back again the next night, and we did. We added an Englishman named Morton who worked on the cocoa project, to whom I loaned a surfing T-shirt and a pair of shorts. I also asked the Uruguayan librarian to join us.

"But I don't know any rock songs or any songs in English!" she oooeeed, eyes wide.

In the end, though, she was thrilled by the invitation. Morton and I spent the early part of the evening talking cocoa over some Guinness stouts. Then we fetched her and Heinz and Harmon and went for dinner at the Beiruth, featuring more Cameroon-brewed Guinnesses. Then on to Maele's. Alas, the maestro, Maele, wasn't there, but the Nigerians and a bunch of other musicians were, plus a covey of teenage girls who danced. While a band rehearsed, we danced, too. Then Dayday got on the mike and said, "Here we have some new friends, so let's jam."

The crowd blasted through "Barbara Ann" and thumped out the hep-

hep-humby-daydy-daydy-hep-hep of "Runaround Sue." The librarian was stoked. Heinz even got into the act, forcibly: we carried him from sidelines to center mike, where he gamely provided some "waah-oooohs" with a German accent. We had brought more Guinnesses with us, and they seemed to magnify both the volume of the vocals and our appreciation of the bizarre international amalgam booming forth from the speakers.

We were still singing when we left, and got into a couple of four-wheelers for the ride home. The stars seemed particularly bright.

Making Plans

The next morning my voice was half an octave lower and my head felt half a size bigger. I had to rally, because people work half-days on Saturdays. After three unsuccessful attempts, I was going to try again to see Don Constantino, the Minister of Planning. He was supposed to be a difficult man—stubborn, sensitive, not capable or powerful but holding what could be a key post. Eric said, "Somehow you have to let Don Constantino see that you could be useful to him, without intimidating or threatening him technically."

Lo and behold! almost immediately after arriving, I was ushered into the minister's office.

Don Constantino was looking good in his dark, pinstriped suit and foulard tie. A handsome man of medium height and steady gaze, his appearance belied the stereotype evoked by his education in heavy equipment repair in the Soviet Union. I wanted to talk with him about the country's planning system and how the proposed World Bank economic rehabilitation project might intertwine with it.

Don Constantino began with some background. "In the Ministry of Planning, the history is very poor. It was a ministry that didn't function. Only after 3 August 1979 [the date of the coup against Macías] did planning begin. Since then, we have made enormous efforts to move forward. Technical assistance has been extremely important to the ministry, and through it we have made strides in training personnel overseas.

"We have had to learn how to do planning, how to develop projects, how to develop strategies. At the operational level, our main task has been trying to coordinate the rest of the ministries, avoiding replication. We don't yet have a planning staff, so we use what the other ministries already have."

Currently, the Ministry of Planning had but four Guinean professionals. There were also several foreign advisers.

I asked how the other ministries worked with the Planning Ministry. Don Constantino said there were occasionally technical meetings. "We meet every three months with people from the ministries and ask why there were these failures on the projects. We are looking for coordination always." There were no high-level interministerial meetings to work on strategies and projects.

"Each ministry is now working on short-term plans. These should be ready by the end of September." What was short term? Two to three years. "The 1982 document prepared for the donors' conference in Geneva was more a series of projects, but without coordination to achieve a common end." This, the only "plan" the country possessed, was not functional.

Don Constantino thought the completion of the short-term ministerial plans in September would make a big difference. "Only with these plans can the Ministry of Planning talk with authority. Only then can we tell the other ministries, 'You cannot do this because it is against the policy.' "

At this point I shared with Don Constantino some experiences from other developing countries. The stories I told had a moral. Successful ministries of planning tend to think of their role as facilitators, not nay sayers. The idea of national planning has evolved. A plan should not be a set of marching orders but a vision of a country's situation and its strategy. The Minister of Planning should be able to help his ministerial colleagues achieve their objectives. His vantage point should enable him to discern policies and projects that overlap individual ministries. He should have benefits to disburse, in coin the ministries will understand— something as narrow as help in preparing projects, something as concrete as budgetary authority, something as visionary as cross-ministerial pro- grams. Otherwise, "planning" can easily degenerate into an unproductive battle for bureaucratic turf.

In this context, I said, the administration of the proposed World Bank project could be more important for his ministry than at first it might appear. There would be a project coordinating committee made up of key ministers, including Don Constantino. The project would have something like ten million dollars. The money could be especially important since the government's present capital budget had to be allocated to counterpart funds for foreign aid projects. And the project offered the chance to think about how to make free-market reforms work in Equatorial Guinea. A good strategy was essential to get the next level of aid from the World Bank—a structural adjustment loan.

Don Constantino listened carefully and made an interesting response. "We have many needs for imports, because of the major change that we have made in the economic system. The World Bank will help us to meet our import needs in the next two years, which will be a time of urgent requirements for imports. The various ministries have been working for a month to tell their needs. The Bank has a large mission here now to do a detailed study of the sectors and their needs. I am a person who likes careful study. Once the study is done, then the task is to do what the study says. If the imports are well planned, then the administering committee does not have to think about strategy. We therefore need a small committee that could make sure the imports specified were handled expeditiously. I think the chairman of this committee should be the Minister of Planning."

"Couldn't the economic rehabilitation project serve as a catalyst for the preparation of a medium-term development strategy?" I asked. Despite the minister's valiant efforts, this did not yet exist for Equatorial Guinea. Couldn't Don Constantino imagine that the committee administering the project would spend some of its time looking at the public budget, some examining a few key market failures in the private sector, and some thinking about the kinds of reforms that might make a strategic difference? Wouldn't such a process abet the government's efforts to do strategic planning?

We talked it over. I tried again to convey with examples from other countries that planning was most effective when it helped individual ministries according to their own lights, rather than restricting them or invading their turf, and when it tried to identify a few crucial themes instead of aiming for full "coordination" and illusory control. I asked again whether the World Bank economic rehabilitation project might be part of such a planning process.

Finally, after a long pause, Don Constantino replied, "This is all a new dimension of the problem. We had been told to get together a list of import needs, that the World Bank would then get them for us. We were not told about these other aspects."

I stressed that I was speaking as a consultant hired by his government, not as a spokesperson for the World Bank. If the minister and his colleagues so chose, the way the rehabilitation project was administered could provide a springboard to a structural adjustment program, which meant increased foreign assistance. Don Constantino liked that idea.

Cocoa

Historically, cocoa has been the motor of growth in Equatorial Guinea, the traditional mainstay of its economy.

The World Bank had funded a cocoa rehabilitation project. Three people of an eventual five-person advisory team had arrived in Malabo. I struck up a friendship with Morton, a cocoa grading and marketing expert, who had worked with a cocoa import firm in London before taking this assignment. He and I tried to work through the costs and prices from production on the farm through the various stages of fermenting, drying, shipping, exporting, and so forth. He was a good teacher. After quite a while, Morton reached into his satchel and took out a typewritten paper.

"I haven't let anyone here see this. I think you might find it of interest."

The document was a confidential November 1984 trip report written by two members of another English cocoa importing firm. This company did business with one of the two private Guinean companies that dominated the cocoa exporting business. The document Morton showed me was amazing in frankness and detail. It referred to price fixing and other scams between exporters and importers, such as pretending that so much cocoa of such-and-such quality was shipped when actually the quality and quantity were much higher. It described bribes to several Equatoguinean ministers. Most remarkably, it detailed the company's corrupt deals with President Obiang and his lawyer.

Reading the document was like a kick in the gut. Even though I had written a book about Third World corruption, seldom had I seen such blatant, almost casual evidence of graft. Morton said earnestly that he hoped to do something in his grading and quality control job to break up the possibilities for such corruption. He wanted more of the money to go to the producers. I admired his attitude.

Since almost all the cocoa is on Bioko, I thought I could learn firsthand about the sector's problems and prospects. One afternoon at six, I met Aurelio, one of the leading Guinean cocoa producers, in his office.

Aurelio was a muscular, very black man with hair cropped close to baldness. Though he was sitting at his desk, his face was as wet as Moses Malone's in the fourth quarter. I introduced myself and observed that it was hot. Aurelio said if he wasn't sweating this way, it meant he was sick. A few minutes into our meeting, the city's electricity went out, so he opened the shutters and door, and we talked in the dim light about the costs of producing cocoa.

Aurelio thought I should visit a cocoa farm, and so the next afternoon we went to his own farm, about a half-hour's drive from Malabo. With us was another cocoa man, a good-humored Spaniard named Guillermo, with lively eyes, a gray beard, and a bushy handlebar mustache. We all sat in the bed of the Land Rover truck and were driven—first on paved road, then dirt, and then on two tracks climbing through that magnificent, dark green forest—to Aurelio's cocoa farm. Down the two mud tracks water was flowing; it must have rained up in the hills.

"See why we need manpower?" Aurelio asked, pointing to the cocoa fields we were passing. "Look at the suckers on the trees. Look at all the weeds. There are squirrels all over here. These orchards are no longer worked. They used to be in Spanish times, but no more. The trees need care, and spraying, and trimming. The old trees need to be replaced with new ones. We need many people just to chop back the suckers and the weeds."

Laborers worked in rubber boots and "monkey suits" wielding machetes and machete sharpeners. They lived alongside the hacienda and the cocoa-drying machine in group housing that appeared designed for horses instead of humans—a series of connected stalls with walls and a roof. In addition to a wage of about $35 a month, laborers received a supply of basic food. If you had a large cocoa plantation of over 400 acres, you would ideally like to employ 1 worker for every 5 acres. But labor was in short supply in the cocoa sector. The imported Nigerians of Spanish times had gone home. Macías had responded to their exodus by forcibly bringing some 35,000 people from Río Muni to work the cocoa orchards. After Macías's overthrow, most of them forsook this occupation, and many returned to the mainland. Consequently, perhaps half of all the cocoa orchards on the island had been simply abandoned—and those under cultivation had 1 worker for every 8 or 9 acres.

The luscious, wet foliage gleamed in the late afternoon sunlight. The cocoa pods were about the size of avocados. Now they were green; at harvest time in the fall, they would be reddish orange. The pods would be picked and then, for quality's sake, the beans would be fermented in large piles for a couple of days. Often nowadays, the fermentation step was skipped. Then came the drying, in huge cement basins the size of a basketball court, with a courtwide mechanical rake moving back and forth to sift the beans, and wood fires burning under the cement to dry (but not roast) them. The drying went on day and night during the season.

We entered the hacienda, an old wooden structure with little romance; but from the second-floor veranda, the setting was spectacular with the rain forest all around and the sun's rays turning pink. And over a welcome beer, we went through the costs of various stages of production. Guillermo did most of the talking, with occasional comments from Aurelio.

Finally, Aurelio yawned. "Well, professor, a student can only absorb so much in a single sitting. I think you've got a lot on paper already." And so we left. On the way back Guillermo offered to show me some documents on production and exports.

A day later I called Guillermo to set up a meeting, and he asked me over for Sunday lunch. His house was on the east side of town. From his lot you could see the twin spires of the Gothic-style cathedral to the southwest and the hospital across the green gulch to the east. It was an old colonial house, with several cars parked out front, some small trees, and a tower emerging from the second floor. I walked around the side to where Guillermo said he'd be. The scene included a little swimming pool, a monkey in a cage, and a thatched roof over a poolside patio. Guillermo had company: the head of Spain's technical assistance to Equatorial Guinea, a Spanish importer-exporter, and a Spanish diplomat. Also present was Guillermo's attractive, blonde wife, Marisol.

This was another world in Malabo, the world of the colonialist. Or better, ex-colonialist, as Guillermo's house was old and rundown, and the setting could not be called opulent. But an African servant was passing out the drinks, another tended Guillermo and Marisol's small son, and a third prepared the fire for cooking. The hors d'oeuvres had been imported from Cameroon and Spain. The style of conversation was the kind one seems to find among expatriates in almost every developing country I know: a combination of gossip about leading figures, complaints about "the system" and "the people," and great cynicism.

Later Marisol and I talked while the four men played dominoes next to us. She looked to be in her late thirties. She had come here four months before, having given up an advertising career in Barcelona to be with Guillermo for more than a few months a year. He had returned to the country when Macías was overthrown in 1979. Like all foreigners, Guillermo was not permitted to own land, but he could manage farms; in his case, he had joined with Aurelio and seven other cocoa growers to try to bust the duopoly that controlled the country's cocoa exports.

"I like being here," Marisol said. "There is time. You feel close to the earth, you can reach down and feel it. The Guineans are a wonderful people.

"On the other hand, there are many drawbacks. It is hard to find food.

There is little to do, little intellectual stimulation. You should bring along a trunk of books. And the people we see here at the house, they are the same." She motioned at the domino table. "They come every Sunday, play the game, relax. It is nice. But the people are the same, the conversations are the same. After a while, it can get suffocating."

After lunch, which was sumptuous compared with what I'd been eating, I went inside with Guillermo and read farm-management studies, export figures, and a paper he and his colleagues had prepared for the government last year. We talked over the problems of the cocoa industry. In the background his son was watching a twenty-three-inch color television. An English crime movie was being broadcast to the Equatoguinean population privileged enough to have a tube. The country had no newspaper or magazines; and indeed, none was available from abroad. But there on the national television station, a blonde woman was being knifed, to die screaming in a London street, crying out in dubbed Spanish.

I thanked Marisol, said goodbye to the Spaniards on the patio, and left the colonial world. Across the street were two shacks, also an abandoned concrete structure; beyond were some beautiful full palms and heavy leafed plants; and then the gorge and that awful hospital on the hillside across the way, evoking an old photograph of the Alcázar of Toledo after a siege in the Spanish Civil War.

The Project Takes Shape

Before our mission left the country, Heinz and Eric wanted to organize a meeting with the key ministers. On this occasion a brief summary of the team's findings would be presented, orally and with written copies.

Three days before the meeting, Heinz came down with malaria and was unable to complete his paper. The pages he did finish, I typed and translated till late at the U.N. office. Heinz recovered strength and, on the morning of the meeting, was slaving away to finish. He worked on the English, while in assembly-line style Eric and I translated and a hired secretary did the typing. We spent the morning transcribing in Eric and Heinz's hotel room, as Harmon napped on the couch. One big question was whether Heinz and the rest of us would finish by the time we met with the ministers. The other was, Would we meet with the ministers at all?

We had, of course, no "appointment." We waited for a call. Finally, at about one thirty, we walked to the Beiruth for lunch. As we were eating, the call was relayed from the hotel. "Please come immediately to the

Ministry of Education, Sport and Culture. The ministers are there and ready to meet you."

After racing back to the hotel and suiting up, we made it over to the Ministry of Education in fifteen minutes. We were taken to a second-floor conference room. The ministers weren't there. They were in the Minister of Education's office. Eric thought they would now make us wait for fifteen minutes. He was right.

The conference room was like a classroom, with aqua walls, fluorescent lights, and—of all things—a large blackboard at the head of the room. The table was high, and the chairs were low. A male secretary came in, wheeling a padded, office type of chair to the head of the table.

Finally, eight ministers entered, all the important ones except the Minister of Finance. Greetings were exchanged, but their faces weren't smiling. Don Ignacio, the cordial Foreign Minister, was the exception. He had a nice smile as he sat in the padded chair at the end of the table and ran the meeting. But the others looked depressed, even sullen.

Heinz began to read his summary, in German-accented Spanish. I watched the ministers. One had his brow knotted in what looked like anger. A couple were taking notes. Most were listening with their arms crossed. Heinz was laying it on them: the need for maintenance, the need for repairs, the need for a change of mentality about capital goods. The ministers looked sadder—and smaller. In the low chairs at the tall table, I realized that Don Constantino, the Minister of Planning, was only about five feet seven inches tall. Alongside me, the Minister of Industry and Commerce, who had looked formidable in his office, was barely able to rest his elbows on the conference table. The Vice Minister of Finance's stern face looked out of place only a few inches above the table top. Equatoguineans were not big; at six foot one, I was usually considerably taller than anyone else. But in this setting the disparities became symbolic: a veritable classroom, with the World Bank's Heinz giving a stern lecture and the country's most important ministers looking like schoolboys forced to sit through a subject they did not enjoy.

Then I realized that the padded chair that had been wheeled in was fully extended, so that the Foreign Minister, at the head of the table, looked like a six-footer. He was comfortably elevated above his colleagues and the equal in height to his three Western visitors.

Heinz finally finished. The Foreign Minister thanked him and asked the others for their comments. One minister complained that the amount of the proposed loan was too small. The Vice Minister of Finance said the project should be administered by the Ministry of Finance and should involve fewer expatriates. Heinz commented back. Then the meeting ended, stiffly. Class was over.

I kept trying to see Don Manuel, the Minister of Finance. No luck. Finally, I decided to work on Esmeralda, his surly secretary. How about lunch? Or a beer? Or a cup of coffee? One morning that week, I walked in and asked whether the minister was in, and Esmeralda said, "No, but you can take me out now for coffee."

Except for Harmon and me, the other team members had departed, and he was busy writing his report. So transportation was no longer a problem. I had a car and driver all day. I ushered Esmeralda into the back seat, and the driver drove us to a brand new spot that featured espresso coffee and Spanish sweets called *churros.* We went inside. The driver, emboldened by our buying his lunches most days, came along, sat at our table, and ordered a beer. I got a coffee. Esmeralda ordered a breakfast that would have surprised Mike Tyson.

Conversation came hard, if only because she kept eating and eating. Finally, she paused and touched my arm.

"What hotel are you staying at?"

Don't have one, staying at a house.

Esmeralda thought that one over. "Well," she said, leaning forward, "let's go away together to Douala." That's the commercial port of Cameroon.

Naw, don't have a visa. Um, let's get back to the ministry.

We drove there. Esmeralda got out and told the driver, "Pick me up at three, that's when I get off work." Then she instructed me. "See you after work. Let's go do something."

I muttered excuses. See you tomorrow, when I come back to see whether I can meet with the minister.

She disappeared, and I got back in the car. I looked at the driver, he looked at me, and we both laughed.

Aside from chasing appointments, I also chased papers. Eric asked me to fetch three documents from the cocoa project after they were signed by the President and assorted other officials. I had to retrieve another paper signed by the Minister of Finance regarding the rehabilitation project. Then there was the contract for my three-week consultancy to the Republic of Equatorial Guinea. For technical reasons, the contract had to be signed by Don Constantino, the Minister of Planning. And all week long, Salvador, the Guinean administrator of another World Bank project, had been asking

Don Constantino to sign, and Don Constantino hadn't done it. Now Don Constantino was asking Salvador what I had done to earn the money. That seemed reasonable. So, the morning before I was to leave, with a two-page outline of my report in hand, I went to the Planning Ministry to brief Don Constantino and get the contract signed. We had an "appointment."

He stood me up. I went to my other stops, looking for the other papers. No dice. Back to Planning. Don Constantino not in. Back to Finance for the second of two interesting conversations in two days with the vice minister. Then back to Planning. Waited in Salvador's office. It was slightly less humid than the tanks at Marine World. Salvador had given the minister my two-pager and the contract. Salvador was worried that he wouldn't sign. Finally, Don Constantino came to Salvador's office to talk to me—not about the substance of my report but about why he had to sign anything. I explained—twice. He said he couldn't sign. Then that he would sign. He left. Salvador went to his office. Salvador returned to say the minister said he'd sign it later.

The sky outside was as dark as a bruise. It began to rain, hard. I left in search of other papers—unsuccessfully. What a day!

I had arranged to meet Florencio and one of his colleagues for a farewell lunch. We sat at the Miramar, Malabo's other restaurant, with a spectacular view of the harbor. A breeze wafted by, and the menu featured sole.

Florencio asked me what I had learned, what I would say in my report. I gave a ten-minute briefing based on the outline I never got to discuss with the Minister of Planning. I outlined five key features of Equatorial Guinea's situation—the fact the country was split geographically, the awful deterioration under Macías, agriculture (not just cocoa) as the motor of growth, the labor shortage, and the devaluation and new currency. Then five obstacles to the country's medium-term development: the failure of certain markets to function (especially for credit, maintenance and spare parts, and labor); corruption; the lack of funds for public-sector capital investments; poor strategic planning in the public sector; and the need for external financing and foreign aid. Finally, how the proposed World Bank rehabilitation project—both the money and the process of administering it—could be used to help address each of those five obstacles.

The economy was in disarray. But it was an economy with a future. It would be a big success just to get production back to where it was twenty years ago. The country had abundant resources in cocoa, timber, coffee, and fishing. It might have oil and minerals. There was plenty of fertile land

and plenty of water. The proposed project had the money and the clout to make a big difference.

I finished. Florencio chewed on some bread, and then smiled.

"I have two reactions," he said. "First, you have an excellent vision. Second, you must come back to Equatorial Guinea. You must help us make that vision a reality."

We were drinking a beer at the end of the meal when Salvador arrived.

"Roberto, I've been looking for you everywhere," he puffed as I poured him a brew. "Don Constantino signed your contract! But he told me, 'Don't you ever do this to me again,' as if somehow I had deceived him."

That was good news—though Salvador reported that none of the other papers I was seeking would be ready before I departed.

"Stuck in Malabo Again"

That afternoon I walked around Malabo and then at six went to Maele's place. A few nights before, Harmon and I had stopped by Maele's house. I had taught everyone another song—"Lodi" by Creedence Clearwater Revival—but improvised on its words to make the chorus "Oh, Lord, I'm stuck in Malabo again." They had loved it. Maele had asked me to write down the words and music and bring it back to work on. A day later I had brought several copies of the English lyrics for Maele, along with the chords and a Spanish translation. But, though he was enthusiastic, his rehearsal went late, and he had said to come back early the next evening.

At six o'clock only a few people were in Maele's main room, devoid of furniture but full of mikes and amplifiers and drums. He got out the lyrics and music and his acoustic guitar. He gave me one of the electric ones. He is a lefty but, lacking a left-handed guitar, he just turned the guitar upside down and played it left-handed. This meant he had not only to learn all the chords and make all the runs on his own, but to reach a long way to play treble runs. He not only did it, he ripped.

We got to work on "Stuck in Malabo Again." We played it five times, just the two of us. I hummed a guitar solo I couldn't play; Maele picked it up and, two times later, had it down. He made suggestions. He wanted to repeat the chorus in each verse. He wanted two instrumental solos, one the Western one I'd suggested and the other an Africanized one.

Other folks began drifting in. The drummer who looked like Michael Jackson. Dayday. A famous singer from the Congo, who didn't speak English or Spanish but listened and liked, soon was joining us on the vocals. Equatorial Guinea's other rock star, Besosso. The female backup singers, who were soon joining on the chorus with a high and penetrating "Oh Lord, I stackin' Malabo agin." We were on the full equipment now. Harmon was helping Michael Jackson get the double pump on the foot pedal to the bass drum. We stopped several times to get the bass run right. We played the song again and again:

> *I came to Malabo by accident, on Air Iberia.*
> *Overslept my destination, Lagos, Nigeria.*
> *I've been here ever since, and till I don't know when,*
> *Oh Lord, I'm stuck in Malabo again!*
>
> *In the Malabo market you can find anything to eat,*
> *As long as you don't want vegetables or fresh fish or meat.*
> *You can buy a can of sardines if you gotta lotta money to spend.*
> *Oh Lord, I'm stuck in Malabo again!*
>
> *Malabo's got brand new money, they call it the C.F.A.*
> *They threw away the old stuff, the worthless ekuele.*
> *But all the cefas are gone now, taken by those foreign men.*
> *Oh Lord, I'm stuck in Malabo again!*
>
> *If Malabo could export friendship, we'd all be millionaires.*
> *Malabo people are very nice, take away all of your cares.*
> *If you go 'way from Malabo, you're gonna leave behind a lot of friends.*
> *So, oh Lord, let me come back to Malabo again!*
> *Oh Lord, let me come back to Malabo again!*

The room now had about forty people, and it was close to eight o'clock. Maele wanted a change in the last verse, where the song endorsed the wonderful people of Malabo and the chorus was "Oh Lord, let me come back to Malabo again."

"Let's have five repetitions of that last line," he said. "That will let the crowd get into it. They can clap their hands, they can sing along. Even though they don't know English, they will know these words if we repeat them. And it's a happy ending to the song."

So we tried it once that way. The crowd loved it. Harmon was now singing alongside one of the teenage high-pitched girls. The Congo guy was doing backup vocals with the two Nigerians. The bass guitarist had it down.

"So how about one more time, the last one?" I asked Maele, and he said yeah. I went around to all the musicians and singers, and we agreed we'd try to do it the best yet, the goodbye version. The crowd was eager, and everyone was laughing and smiling. Then it got quiet.

Michael Jackson gave us a one-two-three-four, and I started the guitar part. Then the bass and Maele came in, and the first verse began:

I came to Malabo by accident, on Air Iberia.
Overslept my destination, Lagos, Nigeria . . .

The place got wild. People sang and danced. Maele's guitar solo was amazing. Michael Jackson got his shot at a drum solo and hit the bull's eye. When we reached the last chorus—"Oh Lord, let me come back to Malabo again"—Maele had the whole audience involved, waving and clapping and singing, and he finished it off with a big guitar run.

It was a celebration. Everyone crowded around. We were shaking hands and hugging and laughing. As we left Maele's, Harmon and I felt a little dazed and very happy.

We wandered across town to a farewell party in our honor given by the Uruguayan librarian. We zoomed into the librarian's about six inches off the ground. We ate and drank, and then we sang. The librarian led the Latins in assorted love songs with vaguely cha-cha beats. By popular request, Harmon and I did "Stuck in Malabo Again." A future top-tenner in Equatorial Guinea, no doubt. Then it was off to bed for a heavy sleep.

The next morning Harmon and I went to the airport at seven. Lots of folks were at the airport to say goodbye or hello, including several of my new Guinean friends and several foreign-aid types. Harmon and I endured a two-hour wait, and finally walked out across the runway to the Iberia jet that visits Malabo once a week. As the plane took off, I thought to myself, there were two things I hadn't found here. I never got to talk with the Finance Minister. And I never saw any surf. No waves at all.

Then I glanced down at the coast of Bioko. Below was a beach at a point I hadn't visited. Lines of surf were rolling in. It looked like a nice left.

The stewardess gave me a glass of orange juice, my first in weeks. Look at it this way, I thought. You can meet the Finance Minister and ride those waves when you come back to Malabo again.

3

Witch Doctors

BACK in Malabo again. It was the end of June 1986, almost fourteen months after I left, and the foliage surrounding the airport was just as I remembered it: the rich greens of ferns and banana and cocoa and the majestic ceiba trees. The airport terminal still looked like a rural storage shed, and the humidity was about the 90 percent that the old Spanish books say is the average for Malabo year round.

It had taken much longer than expected to return to Equatorial Guinea. After we left in May 1985, the reports of the team members were assimilated at the World Bank into an economic rehabilitation project. I was told to be ready to begin work in Malabo in a few months. The Central American management school, INCAE, invited me to Costa Rica to spend those few months writing, and I accepted. The project suffered delay after delay, both in Washington and in Malabo. A few months turned into more than a year. In the meantime, I worked in Bolivia for a couple of months, consulted twice in Panama, made my second trip in two years to Nicaragua, and finished a book on élites in developing countries.

Now at last I was back in Malabo. I had passed a fitful, sweaty night on a bench in the Lagos airport after a delayed flight from Ghana, where I had spent a week looking at their economic rehabilitation project. In the Lagos airport neither food nor drink had been available. At dawn I boarded the Saturday morning Iberia flight. The flight attendants responded to my urgent request for sustenance with the airline equivalent of prison rations. Bread and water. To be fair, the bread did surround a sliver of cheese.

I was finally arriving in Equatorial Guinea as the economist/administrator for a ten-million-dollar project—a sum amounting to something like one seventh of the tiny nation's gross national product. A team of ministers and I would be spending that amount over the next two years to "rehabilitate" the Equatoguinean economy. We would be developing and, it was hoped, implementing an economic reform program for the country. I would have to co-sign every check. I wondered about my reception. Would the new Minister of Finance be at the airport to meet me—Don Bonifacio, who had replaced Don Manuel in a big shakeup in February? Would the Minister of Planning be there, the quirky Don Constantino, who wanted himself rather than the Finance Minister to control the ten million?

My reception turned out to be less grand than some of the scenarios I'd imagined. No one met me. After two hours of waiting for luggage and clearing customs, I snared a ride into Malabo and went to the Impala Hotel.

"No señor, no reservation for you. And there won't be any room anywhere in Malabo. The government is hosting a big conference for UDEAC." This was the Central African economic union that Equatorial Guinea had joined a year and a half before. "Important representatives from neighboring countries have taken all the rooms. The government has decreed it. We even had to discharge long-time guests from their rooms."

So I tried the other hotel, the Ureka. It had a room. No air-conditioning, no water. Since the city's electrical generators were being repaired and rebuilt with German help, we had electricity only from a little after dusk till about midnight. I didn't know what was wrong with the water. The problem was not scarcity. It was the wet season, with up to a foot of rain a week. During downpours the streets were transformed into muddy rapids. I was told to fill the bathtub with cold water during the hour in the morning when the water was running. It was advice I came to value. After walking through Malabo's streets drenched with sweat, I would return to the room, undress, and ease myself into the cold bath. A few minutes later, my body temperature lowered to humane levels, I would lie on the bed, arms and legs outstretched, and wonder how I had ever fancied myself an energetic person.

I spent early Saturday night at the Beiruth restaurant watching a World Cup soccer game beamed in from nearby Cameroon, then went to a rock concert at the Teatro Marfil. This rundown structure had music once every few months. This time the protagonists were Besosso, one of Guinea's two rock stars, and some visiting Frenchmen. To my delight, a French guitarist ripped on "Hotel California"; but the Africans liked it better when Besosso did big rhythm African rock, with three tireless and shapely female dancers shaking in unison alongside him. After a Sunday foray into the countryside, I returned at night to the Beiruth for more televised soccer, now with some newly found acquaintances and fellow beer drinkers. The Spaniards were there in force to see their national team play at eleven at night, and wandered home saddened and besotted after its defeat.

Monday morning was overcast, as most days those months. I suited up and wandered over to the Beiruth for breakfast. Sitting at the bar with a cup of coffee, I read over the legal documents concerning the economic rehabilitation project. I made notes for myself about what I had to do with the Finance Minister that morning, including getting my contract signed. A Guinean fellow about my age, also in a suit, was the only other patron. He sipped a cup of coffee. I asked him whether he'd watched the game the previous night. He hadn't, but chatted about the games he had seen so far and about the sad reaction of Guineans to the Spanish loss. The locals retain not only the Castilian lisp but the sporting loyalties of their colonial masters.

Eventually I asked him where he worked, and he said the Finance Ministry across the street.

"At what?" I asked.

"It is under my direction," he responded.

"Are you Don Bonifacio, the Minister of Finance?

"Yes, I am."

"Well, I was just coming to see you this morning." I explained who I was and what I was doing there.

"Señor Klitgaard! We did not know you were coming! When did you arrive?"

I told him, and he said to come by his office in twenty minutes. I did so, delighted that someone knew of my existence.

The ministry had been cleaned up some, but walking to the second floor via a crumbling staircase around the back of the building, you still looked down on a humble courtyard full of banana trees and chickens and discarded tires and half-naked infants. Don Bonifacio's office was being renovated, so we sat in the Vice Minister's office. I gave him some documents from Washington, a report on my week's visit to Ghana, and the draft contract the World Bank had prepared for me. Don Bonifacio was friendly but distracted. Visitors were announced by his secretary—no longer the redoubtable Esmeralda—and he was able to escape for only a few minutes to talk with me.

Leaving the ministry, I saw across the street Salvador, the Guinean who administered the World Bank-funded technical assistance project. We embraced, and he took me to the Planning Ministry on the other side of town, where I spent the rest of the morning meeting with the Planning Minister. Don Constantino said I would be working at his ministry. He showed me new offices he was building for the people on the technical assistance project. I explained to him that the project called for me to work at the Finance Ministry. That was the first piece of bad news. Later I told him that the World Bank had decided that Don Bonifacio and not Don Constantino would chair the new ministerial committee. Don Constantino disagreed. And I said that Don Bonifacio would be the person to sign my contract. Don Constantino again disagreed.

This set the tone for the first few days of work. I was greeted cordially enough—wouldn't you be nice to ten million dollars?—but the preoccupation was almost entirely with who would sign what and who would convene meetings and where my office would eventually be located. Meanwhile, I learned that all logistical matters had lain in limbo. The government was supposed to provide me with an office, a car, and a furnished place to live. But nothing had been done.

Mysterious Powers

I had heard a lot about Don Milagroso.

"He's the power behind the Finance Minister," an official from the International Monetary Fund had told me in Washington. "Watch him carefully. He is very dangerous. He pulls the strings.

"He is a witch doctor. He is the Darth Vader of the government. He may try to take all the money of the economic rehabilitation project and decide himself what to do with it."

A week after arriving, I was to meet with Don Milagroso. Our appointment was at eight thirty on a Saturday morning. The night before, a knowledgeable friend in Malabo summed up his impressions of Don Milagroso.

"Listen, he could be anything with you. He could be lucid and charming"—the friend held up his first finger—"or he could be stoned out of his mind at eight thirty in the morning"—second finger displayed—"or he could be drunk"—the ring finger. "You could be a minute late and he'd chastise you, or you could be waiting an hour and a half for him to show up. With Don Milagroso, it's a complete lottery."

I had met Don Milagroso briefly on Wednesday afternoon. The Finance Minister had told him of my arrival. In the Gue Gué Restaurant, where I was lunching with a local Spaniard who was advising me about housing, in walked Don Milagroso (the Spaniard said). A young man, about thirty-five or forty, short, round-faced, with a wrinkled brow and a slight mustache, almost boyish looking: Darth Vader he did not appear, nor did his suit and tie resemble the trappings of a witch doctor.

I went over and introduced myself. Don Milagroso was friendly, introducing me to his companions. I said I'd come by and make an appointment, and this I did on Friday, being told to come back the next morning at eight thirty.

Given my friend's warning, I got there early.

Don Milagroso was the director of the equivalent of the central bank, the Banque des Etats de l'Afrique Centrale. Called BEAC, it really was the Equatoguinean branch of the bank for UDEAC, the regional currency union. The other member nations were deeply involved in managing this currency union, with French advisers; but Don Milagroso was the Guinean in charge of the local branch—the country's big money man. He had been director of the country's central bank during Macías's reign in the 1970s. Don Milagroso was then said to be the youngest head of a central bank anywhere in the world.

BEAC and Don Milagroso were important to me for several reasons. My project had to set up several accounts there. One account would provide a rotating loan fund for the Banco de Crédito y Desarrollo, the state development bank—or this was the original plan. The BCD had recently gone bankrupt. Its future was unclear; some said the bank would need to be rebuilt from scratch. Since "my" project's funds would be providing a good chunk of liquidity for the bank, I had to understand the banking system better.

Even apart from the bankrupt BCD, banking was a mess. The only commercial bank was Guinextebank—half Spanish, half government—and it was virtually insolvent. You could go there to exchange two hundred dollars, and the bank officers would tell you they simply did not have the liquidity to cover it. Government employees could not cash their paychecks, and depositors could not withdraw money from their own bank accounts. All the *cefa* francs (CFAF)—usable in the neighboring countries that were members of UDEAC—seemed to have left Equatorial Guinea. It was an urgent problem. People recalled that the overthrow of Macías in 1979 had been preceded by a liquidity crisis where banks could not cash paychecks for eight months.

Perhaps if I could establish a good working relationship with Don Milagroso, we might be able to use some of my project's funds to tackle strategic problems of the banking sector.

The BEAC buildings were modernistic monstrosities. Built under Macías and featured on the back of the old one-thousand *bikuele* bill, the complex included a dome pocked with square windows in a spiral pattern, and a connected white concrete box with waffle-iron windows right out of Silicon Valley. You entered through the dome. It might as well have been a rink for roller skating. Only the space at its rim was used, and much of that, even on Friday, consisted of unoccupied desks. I turned left past a sign in French and ascended stairs that resembled a series of huge dominoes joined at one end and forming another spiral. The second-floor waiting room had high ceilings, and its sand-colored walls were finished in stylishly rough concrete. The chairs were heavy Scandinavian with corduroy, and the coffee table was an irregular triangle of glass. The place had about as much to do with Equatorial Guinea as a retrospective exhibit of de Stijl.

At eight thirty the informally dressed man who seemed to handle appointments said that Don Milagroso would see me in a few minutes. And after a few minutes he led me to the end of a long, glassy corridor, through an opaque door to a secretary's office, and then, after knocking on another door, into Don Milagroso's office.

It was slightly smaller than a heliport. Don Milagroso greeted me in front of a desk as big as a Ping-Pong table, led me on the walk past leather-and-chrome chairs over to a large sofa-and-easy-chair combo, and asked me to be seated.

"Sorry, I have a terrible cold," he said with a snort into imported French pocket tissues. "I am glad you are here."

I told Don Milagroso that I was pleased to meet him and hoped that he and I would be close colleagues working with the economic rehabilitation project. I had come to request his help in setting up the project's accounts at BEAC. Also, I said, I needed to understand the problems of the credit market and of the banking system generally, and I brought up the rotating fund for the BCD.

"As I understand it," Don Milagroso said, "the rotating fund would work as follows." He gave an accurate account. I liked the way he closed: "The purpose of this half million dollars is to make additional loans to small businesses, workshops, and cooperatives, which are starved of capital."

We then talked for a while about the problems of small and medium-sized businesses. Don Milagroso explained that the credit market didn't work for these enterprises. It was a topic in which I had long been interested. We talked over Equatorial Guinea's economic reforms. I expressed some worries. The experience of other countries had shown that such reforms might benefit primarily the foreigners and the already privileged, who were able to take advantage of new markets in a time of scant liquidity. So, I asked, shouldn't special efforts be made to help local entrepreneurs? It was something Don Milagroso had thought about; he had even taught classes for small businesses in the mainland city of Bata. The conversation was full of nods of affirmation. Common ground.

We talked some more about the economic rehabilitation project. We agreed that the project should not just be a source of money for imports but a lever to help reform systems of public procurement and private-sector credit. I wasn't expecting his eloquence or apparent social concern. Don Milagroso's voice was soft, but he spoke with enthusiasm.

"You know, it is very good that you are here," he said. "I know you will find that your ideas are exactly in accord with those of the President. We will have to see to it that you meet with him. He will be happy to hear what you say.

"Has the government set up a counterpart for you in the Ministry of Finance?" he asked.

"Not yet," I replied. But I asked Don Milagroso a question. Since he and I and the Finance Minister and the others should work as a team—and since we were all about the same age—might we not be counterparts to each other?

Don Milagroso smiled and nodded. "Let me give you my private number. Any time you have a problem or want to talk, just call me."

He added further cordialities, and it was clear that our appointment was ending. But he added a final point.

"Your ideas are in accord with the President's," he murmured in a manner I can only describe as dreamy. "And I urge you that if you run into any difficulties here, any obstacles, with me or with the Finance Minister or with anyone, please do not despair. The President knows what occurs." These last words were spoken slowly. "He may not know the reality of what you are experiencing. But you can always tell him what that reality is, and he will listen to you and resolve your problem."

We said goodbye. In the lottery of Don Milagroso, I had surely drawn the lucid and charming outcome. There was a good chance, I thought, that we might work closely together, even become friends. As I embarked alone down that long corridor, I wondered about his eerie remarks about his omniscient and benevolent President. They almost resembled a priest's invoking of the Almighty. Was that what was meant by "witch doctor"?

Stone-Broke

I obtained all the reports and data I could find on Equatorial Guinea's economy. I pored over them. The country's situation was dismal, worse than on my first visit. But, again, I thought the medium-term prospects for growth looked good—at least compared with Bolivia or Nicaragua, where all I could foresee was continued decline.

The first thing that had to be said about the data and the analyses was that they disagreed. The United Nations had one set of estimates; the World Bank, another; and the International Monetary Fund, a third. The differences could be large. Take what seemed like a simple projection. What would Equatorial Guinea's exports be in 1988, two years hence?

In April 1986, the World Bank said $42.4 million.

In February 1986, the U.N. said $34.4 million.

In April 1986, the IMF said $29.5 million.

While one wouldn't be surprised by, say, a 5- or 10-percent discrepancy, the World Bank's estimate of exports for 1988 was 44 percent higher than the IMF's.

Formal economic planning is almost impossible when basic economic parameters are this uncertain. We did not have a reliable idea of the rate of inflation, the size of the economy, or even the population of the country. The mathematical modeling of an economy is always uncertain; in Equatorial Guinea it seemed impossible.

You couldn't believe the government's budget. A lot of spending went on that did not appear in it—until later, that is, when funds supposed to be there turned out to be missing.

In the balance of payments, there were huge entries in the category called "errors and omissions," a kind of catch-all accounting label that enables the books to balance. A few numbers give an idea of how big the errors and omissions were. In 1985, exports were about $23 million, imports about $33 million, and the deficit on the current account was about $8 million. The "errors and omissions" category totaled about $9 million and was the largest chunk of the country's $14-million balance of payments deficit. A lot of this was money that had left the country, often illicitly. Equatorial Guinea's new, convertible currency meant that you could take money out and readily convert it to French francs. Preliminary information from the Central African currency union and the Bank of France showed that at least $2.5 million had left the country in bank notes alone.

Equatorial Guinea did not know exactly to whom it owed how much money or when it was payable. It had recently set up an office to try to sort this out. The IMF's estimates of the debt burden were alarming. In July 1985, the payment of over $45 million of Equatorial Guinea's international debt had been rescheduled by the so-called Paris Club, a consortium of lenders. Though the IMF called this "generous," one of its reports noted that merely to pay the interest on the estimated $118 million of international debts would take up 105 percent of Equatorial Guinea's 1985 exports, more than three times the proportion in comparable countries.

Equatorial Guinea was broke. The consequences were everywhere. Since the country had not maintained the airport, for several months last year Iberia had canceled all flights in protest. The Central Bank had expanded credit too much and too fast, leading to what one report called "a weak loan portfolio"—in plain talk, loans that would never be repaid. And from 1982 to 1984, credit to the public sector, mostly to public enterprises, had gone from 5 percent of total credit to 39 percent. Yet the public enterprises were losing money too, so that money would never be repaid. The energy company was charging for electricity a price only about two thirds of the average cost. Even so, less than a third of the bills were being paid. No wonder the street lights were now shut off, and the city had electricity only a few hours every evening.

What was the good news? You had to keep reminding yourself that the country used to produce about three times as much per person in real terms as it did today. Whereas now the country was importing food and palm oil, in the 1960s it was exporting both. Now we imported fish, then we exported fish. (I had already started unconsciously to think of Equatorial Guinea as "our" country.) Cocoa production was five times higher in 1965 than in 1985; coffee exports ten times higher. We had lots of timber, maybe some petroleum and minerals. We had fertile land, and we didn't have many people. And President Obiang had promulgated macroeconomic reforms to open up and stabilize the economy.

So why couldn't we make great strides in the next few years? It was becoming clear to me that most of the money from the economic rehabilitation project would have to be used simply to pay back some of Equatorial Guinea's international debts. But couldn't we use some of our project's resources to deepen and implement free-market reforms, improve the infrastructure, help the poor? Couldn't this be the basis for Equatorial Guinea's first structural adjustment program?

The Clan

Casa Mota is one of Equatorial Guinea's largest cocoa exporters. It was here long before independence, remained during Macías's ruinous reign, and was now continuing in the post-1979 regime of President (and Colonel) Obiang Nguema Mbasogo. That's staying power. Nineteen eighty-five had been a terrible year for Casa Mota and the cocoa business as a whole. Overall production in Equatorial Guinea dropped from about 8,000 tons to about 5,000. Untimely rains were partly to blame. So was a run on cocoa farms by government officials the year before.

When the World Bank's cocoa project was approved in late 1983, top government officials had foreseen a gold mine. "The World Bank will be giving credit to those with cocoa farms. Let's get cocoa farms." And so in 1984 there were draconian nationalizations of farms that had not been continually occupied during the Macías terror. Most had been owned by Spaniards and Portuguese; now government ministers held title to the choicest farms. The Prime Minister had a beauty near Luba, and the President himself seized nearly four thousand acres near the Malabo airport. These new "farmers" went to the BCD and the Guinextebank, demanded loans, and got them. Often the money they received was squandered on cars and video recorders, not on lime and copper sulphate for the cocoa trees. Yields plummeted. When the harvest came a cropper, the ministers couldn't pay their loans—nor could many other debtors. Casa Mota itself was out CFA 91 million in bad debts to the farmers it loaned to and bought from—about $260,000. Another large cocoa-exporting group—Guillermo and Aurelio's APECSA—had extended almost a million dollars in unpaid loans. Casa Mota and APECSA had in turn borrowed much of this money from the banks. This was "the weak loan portfolio" mentioned in the economic reports; and in this way, the country's credit system had been paralyzed.

I met some of the Spaniards working for Casa Mota, thanks to my friend Morton, the bearded, wisecracking English cocoa–quality-control expert whom I had met the year before. One evening we watched a World Cup soccer game on TV at the massive Casa Mota residence, a lovely old three-story structure near the port. The large second-floor common room had a bar, a dining area, old oil paintings of Africans and cocoa fields, and a color television. About fifteen people in their twenties and thirties were there. They displayed a remarkable combination of gentlemanly politeness and the ability to have a raucous good time. There were plenty of jokes and beers, and afterward some singing of Spanish songs; but also in evidence were courtesy and respect, even a kind of courtliness. The Casa Mota people asked me back a few days later, and before long I became something of a regular at their house. They were domino players but in the Spanish style, and I taught them our American version, which they came to enjoy.

Late one night a bunch of us were playing dominoes upstairs. While playing, we often talked about cocoa, and they were excellent teachers. Now the topic was politics.

"The government is dominated by the Mongomo clan," one of them said. Mongomo is a town located at the eastern edge of the mainland portion of Equatorial Guinea called Río Muni, almost at the border of Gabon, and is inhabited by a particularly fierce subset of the Fang ethnic group. "The President is the nephew of Macías himself. The power of the country is held in the major families of Mongomo and has been since independence. They say that village elders make a lot of the big political decisions, in ways no outsider understands. The objective of most of the Mongomo clan in government is to take care of their family, their clan, and later the broader world of the Fang people. The rest of the peoples of the mainland, or the Bubi people here on the island, may as well be foreigners."

Don Constantino, the Planning Minister, was from Mongomo. Don Bonifacio was not; he was half Spanish and half from a small ethnic group from the island of Corisco on the southwestern shore of Río Muni. Don Bonifacio's Vice Minister of Finance was from the clan and had been charged, it was said, with keeping an eye on him.

"Obiang is trying to build a strong system around himself," another domino player said. The President's birthday is a national holiday, and his somewhat worried-looking portrait hung in every office, store, and home—even in Casa Mota's living room. "But he has to keep the clan happy. He has put many of them in top government positions, even when they are venal and incompetent. And he can't trust them, either. He's afraid of disloyalty."

"That's right," put in a third player. "When the President leaves the country, all the roads are blocked and the soldiers come and make you close and shutter your windows if your house is facing the road. And while he's out of the country they keep guards on the airport and the radio station and the palace." The presidential guard was not Equatoguinean but consisted of some six hundred troops from Morocco. Dressed in fatigues and with brown skin, high noses, and sinister mustaches, they could be seen patroling the entrances to the presidential area of the city, the airport, had suggested. Doubtless, my connection with the World Bank made the locals recalculate.

Still, I liked the place. Gómez invited me back for dinner sometime. I left with a cordial handshake and began to check out him and the apartment in earnest. It turned out it belonged to someone else. Gómez was himself renting it, unfurnished, for about a fifth of the price he was asking from me.

I saw Gómez again one afternoon and asked him whether he was the owner. Eh, no, not actually, he admitted. But there would be no problem in getting the owner to approve a sublet. We left it that he would make a list of all the furniture in the house and arrange an appointment for me with the owner as soon as possible.

Gómez made good on his dinner invitation a few days later, so I brought over a bottle of wine and a quart of beer, and he and Juana greeted me warmly if still with a bit of stiffness. Two little black girls joined us for dinner, one about eleven and the other about three. They turned out to be relatives of Juana's for whom she and Gómez were caring with all the warmth and affection of their own children. The family setting was welcome after too many restaurant meals and too many all-male sessions at Casa Mota and elsewhere. The children broke the ice. Gómez loosened up, and Juana laughed. The chicken was succulent, and his stories about his fascinating, up-and-down career kept my interest.

Four days later I finally met with the owner, a painfully shy young Guinean. He wanted to double his rental charge in order to sublet to me. I explained that I didn't want to pay more than the fair market value of the property. I would keep looking.

So five weeks after arriving, I was without a place to live. No mail had arrived in the country during that period, nor had my air freight, concerning whose whereabouts the airlines expressed complete puzzlement. I had no office and no form of transportation save the soles of my shoes. Oh Lord, I'm stuck in Malabo again.

Don Milagroso and I met in his capacious office to go over the technicalities of opening the project's accounts at BEAC. Don Milagroso stood in front of his desk to receive me. He walked forward and shook my hand. He wore a long-sleeved dark blue shirt-jacket with matching pants.

"Why didn't you call me?" he said. "You don't have to wait for appointments. I told you to call whenever you need me."

I thanked him for that courtesy and asked him if he'd overcome his cold. He had. After a few more cordialities, we discussed banking procedures

and their own barracks in the center of town, alongside which one was not permitted to walk or drive.

I asked what they knew about Don Milagroso.

"Whoa, very powerful," one man exclaimed. "From one of the most important families of Mongomo."

"Yes, powerful and smart," said another. "The other day we were presenting our cost figures to him on cocoa production, trying to get him to understand why the export tax has to be reduced. He saw a place right away where we had accidentally double-counted. Not many people would have seen it, but he did—right away."

Why was Don Milagroso so powerful?

"He has mysterious sources of power." another said. When I asked what he meant, he looked at me furtively. "It's some kind of diabolical thing, they say. He has a power over others from Mongomo. He's always been a force around here, even in the time of Macías. Don Milagroso is very strong."

Witchcraft

Witchcraft was widespread in Equatorial Guinea, as in many parts of Africa. The locals relied on indigenous healers; and I had heard that in other parts of the world, Western doctors were taking native remedies more seriously these days. But a Chinese doctor working in Malabo took a little of the luster off the idea that the witch doctors' medicines worked well.

"We get people in the hospital here that are so messed up with infections and unhealed fractures. They go to witch doctors, and their injuries grow much worse as a result. Sometimes they die. I know that we could save some of those who die from malaria and stomach problems if we could treat them instead of the witch doctors."

I was reading about the Fang and their witchcraft. The interior of what was now Río Muni was one of the last places in Africa to be explored by Europeans. Paul Du Chaillu in 1856 was one of the first to penetrate the area of the Fang. He was surprised to discover cannibalism. Surprised, because despite all the stories about Africa, the French explorer knew that there was little evidence of such practices.

"I perceived some bloody remains which looked to me human," Du Chaillu wrote, "but I passed on, still incredulous. Presently we passed a woman who solved all doubt. She bore with her a piece of the thigh of a human body, just as we should go to market and carry thence a roast or a steak." The evidence accumulated as Du Chaillu traversed Fang territory. Human bones were thrown outside the houses of villagers, mixed with other offal. "In fact, symptoms of cannibalism stare me in the face wherever I go, and I can no longer doubt."[1]

In the 1890s, the English adventuress Mary Kingsley also discovered grisly indicators of necrophagy. Visiting a Fang village, she spent the night in a two-room house. In the early hours a smell pervaded her apartments, and she tracked it down to a small bag hanging from one of the roof joists. She emptied the contents into her hat. "They were a human hand, three big toes, four eyes, two ears, and other portions of the human frame. The hand was fresh, the others only so-so, and shrivelled." Kingsley thought it "touching" that the Fangs should keep a little something of their victims by way of a memento.[2]

Today's Fangs lay heavy emphasis on witchcraft; and according to the only recent Spanish book on their culture, cannibalism still plays a part.

In *n'buo* or witchcraft resides the explanation of any extraordinary phenomenon—animate, physical, or spiritual—in the life of these peoples. It constitutes the great resource and panacea in all actions. . . . The gift of making magic is localized in the *evú*, which according to their stories is a kind of polyp that resides in the stomach of those who have this quality of influencing or manipulating the spirit of the rest. . . .

The *beyem* or witch doctors have to nourish their *evú* with human flesh, assimilating at the same time the qualities of the dead person being eaten. To obtain this macabre meal, they will unearth important people, since the power of their flesh is greater. They eat specific parts, especially the brain and the guts, wherein reside the vital forces. The flesh is seasoned by the expert witch doctors with all sorts of magical sauces, and it is then ingested in nocturnal meetings, almost always in the jungle, under the influence of the forces residing there.[3]

When I would ask about witchcraft or about Don Milagroso's supposed powers, people were evasive. I was told that Macías himself practiced sorcery, that he asked the witch doctors of every village to give him their magical staffs. Macías kept all the staffs together, drawing on their combined powers; and he and his collaborators passed on to the people stories of his supernatural powers. It was said that Macías practiced cannibalism; and a humble electrician in Malabo told me in all sincerity that when Macías had died, the very earth had spewed forth blood.

Property Rights

Perhaps I would need to summon up some magic to f[...] I had moved from the Ureka Hotel to a ramshackle s[...] Impala, which had been vacated by an American radio[...] home for the summer. The technician was worried about[...] ence goers taking over his suite, and I was worried abou[...] in a cocoa field. We had, as they say, a mutuality of in[...]

My new quarters had electricity much of the day, [...] hotel's generator, and there was hot water. But I was eag[...] of my own. The Impala was okay but had its share of inse[...] I walked into my bathroom at the Impala and heard th[...] something falling. I looked around and saw nothing and[...] business. As I was washing my hands, I saw something n[...] corner of my eye. There, running laps around the empty[...] tarantula the size of my fist.

My search for places to live had so far been like my sea[...] Both objects of my desire were scarce and hard to find, a[...] found them, small and unexciting. I heard about a furnishe[...] Spaniard named Gómez wanted to rent. After much uneve[...] around, that sounded great. Since Malabo had no furnitur[...] nished place would save months of hassles importing, clea[...] getting reimbursed, moving in, and so forth.

One remarkable problem in Equatorial Guinea was prope[...] was often unclear who the owner of a piece of property[...] abounded of rip-offs and frauds. You might rent a place from[...] only to find out two months later that it belonged to someo[...] the government.

I had asked a Guinean acquaintance about Gómez. "Hmm, [...] he said. "Don't trust him. Stay away." But why? "I can't te[...] watch out."

So I was watching out when I arrived at Gómez's second-sto[...] walled, two-bedroom apartment. It had wicker furniture, a tele[...] a double bed, lots of light—and a refrigerator and a freezer. G[...] about fifty, with gray hair waving back from his forehead, sad[...] a try at a smile. The mouth of his mulatto wife, Juana, mo[...] naturally. We sat down and talked about the apartment. Gómez [...] he was going to Bata to set up a business. He wanted to rent the a[...] and sell the furniture; or he would rent the furniture and the ap[...] We talked price, which was higher than what his friend who had[...]

and then the economy. He impressed me with his quickness, his responsiveness, his ability to see big and small issues with equal facility.

We ended up talking a lot about training. Next year the donors of foreign aid to Equatorial Guinea would hold a big meeting with the government. The idea was to coordinate the donors' efforts—no small task since each donor had its own aims and bureaucracies, and an important task since foreign aid made up such a large chunk of the country's national income. I asked whether the Guineans would be prepared for this conference and the ensuing negotiations. Was there the risk that whatever the donors decided would be stuffed down the Guineans' throats? Would it be a good idea before the conference to provide some training on economic and sectoral strategies for middle- and high-level government officials?

Don Milagroso was enthusiastic. He talked about his own interest in economic strategies.

"I was in charge of all the negotiations for our integration into UDEAC," he explained. "Before that, I wrote a university thesis on the economies of Central Africa. I would love to work together with you, to share these things with you. Why don't we do this? Let's get together, you and me and the Minister of Finance, and let's systematically go through three subjects. First, the economic rehabilitation project—what it entails, its steps and requirements, its strategic uses. Second, the idea of a series of seminars for people from the Ministry of Finance, BEAC, and maybe other technical experts on economic strategies. Third, what training might be good for other small- and medium-sized enterprises."

We agreed to get back in touch. The more I was getting to know Don Milagroso, the more I liked him.

Who Cares?

One evening, I went with Morton and Everton, the head of the cocoa project, to Guillermo and Marisol's for supper. They lived in one of Malabo's nicest old houses. As we entered the house this evening, Guillermo was playing a computerized musical keyboard. In the large and airy living room, a covered billiard table stood in the foreground, and at the rear was a set of large flowered chairs and couches around a big low table. Dark wood ran halfway up the walls. Two air-conditioners hummed away near the top corners, and a fan turned slowly overhead. In an adjacent, darkened office, I saw the blue glow of a computer console which had been left on, spreadsheet in place. Guillermo had been working out the costs of cocoa production—a topic we had discussed the year before.

A servant brought out beer and whisky and hors d'oeuvres of toasted cheese and ham with figs. My beer sat on the table in front of an elegant ebony sculpture of a hippopotamus on the run. In the corner was a bigger-than-life bust in light wood of Guillermo, which faithfully reproduced his beard and handlebar mustache and his laughing eyes.

I had talked with my Spanish friends Guillermo and Marisol twice since my return—at the previous Friday's Fourth of July party at the U.S. Embassy and at another party on Saturday. They were a wonderful couple. Marisol was attractive and effervescent. She wore big glasses and a contagious smile. Guillermo was forceful and funny and full of tales.

Cocoa was the topic of conversation. On the previous Friday, the government had set this year's purchase price to be paid to farmers for cocoa. The exporters howled. With world cocoa prices down about a third since the beginning of the year, the relatively high purchase price, coupled with the continuation of the 30-percent export tax, would squeeze their profits. "No one will buy cocoa, because you would lose money doing so." When I saw Guillermo Friday night, he had been drinking heavily, apparently in lament. He was still singing the blues.

"We have to make the case that a thirty-percent export tax is too much," he said. "But we can't make that case because no one cares."

But weren't many ministers also owners of cocoa farms, and wouldn't their self-interest induce the right perspective?

"Yes, but they don't care about profitability. They will just default on their loans," Guillermo said, never losing the twinkle in his eyes even while complaining. "They don't pay the banks back, so they make out all right even when the prices are all wrong. They default, and so will I. That's the only way we won't lose our shirts on cocoa."

At dinner the conversation ranged widely. Guillermo and Marisol told amusing stories about the zealous local Cuban diplomats, all true believers or at least true preachers. "We don't have crime or drugs or prostitution," they declared. Marisol thought at least one of them was too smart "really to believe such rot." The malaria epidemic was discussed. Guillermo had contracted a strong case ten days back. Cerebral malaria had arrived, which the locals called *el martillo,* "the hammer." It is resistant to chloroquine, the standard prophylactic, and can cause death or brain damage. I had been shocked at many serious cases of malaria in Malabo. Almost everyone I had met, Guinean or foreign, rich or poor, had either suffered from the disease or had a family member fall victim. A United Nations employee had to go home to Holland for three months to recuperate. Had anyone,

I asked, looked into the cost and effectiveness of a malaria eradication campaign?

"There is no way to stop it here," Guillermo said. "Look at all the rain, and look at the hygiene. These people don't care. Out back of this house we look over the presidential compound. There's a garbage dump right behind the President's house. They just toss things out there, filth and trash, and it festers on the hillside."

After dinner, for my edification as new arrival, the conversation turned to accounts of the anomalies (and worse) of local life.

"We do some importing, you know," Guillermo said. "The government tries to get you in the funniest ways. For example, there are taxes for the 'biological inspection' of gin, chickens, you name it. Allegedly for testing purposes, they insist on taking two bottles of gin per case. Then they charge us a hundred and fifty *cefas* [about fifty cents] per chicken for 'inspection.' If we don't pay, they'll hassle us. The chickens we import are frozen. Unless we pay them a bribe, they ask us to unfreeze them for testing. Then say they can't get to it, and tell us to freeze them back up again. And so on till you pay."

"And you should see their testing laboratory," Marisol put in. "You can imagine—no equipment, not even a microscope. A lot of people sitting around drunk."

"The government has started to charge for electricity," Guillermo noted, "which is fine. But we don't use their electricity. We have our own generator. That doesn't exempt us. The electricity man will say, 'Okay, pay a charge to us for your generator.' Arguing doesn't do any good. For water they have tried to charge us two hundred and eighty thousand *cefas* [about $800] a month! I asked them where they got that figure, and they said, 'You have a small swimming pool, and besides you whites bathe a lot.' No one else in town pays. They pick on a few of us they think have money."

Everton and Morton added their own examples. Everton's tone was more venomous than Guillermo and Marisol's; Morton's more morose.

Inevitably the discussion returned to cocoa. Guillermo despaired of having the government understand the economics of cocoa production and marketing.

"The ministers can't add! Even those who call themselves government economists and planners can't work a simple balance sheet. Take the Minister of Finance. He used to work at BEAC as Milagroso's deputy. Apparently he was good at narrow calculations at the bank. But he can't get the big picture. Milagroso can. He has others do his work, but he can pull it together. He's smart."

Despite the good natures of Guillermo and Marisol, the stories were starting to chafe. Around the globe, expatriate complaining has in common an alienated sense of superiority and a hopeless verdict. Whenever I asked about practical matters, about what could be done to alleviate the problems they cited, Everton or Guillermo would snap back almost impatiently that nothing could be done, that nobody *cared.*

Take cocoa, for example. If one is trying to decide short-run policies toward cocoa, a key question is what things looked like over the longer term. Is cocoa viable in the long run in Equatorial Guinea—even without export taxes? Is cocoa rehabilitation worthwhile, given world prices, local costs, and the lack of labor? Sometimes in conversations with Morton and Everton, I heard no as the answer. But it was hard to get them to address such questions straight on. It was easier to say that no one cared; or that everyone was robbing; or that even if the problem they had just been complaining about were in fact cleared up, there was another problem that made it all hopeless, around which a new round of stories would commence.

Morton in particular seemed defeated. A year ago I had liked and admired his idealism, competence, and desire to make a difference. But then he had only been here six weeks; now he seemed broken.

On the way home Morton and Everton drove by two cocoa warehouses to see whether the guards were on duty. So, I thought, whatever their cynicism, Morton and Everton did care. Good for them. I asked gently how they viewed the cocoa project now. What were its points of leverage, given all the problems we had discussed this evening? Why, after all, were Everton and Morton still here?

"I don't know," said Everton. "There are financial reasons of course. We're paid well to be here. Then some days I feel good about our project. Someone will come through on a farm thanks to a loan you gave him, or someone will tell us we're helping out and doing a good job. Then the next day I feel that progress is an illusion.

"But, you know, you will find that farmer who is producing five hundred eighty kilos of cocoa per hectare* while his neighbors are getting only two hundred and fifty, and he's paying back his loans. He's done it through his hard work. And I think, maybe we can help people like that."

---

*Just under 1,300 pounds for every 2½ acres.

The IMF Descends

The next morning I got word that Don Milagroso wanted me to come to a meeting at eleven at the BEAC. Guy was there, the fiftyish French budget specialist working with the Ministry of Finance. Gaunt and stooping, his posture suggested someone taller than his five-foot-ten. Several Guineans were also present. Also there was a woman I hadn't met, a chain-smoking French ectomorph whose job it was to make sense of records of public spending in the Ministry of Finance.

"I am leaving in three weeks, thank goodness," she told me. "No more here." The two shafts of smoke she exhaled through her nose stood out like tusks.

Don Milagroso strode in, elegantly attired, and greeted us. "The International Monetary Fund mission arrives tomorrow for a two-week stay," he said. "We need to get together and form a strategy, and to assemble data for them. I want your help." He went on with generalities. Guy said he had data together on the national accounts. The French woman averred that the data on spending were a mess. There was more talk about the availability of various sorts of information. As the conversation went on, the idea of "forming a strategy" was forgotten. I asked Don Milagroso what decisions the IMF might be hoping to make as a result of its visit, and its key concerns in making those decisions.

After a while four issues emerged:

The perilous lack of liquidity in the country's banking system, coupled with a more than 100-percent increase in private credit the year before.

The debt burden.

The capital budget: public investment now and over the medium term. (I had yet to unearth the capital budget and doubted that one existed.)

Finally, the cocoa export tax and the budget deficit. If the tax were reduced in order to stimulate production, government revenues would fall. How would the already gaping budget deficit be met?

The meeting closed without resolving how to prepare these issues for discussion and solution. Don Milagroso thanked us and asked us to return the next morning at nine for the opening session with the IMF. I left, amazed that so little had been prepared for an IMF mission.

Don Milagroso's secretary had a message for me. Horace of the World Bank had arrived, was without a place to stay, and was waiting downstairs at the Impala to use my room if possible. Near retirement, Horace was a tall, pale, white-haired Middle Easterner with thick lips and glasses, who had taken over from Eric as loan officer for Equatorial Guinea. Horace had kindly briefed me and helped me in my visit to Washington a month back.

I found him slumped in a small chair by the reception desk, dressed in a wrinkled shirt and tie and a beige Barracuda windbreaker. He was perspiring.

"My God, it's good to see you!" he exclaimed dramatically as I walked in. He allowed as how he was exhausted and frustrated; he was just in from a couple of weeks in the Central African Republic; and if Malabo didn't have lodgings for him, he had might as well leave tomorrow. I told him the government had cabled him not to come, as the UDEAC conference was taking up all the hotel space and all the government's time. Since we had not heard he was coming after all, no one had met him at the airport. Another instance of Equatorial Guinea's truly primitive system of telecommunications.

"What a country!" Horace sighed—he who had previously served in such nadirs as Zaire. I showed him up to my room.

"We need to talk about your project, number one," Horace declared. "Number two, we need to discuss the contracts. We need to get together with the donors. By the way, where is your office? . . . We need to talk with the United Nations. Next week we will be inseparable. . . . Is Salvador in town? . . . Did you have a chance to meet——? . . . Are you taking your malaria pills?"

An almost random walk through the tape decks of his mind. When I could, I left Horace to rest. Later, luckily, we found a room for him downstairs. Unluckily, the sheets and insect population were not to his liking; for the latter, I did some spraying that afternoon and, for the former, provided consolation.

The next morning at nine, the first meeting took place in the BEAC conference room, which was nearly the size of a basketball court. The four-person IMF–World Bank team, sitting on one side of the huge table, included Esteban, Heinz's replacement as World Bank economist for Equatorial Guinea. Don Milagroso was on the other side, and next to him was a slender black gentleman of about forty, a BEAC biggie from one of the other Central African countries. The biggie wore an Italian double-breasted suit of opulent patina. Since he spoke only French, Don Milagroso conducted the meeting in French. Around the table were Guy and the fully cigaretted French lady, several Guineans, Everton, a Uruguayan U.N. adviser at the Ministry of Planning, and an assortment of BEAC functionaries.

Over the past couple of years, Equatorial Guinea had choked down bitter economic medicine, yet the patient now looked as feeble as ever. The currency had been devalued and converted, but the economy had not rebounded. President Obiang had remarked in a recent speech that the *cefa* should perhaps instead be called *suffa,* the pidgin English word for "suffer."

In fact, the government had promised more reforms than it had delivered. The expansion of credit had greatly exceeded targets. Public spending was too high, and the IMF–World Bank team was worried it would skyrocket. This year was Equatorial Guinea's turn to host the regional UDEAC meetings, including an extravaganza with heads of state in Bata, on the mainland, in December. The IMF was concerned that the government had spent and would continue to spend not only "excessive" but also "unproductive" sums—including the purchase of Mercedes Benzes, the construction of guest houses in Bata, and so forth. Because many conditions agreed to with the IMF had not been met, the Fund had let its 1985 agreement lapse—a kind of de-facto cancellation.

This joint IMF–World Bank mission would determine whether enough progress had been made to justify a new agreement.

Gabriela spoke for the IMF–World Bank team. Fortyish, South American, with dark skin, cropped hair, and clean features, Gabriela had worn a scowl and stared at her note pad as Don Milagroso gave his speech of welcome and introduction. Now she unsmilingly thanked Don Milagroso for his hospitality and for accommodating them in the BEAC guest house. She said that she and her colleagues would be asking the government for a lot of help in compiling data and would be reporting back to Don Milagroso in a week's time with points to discuss. Her tone was formal and frigid.

Earlier, when I had met Gabriela in Washington, she had unloaded frank impressions of Equatorial Guinea.

"It's a remarkable place, there's no other one like it. All the power is in the hands of a clique from Mongomo. The country is very corrupt. The leaders are shrewd, if not highly educated. You can't give them an inch or they will sneak away from you. You have to treat them just like little children. You must be very strict with them. Don't discuss or show a lack of resolve, just tell them exactly what to do."

I had heard similar sentiments from World Bank people. A senior economist in Washington told me, "No way your country will get a structural adjustment loan, not till 1993 maybe. They are way far away from mean-ingful reform—they just don't mean what they promise."

The Bank's visiting agricultural expert, a delightful young French-woman named Renée, said of the Equatoguineans: "They won't under-stand analysis, they don't have the ability for that. They will seize on the alternative that is most favorable to their private interests if you try to do analysis. You have to tell them what to do, and do it in the simplest and most direct terms possible."

I had experienced an example of such telling in the final meeting of our mission fifteen months ago, when our mission's leader had sternly lectured a group of ministers in a classroomlike setting at the Ministry of Education. He had simply laid down the law, and the leaders of the country had taken it—sullenly, arms crossed—like so many recalcitrant schoolboys. In order to receive the loan for the economic rehabilitation project, Equatorial Guinea had been obliged to agree to a number of conditions. The govern-ment promised to charge higher prices for electricity, water, and telecom-munications. It agreed that the World Bank would have to approve its public spending program. It agreed to establish a monitoring office for water supplies, to promulgate a health policy based on prevention, and to enunciate a transport policy that gave first priority to repairing existing vehicles and machines rather than buying new ones. These measures made sense, but I recalled how some of them were invented: in a suite at the Impala fifteen months ago, in something of the fashion of "Let's see, what else would be a good idea . . ."

Presumably this IMF–Bank team would promulgate new conditions for the government to meet. They would use their leverage. The outcomes of such three-week visits—parachutings in by Washington-based officials of various backgrounds and training—would perforce become national poli-cies. Or if not, the country would not get another IMF agreement or World Bank loan.

The IMF–Bank medicine is potent stuff. In the short run, it can drive an economy to its knees and foster political unrest. In the long run, it presumably leads to greater economic efficiency but, as one World Bank vice president put it, "with as yet unknown side effects." And even if long-run growth results, there are dangers. If expatriates and the already rich are the ones who take over privatized state-owned enterprises, the ones who have access to credit and international markets, therefore the ones who really profit from competition—then do we have a recipe not only for a kind of economic growth but also, in a few years' time, for a resentful backlash? Might the pendulum then swing back toward the old, failed national socialisms—to the xenophobes, the communists, the racialists, the Macías's? These questions are further aspects of those tensions between aid and dependency, leverage and sovereignty, benevolence and autonomy.

I looked at Don Milagroso, the witch doctor turned head of central bank. If not to him, then to most Equatoguineans, the IMF–World Bank economic prescription must seem mysterious, even magical. Their experts pronounce heretofore-unknown words—*stabilization, liberalization, privatization*—in the fashion of a medicine man's unintelligible but potent imprecation.

My Magic?

For the IMF–Bank visit—as well as for the country's economic strategy—a key issue was the export tax on cocoa. This tax was the number-one domestic source of revenue in a badly imbalanced budget. But world prices for cocoa were falling. If the cocoa tax remained high, producers' prices would have to come down or exporters' margins would have to be reduced, or both; and it was logical to expect an adverse effect on production and exports. Here was a classic trade-off between revenues and production—in a sense, between short-term economic stabilization and long-term economic growth.

On these topics, studies from Equatorial Guinea proved unilluminating. A recent report covering the first two years of the cocoa project combined a few lazy numbers and several inchoate recommendations. The cost estimates recently produced by the exporters were higher than, and in their structure did not jibe with, four previous World Bank estimates of cocoa production costs. (To my surprise, the World Bank's visiting agriculturalist Renée told me she was not familiar with these various studies. "I guess I'd better read them," she said; but she didn't have time before she had to make her recommendations to the government.)

I thought that government officials would be able to make better decisions about the cocoa tax if they had a memorandum summarizing the relevant issues. So I prepared one. The memorandum reviewed and analyzed studies of production costs, examined the elasticity of supply from studies elsewhere, guessed at how much production would increase if the tax were lowered, and summarized the effects of various tax–world-price combinations in terms of government revenues. The memo included tables and illustrative charts. I analyzed the trade-offs and uncertainties but made no recommendations.

Before drafting the memo, I showed my tables and outline to Everton and Renée and went over them with two of the leading cocoa exporters. The memo was then distributed to key government officials, people on the cocoa project, and the visiting IMF–Bank team. I had been up several nights till three in the morning on the Casa Mota computer, and I was pleased with the result.

But others were not. The day after the memo was formally distributed, Renée and Horace were taking off to return to the States, via Douala and Paris; and I was going with them to Douala to purchase a car. Everton and Morton of the cocoa project were at the airport to see them off. It turned out we had a long wait, all flights having been suspended owing to the expected but delayed arrival of President Obiang from Paris.

After completing check-in formalities, I joined the others, who were sitting at a table in the tatty lounge. Outside, the rainy season's sky was dark as slate.

Morton brought up my memo. "Bob, your recommendation to keep the export tax at thirty percent will ruin the industry."

Surprised, I told him to read again: the memo contained no recommendations, just tables and graphs showing the possible trade-offs between tax revenues and cocoa production.

"But that's how the government is going to take it," he said. "They will look at the revenue side and decide to keep the tax."

"The exporters will shut down with a thirty-percent tax," Renée said. "It won't be profitable to export. And cocoa production won't increase in the future."

Everton said, "We won't know the effect of lower taxes on production till we try. You can't study it theoretically. This country is different from the other places studied in the papers you cited."

I found the conversation baffling. Then Horace spoke. The previous day, he had called the memo "a monumental piece of work." Now he said, "It's dangerous for the government to get a recommendation from Renée, from the World Bank, and then have another person from the World Bank give contradictory advice."

Aha! It turned out Renée had recommended a drastic reduction in the cocoa export tax. She was supported by the cocoa project's people. As agricultural people, they vividly perceived the tax's adverse production effects; the loss of tax revenue and the increase in the budget deficit were for them of distant concern.

It was at this point that Renée contributed her remark: "They won't understand analysis, they don't have the ability for that. They will seize on the alternative that is most favorable to their private interests if you try to do analysis. You have to tell them what to do and do so in the simplest and most direct terms possible."

I must have cringed.

"Bob, look, you've written a stimulating paper," Everton said, leaning forward. "But you forget that the price may be so low that they'll leave the cocoa on the trees. If you want revenue, why not a higher tax on alcohol?" Not a bad idea, but tangential to the points at hand. Later Everton, the head of the cocoa project, said, "Listen, we don't give a damn about government revenues. They just waste the money anyway. We want to raise cocoa production."

Later I stood alongside Morton looking out at the tarmac: the black of the bumpy asphalt runway, the dark green of the surrounding jungle, and the dull and threatening clouds. I told Morton I was disappointed at their reaction.

"We were disappointed, too, Bob," he said. "You shouldn't put out a paper on cocoa without showing us at the cocoa project first." I told him I had reviewed all the calculations with Everton and Renée. Morton exhaled. We stood silent for a while, then forced some conversation.

A while later, Renée came to me and joked, "Let's leave aside unimportant things like cocoa and talk about subjects that matter, like whether we'll ever leave this airport." We had been waiting for three hours and the President's flight still had not arrived. Everton began to regale Renée and Horace with stories of Equatoguinean rip-offs, screw-ups, and perversities. His humor was acid. At one point he talked about the United Nations advisers, who were mostly Latin Americans. (Everton was English, a former military man.)

"What would all these unemployable Uruguayans and Argentinians and Chileans ever do if the U.N. shut down here?" he mocked. "They dream up a bunch of silly projects, the main effect of which is to keep themselves and others like them employed."

I recounted a conversation from a dinner Renée, Esteban and I had enjoyed with the wife of a Chilean agricultural adviser. Both she and her husband had formerly served in Nicaragua. After lauding the idealism and motivation of the Nicaraguans, she held forth on the complete lack of same in Equatorial Guinea. I had gently asked her why, then, they were here.

"We are doing it for the money," she had said. "We happen to be from a country where we cannot make money. We cannot go home until we have money."

When asked how she and her husband felt about their everyday work in an environment she regarded as futile, she had cited a few ground-level successes in Río Muni, where they now lived. And at the end her answer came out a little like Everton's own the other night: "At the top, no one cares. They are all robbing and thinking of their clan. But sometimes you feel that you can help particular individuals, that your efforts at that level may make some difference."

Everton took aim. "You know who all these U.N. people are, don't you? They're all leftists fleeing leftists. They were critics, and then when their side came into power they weren't wanted anyway, because all they know how to do is criticize. And you know about her husband and the 'help' he gives, don't you? He's the designer of that big-ticket goat-breeding project! What a waste of money!"

The morning's conversations had depressed me. I was asking myself, Are expatriate experts and the World Bank this protective of their turf, this confident and yet defensive of their prescriptions, this contemptuous? Is cynicism unavoidable in Equatorial Guinea?

Later, top government officials reacted differently to the memorandum. Don Milagroso had told me how important and ill studied an issue the cocoa tax was. He thanked me for it: "This is exactly the kind of thing we need." The Minister of Finance, Don Bonifacio, and the Minister and Secretary General of Agriculture also liked the memo, saying it had clarified the issues and the uncertainties involved. One of them remarked, "I see that you are working on our side."

The Minister of Agriculture complained that the IMF and the World Bank were imposing measures that favored the expatriate exporters. He said that the people working on the World Bank's cocoa project had become friends with the Spanish exporters and were in their pockets, and thus wanted the cocoa tax reduced.

I disagreed. It was no good to see conspiracies all around, I argued. To increase production, everyone would have to be involved—the government, the farmers, the exporters, and the experts—not only on pricing and tax questions but on the structural problems impeding the production and marketing of cocoa. Wasn't the task, I asked, to create a process where all the actors could work together to identify problems, specify alternatives, consider their pros and cons, and jointly devise ways out?

The minister listened intently. He asked me to write him a memorandum about such a process. I did, hoping that the idea would germinate.

I was pleased by the government's reaction. Unfortunately, I didn't have any magic to give—in this case, not even recommendations. I believed in analysis, and I believed in participation. It had been my experience that decisions are improved by collegial efforts to lay out issues, clarify choices, and separate the value judgments and the factual questions. Foreigners like me can help in this, and if one is lucky, in the process the locals learn how to do it themselves. They get stronger. Their confidence grows.

Could this be a form of beneficence that enhances autonomy?

Reception for the President

After four hours, the word came that the plane with the President was about to arrive, bringing him back from the celebration of Bastille Day in Paris. I wandered out onto the dirt parking lot. Standing near the terminal shed and resting my elbows on a low cyclone fence, I looked out at the reception prepared for the chief of state.

Far off to the left, out on the runway, half a hundred native women were dancing and singing. They wore brightly colored African print skirts; some had T-shirts with the President's picture; others, blouses of clashing colors. Most had their hair in brightly patterned scarves. Their dancing had an African rhythm. I couldn't hear much of their song. From time to time in the breeze, I caught wailing sounds, almost laments.

In front of them at the extreme left of the panorama was a military band—not playing yet, but getting ready, as we could hear the jet overhead in the heavy clouds. The band members were milling about nervously, randomly—a garboil of uniforms and instruments.

Next to the band was a long, single-file line of suited men, stretching all the way across my view. These were high government officials, ministers and general secretaries and the like, maybe a hundred of them. It was the custom for them to come to the airport whenever the President departed or arrived. I picked out Don Bonifacio, Don Constantino, Don Milagroso. Then came a group of heavy-bellied top military brass in gold braids and ponderous uniforms. And then an honor guard from the various services.

As the President's jet began to land, the honor guard snapped to attention; so did the top brass and the ministers. The women were rocking back and forth and sighing at the sky. The storm clouds looked as though they wanted to cry. The jet engines shrieked.

Right in front of me stood a Moroccan soldier with a submachine gun. He wore wrinkled fatigues and an olive-drab baseball hat. His eyes were intent. I thought he was looking at me particularly; there were only about fifteen other spectators strung out along that low cyclone fence. He seemed to be looking at my hands. A couple of his colleagues stood poised at intervals down that fence. Off on the other side of the runway, outlined by a clump of trees other Moroccans were protecting the President from any assault from the forest.

Behind the Moroccan in front of me waited a jeep and a couple of Moroccans in civilian clothes. Then a more senior Moroccan soldier with a walkie-talkie. Then the line of ministers and top brass and the honor guard. Then a Mercedes alongside a red carpet and a podium toward which the jet was now easing. The military band started playing the national anthem. Like other national anthems in the Third World, it was music alien to the local culture: military music from nineteenth-century Europe— provincial, both sad and portentous.

The jet's front door opened. A stairway was rolled up to it. A television cameraman was poised at the bottom of the stairs to capture the President's every step for a long feature on the evening news. A few dark-suited black men emerged from the plane: the President's entourage, conscious of their importance, their heads cocked back. Then out came the tall, forty-odd-year-old President himself, upright and severe in double-breasted suit and glasses. It was my first glimpse of Equatorial Guinea's head of state.

He descended the steps, strode down the red carpet in front of the honor guard, accepted the salutes of the top brass, and shook the hands of a hundred officials. He gazed for a moment at the dancing women, then got into the big Mercedes. As he whooshed away, the assemblage went flaccid, like a balloon losing its air, and I walked back to the terminal. Nothing in either the President's demeanor or the scene revealed that a *coup d'état* and attempt on his life had just been quashed.

I went off to Douala that afternoon in ignorance of the planned coup— without even a hint that dissension was in the wind. After four days away, I returned on a Monday and worked all day. No one mentioned that anything untoward had happened. Don Constantino wasn't at the Planning Ministry; he was "indisposed." At BEAC, Don Milagroso was "out."

Not till that night after supper when, over a game of dominoes at the Casa Mota, someone referred to the "recent trouble" did I learn what had happened. Whispering even though we were in a private house, my companions reported what they had learned "from three different sources" about the July seventeenth coup attempt and the events since.

The plan had been to assassinate the President as he deplaned, in full view of the honor guard, the Moroccan soldiers, all the ministers and military men, and the television camera.

About forty high officials had been jailed. (This was many more than had been involved in an abortive coup in 1983, a few days after which five or six plotters had been executed off the Point of African Unity at the eastern end of Malabo Bay.) Don Constantino, the Planning Minister, was one. Also the Minister of Public Works, who was simultaneously the number-two man in military rank—"a charismatic, strong, bloody, violent man," they said. And Don Manuel, the former Minister of Finance. Not the current Minister of Finance, Don Bonifacio, though; nor the Minister of Agriculture. Apparently most of those jailed were from Mongomo.

"It was an internal struggle," I was told that night. "No ideological or political reasons, just some people who wanted more power."

Later, others said that ideology and politics had been involved. One person explained that the conspirators had all been trained in Eastern bloc countries. The North Koreans had backed it, said someone else, and the Russians.

Another version—perhaps not inconsistent—said the conspirators were rejecting the government's economic program.

"They were tired of what has happened with failed policies—entering into UDEAC, the IMF austerity program, the World Bank. They wanted to go back to a government of force, where people are told what to do. The Minister of Public Works is a Macías type. He would have been the new dictator."

Don Milagroso had been involved.

I heard that he was imprisoned. Then someone said he was only under house arrest, that he had been seen over the weekend drinking at the airport bar, of all places.

"*He* wouldn't be in jail. He's the smartest of the bunch. He was around under Macías, you know. People would disappear then for looking at him the wrong way. He sometimes would put on a uniform and strut around town. Don Milagroso is a survivor."

Another version was related to me a few days later.

"It's bad what happened. . . . So many people were involved that it will mean a major disruption of the government. Scores of people locked up! They say that Don Milagroso was the brains behind it. That's what they say.

"And they say he's been treated badly. He's been jailed and beaten there, disfigured. They say you can't recognize Don Milagroso any more."

4

Us versus Them

PARANOIA was growing. In the wake of the coup attempt, the government decreed that no public employee could meet with or go to the house of any member of a foreign embassy without written permission. Soldiers manned roadblocks on the outskirts of town. Diplomats and U.N. employees were forbidden to travel more than fifteen kilometers beyond Malabo without written permission from the Foreign Ministry. All along I had found it hard to get appointments with the officials with whom I was supposed to be working. Now they were almost inaccessible.

Only slowly and inconclusively did the story of the coup come out, and not everyone believed the official version. "There was no *coup d'état,*" said a newsletter produced by the government. "But there were criticisms of the government and subversive talk." The official story was that the perpetrators would meet at the Club Naútico down by the port and criticize the government's economic policies. These hadn't worked, they said, especially the entry into the CFA franc zone—UDEAC, BEAC, and the change of money. Among diplomats, however, the consensus seemed to be that there had been more than criticisms and, in fact, a coup had been plotted. Both versions agreed that the accused had been unhappy with the stabilization and liberalization policies President Obiang's regime had promulgated—the very policies backed by the International Monetary Fund and by World Bank projects like my own. The conspirators had wanted instead a return to a more controlled economy. Some members of the Mongomo clan were supposedly nostalgic for the days of Macías.

The government held trials that were broadcast extensively on the local radio. Taped excerpts were shown on television in the evenings. I was impressed by this open attempt to do justice—or to be seen to do it. Everywhere I went in the daytime people had radios near, and at night small crowds formed around the television sets of the Beiruth and the couple of bars that had them.

You could watch Don Milagroso, for example. He did not look as though he had been beaten. He appeared tired and, behind the large table in the courtroom, surprisingly small. To question after question, he wearily explained over and over that he was innocent. All he had done was talk about economic policy with the conspirators. Economic policy was his job as the head of the BEAC bank, and the people he was talking to were government officials; he didn't know they were conspiring about anything.

"I was the person who did the studies for entering UDEAC. I negotiated the terms." His strained voice then rose in pitch and volume. "How could I have been a subversive about the economic policy of the government when I was one of those who designed it?"

The most bizarre story to come out at the trials concerned the man alleged to be the prime mover. He was a low-level military man with no government job. Disgruntled with government policies, he wanted to foment a left-wing revolution. To discuss this prospect, he had gone to the embassy of North Korea, on the south side of town across from the Ministry of Education and Sports. The embassy's cheerless balustrade was faced by tall walls of rough mud-colored cement. Alongside the gate was a glass-encased exhibit of photographs of things North Korean. You could study the Great Leader Comrade Kim Il Sung from various angles. Often he was with his son and heir apparent. There were also gleaming factories, rice fields of psychedelic green, and, incongruously, several photos of a hypermodern amusement park with a strong resemblance to Disneyland.

Behind this gate the soldier allegedly had requested an appointment with the North Korean ambassador, expressed his discontent, and asked to be flown to Pyongyang for consultations with the Great Leader himself. According to the government's account, the North Korean ambassador was only partially supportive. He said he would try to arrange an appointment but the soldier would have to pay his own travel expenses.

This fantastic voyage never materialized. Nonetheless, the government said, the treacherous soldier had talked up the need for a violent change of government. For this he was executed off the Point of African Unity. This was the customary place for fusillades, I was told, and had been during Macías's time.

But punishing the other conspirators was more problematic. Many people thought that President Obiang faced a dilemma. On the one hand, he had to show strength against subversion. On the other hand, many of the conspirators were from his very own Mongomo clan. Some had great power there, such as Don Milagroso. The President could neither simply kill them nor let them go free. It was said that he went to Mongomo to consult with the elders. "How this country is really run is mysterious," one diplomat commented. "The elders of the tribe may make a lot of the important decisions. How much power does the President really have?"

And so some explained the less-than-coup charges against the conspirators: a coup attempt would have demanded the penalty of death, which was tribally impossible. So merely "subversive talk" had been perpetrated. All of the accused were found guilty; the soldier was executed; and the penalty for most of the rest, including Don Milagroso and Don Constantino, was two years' imprisonment.

Many people did not buy the government's case. Some maintained that an assassination had been plotted. Others went to an opposite extreme. The charges had been fabricated to enable the President to put the clamps on political rivals from Mongomo. I was learning that you couldn't be sure of what you heard in Equatorial Guinea: for every event, trivial to monumental, you were bound to find four different versions. What was clear was that the government was in shock, and my work on economic rehabilitation would suffer.

Settling In

Getting things under way had a personal side: finding a place to live, transportation, an office. Finally, there was progress. Morton of the cocoa project knocked on my door one day with a suggestion.

"I have a house for you, Bob. It's a big old wooden house from colonial times, in the middle of town, and the people want to sell their furniture, too. A Spanish couple, they're leaving the country and want to sell out."

How much? I was getting used to exorbitant rents.

Morton laughed, "Only twenty thousand *cefas* a month!" That was about sixty dollars.

How's that?

"The house belongs to the government. It gets assigned to people at the government's behest. The current residents have the house because it used to belong to the family. They came back in the early 1980s and tried to reclaim their lands and start a carpentry business. But now they've decided they can't make it, and they're going back to Spain."

I was already imagining the problems of getting a government dwelling adjudicated to me. But it was worth a try. The next afternoon I went to the house to talk.

Located one block from the cliff overlooking the harbor, the wooden structure was imposing if borderline dilapidated. It occupied a large corner lot and from the outside I saw three stories of faded dark green wood. An enclosed veranda, or *pasillo,* extended all the way around the second floor. The *pasillo*'s floor, supported by pillars, formed a roof over the sidewalk below. Every fifteen feet or so along the *pasillo* shutters swung out over the street, and the *pasillo*'s walls were of green thatch, allowing for the passage of light and air.

The ground floor consisted of abandoned storerooms and shops. The second floor was the living area. The third floor turned out to be one giant room, completely unrehabilitated, which the resident said had once been used for dancing. Over its long history the building had served among other things as the Portuguese embassy and a social club for Spaniards.

I entered the house via a dark, narrow stairway with a low beam threatening to anyone over five-foot-six. I came out on the *pasillo.* Looking left, I could see a slot of sea above the tin roof of the warehouse. On the right I looked through louvered double doors into the dining room. The first thing I noticed was the floor, which was of pine so old and untreated it looked like a stable. The walls were of faded white. The doors and accents were painted in a teal color that resembled moldy meat.

But I was charmed by the overhead fans, high ceilings, decorative ironwork doubling as beam supports, and locally made furniture, all of which lent a distinctive colonial aura. The feel of the place was not exactly African. It made me think of the Caribbean—say, an abandoned planter's house in Haiti. My host said the house had been brought in prefabricated, in pine, from Canada of all places, maybe a century ago.

We walked around the house. It was huge. The main house had four bedrooms, a study, a living room, and a dining room, plus a bathroom for the maids and a storage room. A wing of the house proceeded down a street-side *pasillo* and contained a pantry with two refrigerators, a freezer in the *pasillo* itself, a handsome bathroom done in deep green tiles to shoulder height, and an old kitchen walled in white and caramel brown tiles. At the end facing the sea was an area for a small washing machine, clotheslines, and a utility sink.

Sitting at the dining table, I could see a slice of the ocean framed on the left by the wing with the kitchen and on the right by a neighboring house in white and a distant coconut palm. Also in the distance were banks of dark green trees. The afternoon sea breeze was delightful.

The house had no glass. The windows had louvered shutters, which opened outward like doors, and coarse lacelike curtains in white. The air just flowed in. I felt the tropics all around. I loved it.

We talked. The resident explained his situation: he wanted to sell everything in the house. Unusual furniture he'd made himself of heavy Equatoguinean hardwoods. Glassware, pots and pans, dishes, utensils, flatware. A huge safe. All the appliances. A two-thousand liter water tank on the third floor. Bookshelves, a rustic bar, a TV, four beds, armoires, the whole lot.

Apart from the house itself, this was good news. Buying these things in Malabo would be impossible; importing them would take much time and trouble.

I told him I was interested, but had to see whether we could actually get the house adjudicated to me. He said that I enjoyed a crucial advantage: I was employed by the government of Equatorial Guinea.

"The rent here is so low because it's based on what government officials can afford. They won't let a diplomat or a U.N. person live here. The house can only be adjudicated under special circumstances. I can't transfer the house to you myself, the government has to. But we can go together and try."

This we did. The process had ups and downs and round and rounds too laborious to recount. But finally, finally, all the papers and appraisals and adjudications were signed and sealed. And I moved into the Casa Verde, "Green House."

The residents bequeathed me a few other treasures. Chispa was a black dog with long wiry hair, a tail that curled up, and soulful brown eyes. Her face resembled a wolf's, with her own distinctive flourish of odd and unruly whiskers. Chispa frightened the locals with her enthusiastic barking from the holes in the *pasillo*'s thatched walls and from the warehouse roof. But she took to me from the start.

I was also blessed with two maids, whom the residents had praised for diligence and honesty. Both were in their early twenties. Celestina was the cook. She was three months pregnant with her second child, unmarried, round-faced but not unattractive, reserved. In the Spanish system, the big meal was luncheon, served at three in the afternoon. Celestina's job was to prepare it and clean up afterward.

Consuelo cleaned the house and did the laundry. She also came in the morning to prepare breakfast. She and Celestina did the shopping for the house. Consuelo had a pretty face with deep black skin and high cheek-bones, a lovely smile, and a sunny disposition. She was thin, almost ane-mic. Consuelo was married to a soldier and had two children.

The next step was redecoration. Since it proved infeasible to sand and seal the aged planks of the floors, they remained stable-like. I repainted the interior and the enclosed *pasillo.* Eventually the faded white was re-placed by bright white, the moldy meat color by the original dark green of the house's exterior. The *pasillo* was done in dark green with white shutters, doors, and ceiling.

I purchased plants and two large, colorful reproductions of old Guinean maps. In the study were my computer and files along with African fabrics on the tables and decorations on the walls. From Douala, I brought back a fabulous tribal chief's chair carved and hollowed from a single massive trunk of black wood. Its rich old patina now graced the living room. In my bedroom, which contained the house's only air-conditioner, I put up over the double bed a frame of white wood for a huge white mosquito net. It was like sleeping inside a cloud. At the top of the stairs I hung my large white Nicaraguan hammock diagonally across the *pasillo,* from which I could catch the afternoon breeze and gaze at the sea.

When most of the redecoration was done, I invited Morton and the fellows from Casa Mota over for a celebratory dinner.

"I have always liked this place," said one Mota man with twenty-five years in the country. "Now it's the funkiest home in Malabo."

Transportation was a problem. In July, I had gone to Douala and checked out cars. After getting specifications and duty-free prices for four makes, I returned to Malabo, and the government's choice was a short wheelbase Toyota Land Cruiser. Four-wheel drive, no frills except big tires. I began the acquisition process via the World Bank—the first of many imports to be financed by our project.

But getting it was still months away. Slow mail service to Washington. Paperwork at the World Bank. Paperwork in Cameroon for the duty-free export. Arranging the shipping on the antique ferry boat that came once a week from Douala. In the meantime, I needed more than my legs.

How about a motorcycle?

I had ridden a motorcycle once. It was in Bali, twelve years before. A young Balinese entrepreneur had a Honda for rent. He explained the gear shift—I guess gear shifts vary from bike to bike—and I knew where the throttle was. So without admitting I'd never driven one before, I paid him, cranked up the motor, and blithely drove off—directly into a nearby bush.

"Where's the brake?" I inquired as I picked myself up.

The entrepreneur observed me suspiciously. But it was a tribute to the strength of the dollar in those days that, after answering my question, he simply let me drive off down the road. With no further trouble, as it happened.

Morton once again provided the key clue. His cocoa rehabilitation project had some new motorcycles for sale. Why?

"We accidentally bought racing bikes."

The mistake was innocent enough. The project wanted transport for the Guinean loan officers, who would be appraising the credit-worthiness of distant cocoa farms. Cars would be too expensive. So motorcycles were sought. What kind? Obviously something that could go off the road. What brand? Well, how about Yamaha, that's a good make. What size? Relatively small. So far, so good. Then came the crucial error. What model? Aw, get the top of the line.

The "top of the line" turned out to be a full-race motocross bike. Six of them eventually arrived in Malabo: racing white with red saddles, angry tailpipes, exotic "monocross" suspensions, aggressive air coolers, and high-revving motors that jerked the ultralight machines into fits of scary acceleration. The clutches turned out to be poorly adjusted: slack, then pop. (Only after months did we learn what was wrong and have the clutches fixed.) Within weeks two Guineans had crashed. Malabo's resident biker, a spacy American mechanic who looked right out of a James Dean retrospective, himself drove a monster street bike. Of the new Yamaha, he drawled, "Mmmm-*hmmmm* . . . that's a ma*chine!"*

Presumably in fear of future medical bills, the cocoa project decided to sell three of the bikes. I went to the project's warehouse to try one out. The mechanic rolled out the least used of these gleaming two-wheeled projectiles. This time I admitted my novitiate status. We carefully reviewed the six-speed transmission, the throttle, the kick starter. I took particular care to appraise both hand and foot brakes.

The rest of the warehouse personnel came out to watch. These bikes had a reputation.

The mechanic said, "Give it a go." I noticed that there was no nearby bush to catch me.

But off I did go, stiff as a hood ornament, slow as a sigh. Upon returning from this brief maiden voyage, I explained to the onlookers that it was good with new bikes to keep the RPMs low. They were not fooled. They smiled sympathetically.

I bought the bike. That evening I had dinner with several Spanish sailors whom I'd gotten to know. I showed them my new missile parked outside. You guys ever ride a motorcycle?

"Yeah, I used to, but too dangerous," one said. "Make sure you put up the kickstand each time. One can forget. My brother forgot once, drove off, turned the bike, and crashed. Broke his leg."

Before going home I checked the kickstand twice.

On the next several afternoons I practiced with the bike on the smooth four miles to the airport, the country's best road, no traffic, loads of dark green trees as scenery. I practiced braking, turning. The problem was accelerating. The clutch was as sensitive as sunburn. And a quarter-inch turn of the throttle sent the motor from purr to full attack. One time I'd stall, the next time I'd scare myself to a gasp.

After a week I thought I had it down. I was visiting the Chamber of Agriculture and Forestry, a handsome old building near Casa Mota on the city's main street overlooking the port. As I came out my sailor friends were emerging from a bar up the street.

"Hey Roberto," they yelled down to me. "How's the machine?"

Fine, I replied, mounting up. I kicked on the motor, revved it powerfully a couple of times in neutral, then shifted into first. The clutch popped. The bike screamed. The next thing I knew the front wheel was up in the air and the motor was roaring and I was holding on for survival. Fifteen yards later, the front wheel touched down. Flying past the sailors, I heard them laughing and yelling "Show off!" My recollection is that I mustered a smile.

Another problem was where to work. The Ministry of Finance had no office for me. The Ministry of Planning had some offices under construction, but for nonpayment the firm had stopped work, leaving unfinished walls, a tin roof, and curious orange bars over the windows. So I worked at home. I would show up at the Finance Ministry early in the morning to see whether the Don Bonifacio wanted me. He wouldn't be in, or would be too busy. Rarely a message for me.

Eventually I was involved in some work getting ready for the autumn visit of the International Monetary Fund. Don Bonifacio discovered I was helpful. One day he said, "Roberto, I want you here in the ministry where I can call you quickly when I need you."

I explained that office space was scarcer than snow.

He pondered this for a moment. "Use the conference room," Don Bonifacio said. He walked me to it.

The conference room was just across from the minister's office. It had an air-conditioner but since there was rarely electricity this was only disconcerting. A long wooden table with an insufficient number of chairs graced the middle of the room. The walls were bare and the floors littered with cigarette remnants. The only other piece of furniture was an out-of-order photocopying machine.

Dutifully I began daily to bring in my battery-powered laptop computer and install myself at the window end of the table. Unfortunately the room was long and low and perpendicular to the street's flow of air. It was probably the hottest room in the building. Ten minutes after arriving my shirt front would be soaked. By eleven o'clock I would feel a dull pressure pain beneath the top of my skull.

After a few weeks I went back to my old system, showing up in the morning, then working at home. If the minister needed me or seemed likely to, I would perspire away in the conference room. But he didn't need me much.

Indeed, this was the main problem: he didn't need me because the economic rehabilitation project itself was not under way. The World Bank refused to "make the credit effective" until certain conditions were met. A clause in the project agreement said that Equatorial Guinea's public investment program had to be approved by the Bank before the credit would be effective—that is, before the first installment of money would be transferred to our account. It was the fall of 1986 and this had not yet happened; we didn't know when it would. All our project had were some "project preparation funds" to cover salaries and housing and local expenditures.

Furthermore, two of the three ministers on the project's coordinating committee were out of commission. Don Constantino, the Planning Minister, had been sacked and was in jail. His replacement had not been named. I still had not met the new Minister of Industry and Commerce, Don Camilo. He had been seconded by the President to Bata to head up the preparations for December's summit conference of the six leaders of the UDEAC countries. This very conference and its likely extrabudgetary expenses, which were not yet documented or even admitted by the government, were among the reasons the Bank would not make the project effective.

So I spent my time getting to know some of the characters in Equatorial Guinea's drama. The attitude of "us versus them" was pervasive. "We are giving," I kept hearing from everyone I talked to, "but they are only taking."

"Out of the Trees"

I met with a well-liked young diplomat from the Spanish embassy, who was said to have a deep knowledge of local politics and commerce. I wanted to learn more about the obstacles to foreign investment. Even after Equatorial Guinea devalued and converted to the *cefa,* even after all the economic reforms, investment was virtually nil.

Our appointment was at the Spanish embassy, an unattractive one-story prefabricated building whose only distinction was its potent air-conditioning. An Equatoguinean with a Madrid accent ushered me to the diplomat's office. He emerged effusively from behind his large desk, passed before the Spanish flag draped from a staff against the wood-paneled wall, and after a broad smile and a two-fisted handshake, sat me on the couch and himself on one of the lounge chairs alongside. His cufflinks, smile, and elegant tie gleamed with various degrees of intensity.

I explained my interests.

"Investment, ah. It is terrible, there is almost none. The government talks about investment, then nothing happens. For example, a company was invited to set up a joint venture to sell fish from Spain. No Guineans showed up. It is always the same story.

"Now the only people who invest here are those with the easy businesses. Selling liquor, where people do make money. Importing food, although this is harder. One big Spanish firm was pressured by the government and finally closed down. You know, things like the veterinarian from the Ministry of Health needs two entire carcasses for inspection. Smuggling petroleum products is attractive, too. The presidency is involved in this."

A little later, he said: "I have been here for two years, and my little conclusion about Equatorial Guinea is that the Guineans really do not care about the country. They want to travel if they can, and eat, and have a little money. There are quotas for different businesses for the various ministers. They get a share, this is all that matters to them.

"It is very difficult to do business here. If you want to work here, you've got to pay an extra quota. Some to the customs people. Some to the ministers. Some to get anything done in government. I call it the revolutionary tax. An unofficial surcharge, you might say. How much? Well, for a small investment one had better think of fifty percent for the revolutionary tax. On a larger investment the percentage would be smaller."

I asked whether there weren't some bright spots on the scene.

"All the ministers are dirty. Your man Don Bonifacio, he took a loan for a house in Spain and has not repaid. Look, Roberto, you have to understand this. These people are just barely out of the jungle, just barely out of the trees."

While saying this the diplomat was under perfect control. His voice was pleasant and modulated. His black hair was combed straight back, and his shoes were buffed. King Juan Carlos in the large photograph above him was only slightly more regal. Yet listen to what he was saying.

To be fair, he was almost equally jaundiced about the Spaniards in Equatorial Guinea.

"There are many shady dealings within the Spanish Cooperation," he said. This was the Spanish aid agency, whose offices were also in the embassy. "For example, they give their construction business to a firm owned by three Spaniards and high government officials. A quarter of all the profits go to the officials. The foreign aid people themselves get kick-backs from the company on expenses for repairs to their own houses, fixing leaks and the like.

"Do you know how we award scholarships to Spain? Well, it is not on merit. It depends on who your parents are. Any new minister comes in first thing after being named and asks us for scholarships for his kids. And we give them to him. I would say ninety-five percent of the scholarships we give, which are mostly at the high-school level, go to the sons and daughters of government officials." He paused. "It is a shame, you know?"

Later he brought out files on local Spanish businessmen (no women). These contained photos and summary descriptions on the first page and no doubt many details on the pages I couldn't see. He told me about some of the key players. The photos were almost uniformly mug shots of porcine middle-aged men with scowls.

At the end he said, "Watch out what you investigate in this area, Roberto. I am your friend. These people"—he glanced at the files—"are *gangsters.*"

"Why Invest?"

I pursued the investment question with the French. The French ambassador had recently arrived. We met in his small, electricityless office in the colonial house that served as embassy. The location was ideal: halfway down the narrow point on the west side of the harbor with a beautiful view back toward the colonial center of Malabo and, on a clear day, of the magnificent cone of the thirteen thousand-foot Mount Cameroon some thirty-one miles across the ocean on the mainland.

The ambassador worked tieless and in shirtsleeves. His large face was crowned by an ample mane of graying hair and featured a dour and fleshy mouth, arresting blue eyes with a sign of sadness, and sagging heaviness along the chin. The ambassador spoke only a little Spanish, which he immediately employed to plead ignorance on the subject of my inquiry. But, prodded, he offered some observations.

"There are many obstacles to foreign investment. There is no bank. There is no telex. There is no security of property, of work. Everyone comes to you to take money, this is the problem.

"Many foreign investors come with energy and enthusiasm, only to find little by little a climate without security of money, property, or justice. They get discouraged and leave." He went on to cite four examples.

Later he said, "There is opportunity here. Everything is to do. Let me give you an example. Even the poorest country has a beer company. Here they did a feasibility study, and there is a market. But there is no water and no electricity. It is hard to make beer without water and electricity."

The French embassy no longer had an economic officer, but the ambassador told me that the former economic attaché was now working in Douala. A month later I went to Douala and tracked him down. We talked in an air-conditioned restaurant slightly warmer than the summit of Mont Blanc.

Thin, blondish, bespectacled, in his early thirties, the former attaché was friendly and smart. He said his current job in a French-Cameroonian commercial firm was a godsend after his work in Malabo. That had been full of frustrations.

"One could not accomplish. You ask about foreign investment. The obstacles were many. So many."

In theory at least it should have been an exciting time for the attaché. During his tenure Equatorial Guinea had converted its currency to the CFA franc and become a member of the French-inspired Central African currency, banking, and customs union. A torrent of French investors had been expected.

"During the first months of 1985, right after the big switch to the *cefa,* we must have had an investor a day from France or one of the UDEAC countries visit the embassy. Mostly in commerce, but also some productive types. After all was said and done, only a handful actually invested. And as it developed, not one of them was successful.

"One person paid cash for the Club Joy, you know that beautiful estate in Ela Nguema overlooking the sea? Well, it turned out that the person who sold it was not the rightful owner. The investor lost his money.

"Two commercial firms came in and have since gone under. One employed three and then two expatriates and only turned over about twenty-five thousand *cefas* a day." That was less than seventy dollars then. "And the government would requisition things from them. 'We need your truck tomorrow,' they would order. And they would have to take IOUs from the government that would never be paid."

"Another classic case occurred before my time. A French group bought a big cocoa farm in 1983 or 1984. A little later the government 'renationalized' it. 'You didn't really buy the land,' they said. 'The transaction was invalid.' The property now belongs to some of the ministers themselves.

"The investment code? No, that was not really a problem. On paper, that is. The new regulation is okay, but the Guineans themselves do not know it. Once a week it seemed I had to go to Industry and Commerce and explain the regulations to someone. An office was set up in the presidency dedicated to investment. Foreigners arrived in Malabo and went there and said they never found anyone in the office. I was told that this office did not even possess a copy of the investment code. It was said that despite being close to the President this office had enemies in the government."

He categorized the problems foreign investors faced.

"I suppose the most serious was banking. When Milagroso was the head of the Central Bank and later the BEAC, the Spaniards could convert their money and transfer it out of the country whenever they wished. But for the French there were problems one after the other. We complained. A meeting took place between Milagroso and all the French firms.

"Milagroso told them, 'We lived well before you and will live well after you. The day you make too much noise, you leave.'

"The problem was that suppliers in France were not being paid. Finally the local firms gave up and left, because the context was too difficult.

"Too many problems, Robert," he sighed. "The cost of doing business is high. The cranes at the port are under a Spanish monopoly. It has too little capacity, and it gives different prices depending on if one is a friend or not. The rents for buildings vary so much. We simply could not find buildings or housing for some firms. One never knew who owned what. One's expatriate workers would cost a lot, and they would come for two months, would get discouraged and would not stay. Banking and insurance costs are maybe seventy percent higher than in Cameroon.

"Then there is the electricity situation, intermittent and expensive. No technicians either. No one can repair a generator. One company lost the power for its cold storage and ended up having to throw an entire container full of meat off the Riaba bridge. There are no electricity meters so one might be asked to pay a million and a half *cefas* a month even though one had the generator going for twenty days.

"On the other hand, one paid virtually no taxes. I do not think they had a tax code. I gave the government the text of the Cameroonian code."

I asked him gently about corruption. He had already alluded to several versions.

"Bribery is small in price compared to other African countries," he said. "It is less than in Cameroon, for example. Here you must bribe two hundred thousand *cefas* for a work permit compared to fifty thousand in Malabo. To move anything here costs you a hundred thousand. In Malabo, maybe five thousand. And here if you get stopped by the police for any reason it will cost you. In Malabo, they might ask for a cigarette. Hell, in Malabo on my own I would give policemen a few thousand just to establish good relations and you know, they would salute me when I drove by!

"No, I don't think corruption in the bureaucracy is the big problem. At higher levels, yes. One sees complete amateurs given big timber concessions because of arrangements at the top."

He talked of one foreign investor who "is the laughing stock of wood people in Africa." Among his many errors, the former attaché said, was importing fifty Caterpillar tractors from Gabon second-hand and learning that after a month only two of them functioned. This man had about a fifth of the land area under concession in Río Muni, and he was losing money.

"So many problems. You know, Robert, even under the best of conditions the economy in Equatorial Guinea is so weak and so small that there is just not much money to be made. Plus payments and regulations fluctuate, so it is risky. People also recall Macías and fear the political risks.

"I have to say," he concluded, "that I encouraged many investors not to come."

"They're Not Chinese"

One night I was having dinner at home with a friend when the buzzer rang downstairs. It was an economic officer from the Chinese embassy, who asked in good Spanish for the house's former owner. I explained that he no longer lived here and introduced myself. He was friendly. I asked him to come upstairs. He did. Soon we were all talking and as there was enough for three, I asked him to stay on for supper, and he accepted.

We talked about what each of us did. He was interested in the possibility of China supplying imports under our economic rehabilitation project. He surprised me with his frank remarks.

"We are not a communist country any more," he said, referring to China's recent economic reforms. "We have learned from our many mistakes over the last two decades. Sometimes I see the goods that China exports to the rest of the world, and I am ashamed. We can produce the best quality, and this is what we need to do."

A few weeks later I called him and asked to talk with him and his colleagues about the Chinese aid effort. As with other donors I wanted to learn what they were doing, what problems and successes they had, and how the economic rehabilitation project might complement their efforts.

The embassy of the People's Republic of China stood massively and incongruously in the middle of fields of reeds on the empty road to the airport. The building was white and rectilinear with Oriental latticing. It was topped with antennas and other communication equipment and surrounded by a large wall. Access was controlled by a guard post. A huge red Chinese flag waved high in the wind.

During the reign of Macías, the Chinese had been big in Equatorial Guinea and still had a significant presence. Their aid projects were highly visible. The Chinese set up the electric power plant near Bata. They built and were helping to manage the telecommunications system in Malabo and on the continent. They laid a modern beautiful road on the continent from beyond Niefang through the hinterland to Mongomo, the home town of Macías and of the current president and his clan. This road, probably the best in the country, was used by only a few vehicles every day. Chinese doctors helped run the hospitals of Malabo and Bata.

We met in a sitting room at the embassy. On one wall was a ten-foot-long Oriental brush painting of a hawk on a tree. Around the room were placed heavy couches and chairs in lime green with embroidered lace on the arms and at the back, light blue walls and curtains and screens, and various Chinese objets d'art in the bookcase. There was a huge Japanese television set and a coffee table full of Coca-Colas, but nothing remotely African could be detected in the room. The economic officer was around fifty with a large head, thick features and heavy peasant folds of skin, and a ready smile. He talked incisively about the Chinese experience in Equatorial Guinea.

"One of our first efforts was to bring telephones to the country," he said. "At one point, twelve districts had Chinese communication equipment which we set up. We couldn't send too many technicians to work in the districts—there was no place for them to live, and anyway we didn't have enough money—so we established two groups of Chinese technicians, one in Malabo and one in Bata. But there have been so many logistical problems. Systems broke down, and the Guineans wouldn't fix them. Systems were then taken apart and robbed, and the equipment sold somewhere. The people who were supposed to take care of the equipment didn't. They weren't paid a decent wage, and they worked on their farms instead. So the whole system broke down. President Obiang asked the Chinese government in Peking to set up the system again. He was told no.

"Telecommunications in Bata is now an urgent priority. And as a member of the regional economic grouping UDEAC, Equatorial Guinea should theoretically have four lines between Cameroon and Malabo. In practice we have none. The problem is administration and not equipment. Here the administration doesn't function. For half a year the authorities in Cameroon asked the Guineans to pay their telephone bill. Equatorial Guinea paid nothing, so finally Cameroon cut the lines.

"Our other projects run into similar problems," the economic officer said. He talked of the port in Bata and the roads. Then he spoke of the Chinese experience in the energy sector.

"In 1982 we turned over to the Guineans the hydroelectric center which we had built. It was theirs to run. We agreed to provide a few teachers to train the Guinean technicians. After the ceremony the Chinese delegation spoke to President Obiang about the administration of the facility, how it could make money if it were well run. He said, *'De acuerdo.'* But in reality ever since then the administration has been very bad. Several problems have occurred. The Guinean technicians lose interest in their work. So the Chinese cooperators, who should be instructors, end up running the facility. They are not supposed to do this, but if they don't do it, the center won't work. In Bata most users have no indicator of how much electric current they consume. They don't even have light switches, you just plug in the light bulbs. So every once in a while the Guineans try to charge people for the electricity, and they go with soldiers and guns to the houses of typical folks and say, 'You must pay five or ten thousand.' They never go to the houses of government officials. This all results in side payments and harassment. No one charges the high officials. This is a problem of politics, not of foreign aid. After three to five years the Bata plant will need big repairs. The Guineans think the Chinese will do it again for them, or maybe they don't think at all. They're just glad to have electricity.

"So you see on our shoulders there are always placed burdens. My personal opinion is that without a change in politics here, there will be no progress.

"All countries have corruption, especially poor countries. But here there is no law, no control. A while back children were dying here of cholera and measles because there was corruption in the Ministry of Health. Many babies died. In China men responsible for such corruption would be shot. But here, no. Now the former minister is the ambassador in Cameroon. He was displayed in the independence day parade. A good friend of ours here in Guinea told us, 'We Guineans don't like to work with you because we don't make extra money on things. With the other foreign aid donors we get payoffs.'

"Have you noticed the way people wear a shirt here? You haven't? Well, they wear it, and they wear it, and finally they get a hole in the shirt, up here, and you can see flesh through there. In China we mend such a hole. Here no. You can see meat but no problem. They keep wearing the shirt. Then they get another hole over here, and another one over there. Finally they just throw the shirt out. It's the same with their ports and all their other facilities. Everything is given to them, they don't take care of anything and don't have to."

Later, with the economic officer's help, I met with the principal economic secretary and one of his assistants, and on two other occasions with the head of the Chinese medical team and the head technician in telecommunications. I asked them for their analyses of their sectors' problems, what equipment was needed and why. They didn't speak Spanish, so everything went through interpreters. The verdict in each case was about the same: "We need lots of spares and medicines and equipment, and the Guineans don't manage what they get."

I asked the head Chinese doctor if we couldn't follow China's example and try to eradicate malaria. Perhaps my project could provide the money and the Chinese could teach us how to do it.

She gave a long answer in her soft voice, her fine features wrinkled into a frown. The gist of it came at the end.

"The problem here is hygiene and culture. People don't clean themselves and take care of their environment. It is not just a question of spraying the mosquitoes. Guineans are not like the Chinese."

"Under the Circumstances . . . "

Business was difficult in Equatorial Guinea. Two examples came to my attention in a single day.

My friends at Casa Mota invited me to watch the loading of a big shipment of cocoa at the port. I went in the afternoon to the Mota offices and everyone was frustrated.

"The boat already left," one of them explained. "It couldn't wait any longer and went over to Bata for a shipment of timber. If it picks up a big load there, we're sunk."

Why did it leave?

"We couldn't get the shipping papers signed. First at the port, then at the Ministry of Industry and Commerce. No one was there. It rained this morning, you know, so the guy never went to work. Emilio tried to track him down at home, but he wasn't there. He's still out looking for him."

I went home for lunch. After lunch my friend Ottar came by. He was the tall, phlegmatic young captain of the *Trader*, the old ferry that had flunked safety tests in Norway and somehow ended up plying a weekly Douala-Malabo run. I gave Ottar a gin and tonic and asked him what was new.

"This has been the worst day for me, Robert," he said in his deep voice.

He didn't follow up this remark. I asked what had happened.

"I have been to see the President."

Another pause. Of the country?

"Yes, of the country. It started in Douala. Before the owner left, he told me not to accept on credit any shipments from the government, since they owed us so much money. In Douala, a Guinean official told me to take over a bunch of Mercedeses that had been transhipped to Douala from Europe. I said I couldn't and told him why. The guy came on the boat to Malabo with us.

"After we arrived, an official from the Defense Ministry came to talk to us. Again, I said that I had orders not to deliver anything more until the bills were paid. He left angry.

"So today a bunch of soldiers showed up at the boat waving submachine guns. Their leader said I had to come to the presidential palace right now. So I did, with our Guinean representative. We went up behind the gates above the harbor. I was taken right into the President's office.

"The President asked if I spoke Spanish. I said I did but would like the interpreter anyway. Then he set into a tough lecture that I had to bring the Mercedeses to Malabo from Douala and then on to Bata for the UDEAC conference. He would pause for the translator to translate, and then before I could get a word in, he would go right on.

"He said that if we didn't take the cars, he would nationalize the boat right now and expel all its foreigners from the country.

"Under the circumstances, I have no choice but to take the cars."

The best part of Ottar's story was what happened next. The Equatoguineans are sticklers for formality. Ottar had come directly from the boat dressed as he was, which meant a shirt and pants—nothing formal. Before he left the President's waiting room, Ottar was given a piece of paper saying he was being fined CFA 100,000—about $335—because he had come to see the President without a coat and tie.

I asked Ottar whether he was going to pay it.

"Nooooo," he lowed. "The President promised me he would pay us in ten days, and I know he won't. I'm not going to pay either."

"Useless Experts"

It wasn't just the foreigners who exhibited an us-versus-them attitude. The Guineans had their own versions.

Despite a cherubic face and a mischievous smile, Eduardo looked to be in his early forties. He wore his hair in a slight Afro, unusual here, and equally unusual, he was an engaging and relatively open government official. He had a sense of humor. He needed one. Eduardo was a director general in a Planning Ministry that was, among the many unproductive ones I had seen in the developing world, a real dinosaur.

On Eduardo's desk sat a shortwave radio which delivered every day at noon a half-hour of Spanish-language world news picked up from the Voice of America's transmissions to Latin America. In recounting his adventures traveling in the United States and the Soviet Union, he revealed a nice sense of wonder but also a critical eye about both systems. He made sophisticated assessments of capitalism and communism, their strong points and weak. Over the first few months, Eduardo and I had enjoyed beers a couple of times and once a lunch at my house. We had also discussed the country's draft development plan, which was being crafted mainly by United Nations advisers.

Like me, Eduardo was skeptical of the foreign experts.

"These *expertos,* they are paid so much and they do so little. It is our plight as a small and forgotten country that many times we are sent 'experts' who are not capable enough to get jobs in their own countries. They are sent here at exorbitant salaries. You know, on many projects we do not get the aid unless we also take an adviser."

I knew. That was the case with my project. One "condition of effectiveness" was the employment of an "expert" with my job title.

"Once I was negotiating an investment project with a donor agency. They said we needed three advisers, and the advisers' salaries constituted over half the budget of the project. 'You need these experts,' they told me, 'because you people do not have the analytical capacity.' Analytical capacity!" Eduardo flashed that smile but shook his head.

"So I said, 'I agree with you,' " he quoted himself in his sweetest voice. " 'We do not have the analytical capacity to do this job. But then should the project therefore not contain provisions to create that capacity?'

"They could not see it. Training was not included in the budget, they said. So I asked, 'How can we develop the analytical capacity without training? Or do we just not have it up here?' " Eduardo patted his Afro.

He said the foreigners laughed, and as he told the story, Eduardo laughed. But the story wasn't funny. The donors hadn't come through with the training. And few aid projects in Equatorial Guinea include internal training for Equatoguinean officials. The foreign experts do not instruct, they just do a job. Indeed, contrary to the usual practice in foreign aid, most expatriates do not have local counterparts who might absorb skills through on-the-job training. The result will be unalleviated dependency, with expensive foreigners perpetually justified by the "lack of local talent."

"Foreigners have not helped us," Eduardo said. "We have had many bad experiences. First the Spaniards, then the Russians and the Chinese. Now the United Nations and the French and the World Bank."

He and I knew one bad experience well. The Planning Ministry had received a World Bank-funded "macroeconomist" from South America who, I was told, had done nothing for a year. I couldn't believe he could be as bad as people said, so I began meeting with him twice a week to find out what he thought of the economy and its problems and what topics most interested him. After six sessions I gave up. The man never moved forward. Once when we were talking about cocoa economics, he drew a graph that made it clear he literally did not grasp supply and demand. The Ph.D. in economics his German consulting firm claimed for him had to be as bogus as the orange tint in his hair.

Eduardo continued. "The foreign experts come, they get discouraged, and they take it as easy as they can. You know, after we had the *golpe de libertad* in 1979, the United Nations sent a mission here to assess our needs. They said we would require many experts, but before they could send us anyone, new houses would have to be built and cars imported. No matter that we needed emergency aid, the new houses would come first. That took two years.

"The foreign experts make sure they have their air-conditioning and cars and trips to Douala, and then many of them do not even come to work." He was unconvinced about the motives and results not only of international capitalism and international socialism but also of international aid.

101

The only justification for foreign experts, Eduardo and I agreed, was as teachers, as builders of analytical capacity. He and I planned a short course for local officials on strategies for improving the overall economy as well as for particular sectors. He was enthusiastic. "You are the first adviser who wants to teach us," he said at another meeting. We planned to study twelve case studies from other countries, which I had brought with me. He had talked about the idea with my old friend Florencio of mining and the Director General of Agriculture, and both had been supportive.

"I like the way the course is practical," Eduardo said. "I know just the people who should be invited. The directors general from the technical ministries. It will fit right in with my efforts to generate more cooperation among the ministries at the technical level."

He set to work organizing the seminar. Every week or so I asked him how it was going, and he said it was moving. Unfortunately, a new Planning Minister had still not been appointed, and I thought this might have contributed to the indecision. But then a new minister, Don Diego, was named. The thing still dragged on. I left Eduardo unanswered notes.

Finally I saw him one afternoon and asked him what I could do to help.

Eduardo seemed uncharacteristically stiff. "Roberto, people ask, *why* do you want to give this course? What is in it for you? Why aren't other advisers from other countries also giving the course with you?" He didn't look me in the eye.

Surprised, I went over our earlier conversations. The need for training. The need for practical examples. The need to foment cooperation among the technical people in the ministries. I told Eduardo how well such seminars had been received in other countries where I'd given them. Of course, other advisers could be included if he and his colleagues wished.

Eduardo listened and paused. Finally he raised his eyebrows. "I don't know, Roberto. People don't understand why."

Even Eduardo, with his yearning for better training and his friendship for me, had fallen under the spell of the country's paranoia. I never heard another word from him on the subject. And a month later, he was transferred to a job in Cameroon.

The Bata branch of the Chamber of Agriculture and Forestry of Bata had coffee as its principal concern. Coffee production had decayed, and much of what was still produced was smuggled out to Cameroon and Gabon. The head of the Bata branch of the Chamber was eloquent in describing the coffee sector's problems: quality, credit, marketing, labor. After half an hour I thought he was one of the smartest Guineans I had met.

Then came his deeper analysis of the sector's difficulties.

"The World Bank project in cocoa, they have been getting into coffee as well. Selling it through the Chamber in Malabo. They have been making deals with their friends and former employers in England and getting payoffs on the side." He fumed on.

I didn't buy it. I asked him for his evidence.

"How else would it happen that . . . " He then listed a range of problems, but particularly the fact that coffee had been sold at one price and then the international market had gone up. He said the country had lost a lot of money, and the company gained a lot, from this "exploitative contract."

I talked about the inevitable ups and downs of world prices. He shook his head.

"We always get into trouble because of the foreign advisers," he said. "The FAO project, for example, is stupid."

He elaborated, and he had a point. As I had learned from others, a warehouseful of much-needed agricultural tools and equipment had languished in Bata for two years. The United Nations Food and Agriculture Organization had canceled the project but couldn't decide what to do with the tools.

But he had drawn a conclusion. "Foreign aid projects are no help at all."

"Cheated of Charity"

Sometimes in the late afternoon I would jump on my motorcycle and head into the jungle. My favorite route was the dilapidated road that dead-ended in the mountain village of Basilé, a half hour's ride from Malabo. Within a mile I was in the forest. Reeds thicketed the roadside, above them wildly overgrown and abandoned cocoa trees, and then towering trees of many varieties. The late afternoon light created dramatic shadows and deepened hues of already deep green. When I stopped and turned off the motor, I was surrounded by the cacophonous chirping and whirring and drone of multitudes of insects. No people or papers here, just an extreme density of life. I found this soothing.

At the end of the road is the small Bubi village of Basilé. Small clapboard houses, small children waving, small vegetable gardens with tiny enchanted scarecrows meant to frighten neighbors rather than crows.

One of Basilé's two landmarks is a huge modern concrete house overlooking Malabo. Its water tower resembles a miniature nuclear power station. A sign on the gate reads:

THERE ARE NO CHICKENS OR EGGS FOR SALE; DO NOT INSIST—
THE MANAGEMENT.

The sign was moot, for the house and its accompanying American-sponsored chicken-breeding project had been abandoned a few years ago.

"What happened was classic Equatorial Guinea," an American diplomat told me. "Government officials or soldiers would show up at the project and demand chickens. You know, for a party at the minister's or someone at the presidency. Finally there were just no chickens left to lay eggs. The project shut down."

Now the Germans were looking into the house and associated facility, with the idea of inaugurating experiments in goat breeding.

Basilé's second landmark is its church. It crowns the very end of the road, and the reeds and the jungle commence only a hundred yards farther on. The church is a beautiful structure built in 1905. Inside, the ruined wood of its graceful Gothic vaults looks centuries older. Adjacent to the church is a pleasant concrete building that houses most of the nuns.

Across the way stands the School of the Immaculate Conception, a large white structure whose surprising garden contained the only succulents I had seen on the island. The windows of the two-story building are framed with bright green shutters. Entering the school the first thing I noticed were the shining linoleum floors. I was surrounded by the faint fragrance of witch hazel. In this school about two hundred girls from all over the island studied, and it was evident that the nuns kept them busy cleaning and polishing as well as learning. I came to believe it was the neatest and most refreshing building in Equatorial Guinea.

Madre Josefina, the mother superior, greeted me with a brilliant smile. All of four-foot-ten and black like all the nuns, she was as jolly as a Christmas elf. And full of questions. Where was I from? Wasn't it dangerous to drive here on a motorcycle? Would I like to see the school? How long had I been in Equatorial Guinea?

Madre Josefina took me around the school: its austere classrooms with locally made seat desks; the wardlike dormitories on the second floor, each with fifty beds made so tight you could spin a coin on the blankets; and, below the area where the laundry was hanging, the rabbit hutches and chicken coops. She told me about the school and its students. A primary school, it nonetheless enrolled students up to eighteen years old. During the Macías years, schools were closed and some girls didn't start until they were ten or eleven.

She presented several of the other nuns, who shared her radiant smile, possessing what in Spanish is called *alegría,* or "joy." I have always imagined that people touched by grace share an *alegría.* Whatever their brand of belief, you can see it right away: a kind of magical projection of energy, delight, and selflessness.

Madre Josefina showed me her small office on the second floor, and then we went across the way to the church. I admired its architecture.

"Do you see the roof up there, Roberto, and the sagging walls? Five years ago we received a charitable donation to repair them. We contacted a Spanish construction man. He looked at the church and gave us an estimate." The figure was the *bikuele* equivalent of about fifteen thousand dollars. "He asked for the money in advance to import the materials we needed. But then he went to Spain and never came back."

Couldn't he be tracked down through the Spanish government?

"We made remonstrations but nothing resulted. We were simply cheated of this charity. Many people have now told us we were foolish to trust the Spanish businessmen. So many came after the *golpe de libertad,* but so many quickly left after taking loans and not repaying them."

I went to Basilé frequently. After a while I tried to think what I could do to help the school. Money, yes. But something more valuable. One day Madre Josefina and I hit on an idea. How about once a week inviting a different member of Malabo's international community to make a presentation to the students about their country? One week a Nigerian, then a Russian, then an Argentinian, then a Finn. Madre Josefina and the nuns loved the idea, and I drew up an outline.

But the school's two lay teachers were not so sure. One afternoon I met with one of them. "Why do you want to do this?" he asked with a grim face. "What do you hope to gain from it?"

I never got used to the suspiciousness toward foreigners. But we talked and talked and finally I think he realized this was an innocent venture that might do some good for the students—and for the insular international community of Malabo. The teacher liked the latter point. In fact, he became enthusiastic.

"But it is essential to make a formal proposal to the Ministry of Education and get their approval," he said. I refrained from shaking my head. I went home and drafted a proposal. A week later the school read it and changed it, and it was delivered to the ministry.

Months passed. I often went to the ministry to check on the proposal, and Madre Josefina said she went there twice. No action. Paranoia, then bureaucracy.

IMF Meeting

The attitude of us versus them was not absent from negotiations with the IMF and the World Bank.

The Fund came back to town in early November 1986. The meetings opened in the same place, the BEAC building's cavernous second-floor conference room. But most of the faces had changed. Don Milagroso was in jail, and his colleague, the French heavy, was not in attendance. The IMF people were all new. The athletic Italian, Aliardo, had gray hair, glasses, a bulbous nose, and great repartee in Spanish or English. The team also included a charming Englishwoman and a young, wispish American who recalled Huck Finn. Esteban of the World Bank was back, now like an old friend to me, again joining the IMF mission in another example of growing Bank-Fund togetherness. The Guinean side included four blacks and six white advisers from Finance, BEAC, and Planning. Guy, the senior French adviser, was there. But the woman with the cigarette-smoke tusks had long ago departed to France. Don Bonifacio was sick with malaria.

In his stead, the director of the budget, Don Fausto, offered words of welcome. Since the head of the IMF team was not due for six days, it was Aliardo who offered a response.

"We are here first of all to get information," he said. "We are particularly interested in budget data, debt information, balance of payments, and public enterprises. As this last is something we have not studied in detail in the past, we wish your help, Don Fausto, in arranging appointments with all of the public enterprises." He then explained that negotiations would not begin till next week. Then Dugan would arrive. The head of the mission, Dugan was presently negotiating in Malawi.

"Appointments with people from all the public enterprises" proved a troublesome concept to Don Fausto. He was a large man as Guineans go, amiable, strangely hirsute (mustache, sideburns, and a fur ball under his lower lip, hairless arms), not sharp-looking in a gray bush suit. His problem wasn't personal, as it turned out, but logistical. First there were a lot of people to try to see in a short time, and then, well, the idea of an appointment was difficult. Could people be asked to come to a certain place at a certain time?

Aliardo insisted, so Fausto did his best. And to Fausto's surprise, most people actually did come to BEAC for the appointments. The next days were full of one group after another being quizzed by the visitors about their balance sheets, plans, and performance.

For example, two days later I sat in on the examination of ENERGE, the state-run electricity company. Two Guinean functionaries had come, along with Gracián, a young South American "expert" paid for by the United Nations. Gracián's blazer and shirt recalled an airline pilot. The knot in his necktie was the size of a small apple. I knew Gracián. He loved to talk, to use formalities, to pause and gesture and say things like "Well, you understand, one could say there are three reasons, interrelated of course. . . . "

Esteban asked the group some tough questions about ENERGE. The Guineans looked at each other blankly. Then Gracián allowed himself to speak. *"Bueno, pues . . . ,"* he harrumphed. But before he could get rolling, one of the Guineans interjected to Esteban, "We didn't know you were going to ask such questions, and we don't have the data with us."

Don Fausto said, "You should have known. I told the secretary general personally what the topics would be and he told the director and he told you."

"No, I didn't get the news," came the response. Don Fausto repeated himself. Then there was silence.

Finally Esteban spoke. "Well, can we hear something about the big picture at ENERGE?"

Big pictures were Gracián's bag. He cleared his throat. "Well, it was thought, or it is thought, that if a company were to fulfill the conditions that an independent company should fulfill in this country, then on this basis it should be an independent company."

That was his first sentence as verbatim as I could get it. Gracián kept on rolling. There were many needs, he expounded. New legislation, for example. Moreover, "It is needed to follow steps that are necessary for . . . and also certain economic steps such that the country could move forward economically as it ought to, things that should be studied in great detail, of the economy."

Finally there was silence. Gracián held his tie in his left hand, pursed his lip, fidgeted with his chin. I wondered if my note taking was stimulating him to talk all the more. Then he was off again, concatenating clauses. My concentration seeped away.

But suddenly the Guineans were disagreeing with him. No, there had not been a new decree in mid-1986, they said. Gracián looked troubled. "But ——" he began. One of his colleagues interrupted him and explained. Gracián frowned mightily. Then he could not be restrained. With the forefinger of his right hand gesturing like a master scolding his pet, he said, "Let me see if I understand well what you are saying . . . ," and repeated.

This went on for another five minutes. At the end, it turned out Gracián was wrong about the decree.

So it went. But some facts did get established. Three of the four electricity-generating machines were not working. The European Economic Community was to provide a massive new generator by April 1987. A new electricity transmission network was being constructed. The old one fell apart because of lack of maintenance, though the EEC was rehabilitating part of the network.

ENERGE planned to install electricity meters in homes and offices within nine months. A guess on the basis of billings was that about a third of the electricity was used by the government, another third by government officials in their homes, and about a ninth each by foreign embassies, private residences, and industry-commerce-services. The company was losing lots of money. It cost 170 *cefas* to generate a kilowatt hour, but the average tariff charged was only 73 *cefas* per kilowatt hour. About 90 percent of government offices did not pay their electricity bills, and it was almost official that government employees did not pay either. As a result, ENERGE was being paid for only about 30 percent of the electricity it was billing out.

No wonder, then, that ENERGE was providing juice only from around noon to three and then in the evening from dusk till midnight. The rest of the time, people sweated in the dark. The underlying problem was not generating capacity: it was the economics of high costs and low billing rates. For each additional hour of electricity supplied, ENERGE would simply lose more money.

A hydroelectric project for the island was under negotiation. If approved, it would come on stream in 1990 and provide electricity on the island at much more reasonable rates. The World Bank was fighting the project, saying its capital costs were simply too large for the country to bear. The government adamantly wanted it. No matter what, though, it was clear that Equatorial Guinea would have to come up with a strategy for pricing and charging for the electricity generated. Government salaries were so low that the minimum wage, if spent entirely on electricity, would barely cover two lights, a fan, and a refrigerator. It was hard to collect from people who were paid so little. But unless the EEC or the Germans or the Chinese or somebody else was willing to pay, the electricity company would soon be out of business.

The last session with the IMF was high drama. It had been preceded by fact finding and rocky negotiations. Would we get the long-sought agreement with the IMF that would not only provide the needed funds but also go some way toward justifying Don Bonifacio's and the government's economic program?

Several days before, Dugan had arrived. An Irishman in his forties, with hair flowing back like a Shakespearean actor, a quick mind, and an encyclopedic memory, he was as good a negotiator as I had ever seen.

"Fine, the point is noted as one under disagreement," he would calmly say in French at an impasse. "Let us move to the next point."

Pitted against him was Don Bonifacio, weak and puffy from malaria but—to my pride and, I admit, my surprise—remarkably eloquent, persistent, and adroit. Don Bonifacio had a university degree in economics and was considered one of the only intellectuals in the government. During these negotiations, he had been showing his mettle.

That last evening at eight o'clock in the BEAC conference room, everyone was tired and testy from days and nights of work and negotiation. In the evenings it had become the custom to dress informally; no one wore ties. The contrast with daytime's elegance lent a tone of scruffiness and desperation to the proceedings.

The meeting began. Don Bonifacio produced new data saying that government revenues were actually 15 percent higher than earlier estimated. This would close the gap the IMF team had identified; Don Bonifacio hoped it would justify a favorable IMF decision.

Dugan responded that the team would have to study the figures. He proposed that expenditure cuts now be discussed.

Don Bonifacio said there was no way to cut expenditures any further, so let's talk about revenues. They are 15 percent higher, so that should be good enough for an agreement with the Fund.

Dugan said the mission would have to study the new figures in Washington. For a while he and Don Bonifacio parried inconclusively on possible increases in taxes. The negotiation was going nowhere.

Then Dugan gave a little speech, as usual in French. It signaled we had reached the end. The government would need a sound adjustment program for many reasons, Dugan said, such as renegotiating its debts with the Paris Club. The government had made a great deal of progress. The reasons the Fund could not finalize an agreement were partly beyond the government's control. Nonetheless, further domestic austerity measures were essential. We will leave a letter describing these measures and a timetable.

Don Bonifacio listened grimly.

Dugan went on, softly and slowly. "In my experience, in many negotiations it is difficult to finalize agreements, especially when exogenous factors are so important. There has been much progress in Equatorial Guinea. Let us then leave with you a procedure and a schedule of work needed to finalize an accord. I propose that we have new discussions in January."

Don Bonifacio was stunned.

"I cannot believe after so many negotiations since April, all the tourist trips to Washington, that we cannot arrive at an accord. It seems incomprehensible, after all these efforts, that there is no agreement." Exasperated, he accused the IMF of not negotiating in good faith. Don Bonifacio was trembling when he finished—a result, I supposed, of anger, strain, and illness combined. Negotiations that had been courteous though tense now reached a boil. I wondered what Dugan would do.

He let silence reign for a moment. Then he spoke, as calm as a pond in the morning.

He expressed regret that the minister could have interpreted the Fund's stance as anything but helpful and sincere. He pointed out he was going tomorrow to Paris and then to Madrid in order to plead in both places Equatorial Guinea's case. "That is not a vacation."

"Sincerely I do not see that good will," Don Bonifacio replied bitterly. "I do not think you should want financial equilibrium in the first year. It is true there remain problems, such as Guinextebank, but they worry us, too, and we have taken measures. Don't you like them? We have been beating everyone up, waiting for you so we could finalize our budget, and now you say we cannot have an agreement, after all our efforts. None of this seems to have even any relative value for you. I know this is a new IMF team but you should know the history and not come in empty. Maybe that is why, you do not know the past of what we have done, you act as though you know nothing about what we have already accomplished."

The exchanges continued in this vein. Dugan may have a deeper agenda on our behalf, I reflected. If he went to Paris and Madrid without an agreement, he could put pressure on the French for more budgetary aid and on the Spanish for a favorable resolution of the bankrupt Guinextebank. But with an IMF agreement, both the French and the Spanish might relax and say, "Well, then we're not needed."

Don Bonifacio still wanted a deal. He proposed we meet again at eleven at night after the Fund drafted its letter and studied the new revenue figures.

Dugan demurred as soothingly as possible. It was not unusual, he said— indeed, it was normal—not to reach agreement on a mission. "You cannot give us new figures the night before we leave and expect us to negotiate." His voice and manner stilled some of the turbulence.

After the meeting, Don Bonifacio and I ended up back at the Finance Ministry and—unusually—we went across the street and had a beer together at the Beiruth. We sat at one of the outside tables off in the shadows. Cockroaches clattered below, and a skyful of stars glittered overhead.

After a while Don Bonifacio said, "Roberto, I can ask you this because I can see you are more independent than the rest of the advisers here. Do you really think that the IMF is negotiating with us in good faith?"

He recounted his complaints, his disappointments. He had hoped to get an agreement, and I discerned he had banked on it in his conversations with the President. The negotiations' failure was perforce his own, and his frustration and fatigue were part of a well-known recipe for imagining a conspiracy. I suspected that the theory was not originally his own but that of important figures in the government. "*They* are against us, not on our side" went a popular pattern of explanation. The failure of these negotiations with the IMF were only one instance of the foreigners letting *us* down. For example, look at the economic rehabilitation project: the World Bank still hadn't made it effective.

In his disappointment with the failed negotiations, Bonifacio was wrestling with the conspiratorial argument.

"Roberto, sometimes I don't think the IMF and the World Bank are trying to help us." He paused and looked me squarely in the eyes. "I think they are trying to sink us."

"No IMF agreement, no economic rehabilitation project," Horace of the World Bank was yelling over a terrible transatlantic telephone connection. He couldn't resist adding a dig: "What do you think about that, Mr. Optimism?"

I reminded Horace that "cross-conditionality" between the Fund and the Bank was forbidden by both organizations. You couldn't make a World Bank project depend on an IMF agreement.

Horace said they weren't. The Bank was simply living up to two clauses in the project document. One clause said a rotating loan fund would be created at the Banco de Crédito y Desarrollo, the government's development bank. But the BCD wasn't functioning, so that was out. Another clause said the World Bank had to approve the public investment program. But the budget hadn't been finalized because the IMF money hadn't come, so there was no investment program to approve.

I didn't buy it. If the IMF and Equatorial Guinea had reached an agreement, the Bank would have made my project "effective." If that wasn't cross-conditionality, it was a snappingly vicious circle.

Horace was unsympathetic. "If it were up to me," he shouted, "your crazy country would get no money at all."

Meanwhile, our project had exhausted the meager "project preparation funds" approved at its signing. I was personally out of pocket about ten thousand dollars for project-related expenses, and my salary had not been paid.

5

Beginning to Move

EARLY in October, before the IMF visit, Ottar had come by the house one afternoon and asked whether I would like to go to Bata with the *Trader.*

"We have to take over four Mercedeses for the President," he said. "We'll be there for a week, staying through Independence Day, October twelfth. How about it?"

I could take over my motorcycle and see some of the interior. Everyone had told me how different Río Muni was from Bioko. Río Muni had beautiful beaches, fewer insects and diseases, more exotic animals like parrots and gorillas and elephants. The mainland portion of Equatorial Guinea is twelve times as large as the island of Bioko, so there was plenty to explore. Moreover, Río Muni has three quarters of the country's population, most of its coffee and timber, and most of the potential for food production and fishing and mining. Nonetheless, most foreign aid projects remained on the island, near the capital; and some top aid officials never visited the continental interior. "No hotels," one of them explained.

Transportation between Malabo and Bata was limited. The thrice-weekly air flights were too small and too expensive to satisfy much of the demand. The large government-owned boat *Acacio Mañé* went once in a while, sometimes every couple of weeks but maybe every couple of months. Whenever it did go, it looked like a refugee ship, its decks swarming with an antlike profusion of people plus cars and boxes and containers and produce. The *Trader* had never been to Bata before, but soon the news was all over town.

On the evening of our departure, I went down to the old dock at six o'clock to put the bike on board before the eight-o'clock departure. The entire area was full of people and trucks and cars and soldiers. Hundreds of men, women, and children were pushing to get on board, but they were hardly moving because police and soldiers were inspecting documents and baggage. Hundreds more were on hand to say goodbye or simply to be part of the big occasion. I had seen nothing like this mob scene in Equatorial Guinea.

Ottar and Sigurd, the chief engineer, were observing the turmoil from the top of the boat. Seeing me enveloped in the bodies and baggage, Ottar came down to talk to the police and help me and my motorcycle get on board.

Eventually I joined him and Sigurd on the top deck. It was now dark, and large powerful lights shone from the boat onto the teeming crowd. Something happened in the front of the line, and a policeman started shouting abuse. Suddenly he and a colleague pulled out clubs and began beating people over the head. In the surreally sharp light, blood spurted, red and bright as nail polish.

"Wellll, Robert," Ottar lowed, "how do you like your adopted country now? These people *are* savages, don't you see?"

Sigurd laughed and swigged some beer. "They're different, Bob, and don't you forget it!"

The boat finally left at ten that night, and we did not arrive till the next afternoon at two. Docking at the port south of Bata was difficult. The sea was choppy, and the dock was exposed to open ocean: no breakwater, no enclosed bay like Malabo's. The tide was low, so we had to climb out on ladders. The cars, and eventually my motorcycle, were hauled up in giant nets by cranes on the dock. While waiting for my bike, I carried the surfboard to the beach at the end of the pier. White sands projected as far south as I could see. (A few days later I took the bike down that beach and drove twelve and a half miles before hitting a river.) But if Río Muni were bordered by beaches as fine as any in the world, the waves were weak. During my stay I explored every day, and every day I found baby shore-breaks and nothing more. I paddled out and splashed around in some two-footers.

After a shower back on the boat, I fetched my satchel and took the bike the two and a half miles into Bata. It was another world from Malabo and the island. For one thing, although it was the rainy season and storms blew in almost daily, the air was much less humid. The canopy of the sky was higher and wider; faraway mountain ranges of clouds, as white as whipped cream, were set off by a bright blue sky. The horizon was broader, too; the sea looked endless; and at dusk spectacular sunsets burned red and pink and orange.

Bata itself reflects a sense of wide-open spaces. The main avenues are broad and bordered by trees; some of the sidewalks seem like promenades. Buildings are low and white and mostly cement: no plantation-style dwellings like mine in Malabo. Bata seems a little less dilapidated than Malabo—probably a reflection of the drier climate.

In Malabo views of the ocean are mostly blocked by buildings and trees. In Bata, you can drive along the beach for miles. The city rises gently from the sea, so ocean views are everywhere—unlike Malabo, which is fairly level after the cliffs from the harbor.

On the north side of Bata, where the beachfront becomes a bay, I came upon an old pier sticking out like a lame leg, its tall concrete piles raising it well above the ocean. On the bay side a couple of small boats sat wrecked and rusting. And perfectly shaped one-foot waves were wrapping around the base of the pier and peeling across the bay—a great break if you were six inches tall.

Driving along the bay, I came to the crossroads to the interior. Here I found an informal bus station, along with rickety "hotels," places to eat, dusty stores, and much milling about.

Continuing along the sea, I drove by spread-out cement houses and the prefab dwellings of Spanish technical assistance. The last structure before the airport was a strange, abandoned hotel, the wings of its futuristic but half-finished construction sweeping seaward like concrete tail fins. Someone had visualized a unique tourist retreat, and the beachside location was perfect. But the dream had died, and the hotel's rusted rebars protruded like a skeleton's ribs.

I made my way back into town to the Hotel Rondo, which I found down a dirt road and then a kind of path. This was supposed to be the friendliest place to stay and, unlike the more modern Panafrica Hotel on the beach in town, it served food.

A dining area greeted me: worn-out easy chairs, then tables and chairs, the kitchen in the distance, and through an opening to the yard a view of chickens wandering. The area was covered in tin sheeting, and iron rebars had been artistically fashioned to form a sort of airy wall. Doña Modesta welcomed me, and I brought her greetings from a cousin in Malabo.

"Chico!" she cried upon hearing his name, and soon I felt like a member of the family. I was introduced to four generations of women. Two great-grandmothers were sitting on the settees. These *abuelas* eyed me with suspicious, squinting eyes but then smiled broadly when I came over and shook their hands. Modesta herself was a grandmother—I guessed she was forty-five. Emilia was twenty-five or so and had a brood; the attractive Mónica at eighteen decidedly had brood-making potential. A host of children gathered around to meet me, including Emilia's four-year-old Wendy. The little girl shyly tucked her chin down to her neck and looked up and sidewise at me, but averting her eyes in embarrassment when I looked back; it was the beginning of a mutual crush.

They took me to one of the ten small rooms with a bed and a sink and a fan and showed me the showers and toilets at the end of the dark hallway. Since half the rooms were taken up by Emilia and her husband and their kids and Mónica and Modesta herself and her husband, the place had an authentic family feeling.

While I had a beer and talked with Modesta, a girl walked in carrying on her head a fish as big as her leg. Later I met Modesta's husband, who was a member of the city council, and we talked into the night about local events. The fish turned out to be delicious.

The next morning I awoke to heavy rain. After breakfast when it was only drizzling, I went by motorcycle the mile or so from the hotel to the center of town. I had a lot of appointments.

First I went to the Chamber of Agriculture. No one there. Then down the street to the Ministry of Mines and Hydrocarbons. No one there either. Then up the hill and down the other side to the Ministry of Finance. "The regional administrator just left, *señor.*"

I was starting to see why people said that official life on the mainland was more relaxed.

It began again to pour. I waited under the eaves and watched the gray rain patter on the tall trees. Finally the regional administrator arrived. He received me in a large gloomy office—there was no electricity. I had a note from the secretary general requesting his help in studying problems of customs collection in Río Muni. A better-functioning customs office could help close the gap between revenues and expenditures. Proportional to the value of its official imports, the Bata customs office received only a third to a half of the revenues of Malabo. No doubt there was more smuggling in Río Muni, too.

The administrator agreed that there were big problems. He was bald, which was unusual in Guinea, and had a large, intelligent face. Like most officials on the continent, he did not wear a necktie—a wise and welcome change from Malabo's dress code. "We have many constraints here," he explained. "We cannot offer our workers adequate salaries, and it is difficult to penalize transgressors. For details you should see the regional customs director. His office is there, across the street."

I thanked him, circumnavigated the roundabout, and entered an old cement building painted an unnatural aqua blue. Owing to the overcast sky, light was sparse inside the building. I entered a large bullpen divided by an angular counter of dark wood. The regional customs administrator was beckoned. He greeted me, and I was surprised. I had expected his job to be so sensitive, or lucrative, that only a suspicious and probably corrupt old-timer would hold it. But the director was only in his early thirties and so short as to seem boyish. Far from being defensive, he was eager to please.

"Here, let me introduce our experts to you," he said proudly, leading me next door. In a dark room among plenty of scattered papers sat three very black men in three-piece suits. The director spoke to them in French and introduced me. I bade them good day in Spanish. They did not seem to understand. I asked the director where they were from. "Other countries of our regional customs grouping," he said. "This man is from Chad, that one from Gabon, and this other one from Cameroon. They are helping us adjust our system to the UDEAC norms." French speakers, then, and the director later told me that none had learned any Spanish. What do they do amidst those piles of papers? "They help us," was the director's vague reply.

We went to his office. Its walls had cracks like tectonic plates. There the director described his problems or, as he put it in terms I did not expect, his "strategic difficulties."

"I've been on this job for one year," he said. "We have strategic difficulties. First are the warehouses. You probably saw them out at the port. They are supposed to be under our control. We are supposed to take incoming shipments to the warehouses for customs assessment and processing. But the warehouses have been taken over by the Ministry of Public Works. You see, we had a big agricultural project with the Food and Agricultural Organization of the United Nations. They gave the country a large amount of agriculture inputs—tools, sacks of lime and copper sulfate, rubber boots, and so forth. We were ordered to store these goods in a warehouse when they first arrived. But the project was then canceled for reasons I do not know. The goods are still in the warehouse, unused. We can't get rid of them. Another warehouse is full of Chinese-donated goods and cement for the port, so we can't use that one either. As a result, when imports arrive we have no place to hold them. We let people take them directly from the port and ask them to bring us the documentation here for processing. This leads to much more underinvoicing and payoffs.

"A second problem is our long frontier with Cameroon. The road runs right along the border for many kilometers [about 50 miles]. This makes smuggling easy. We have vehicles to patrol these areas, but most of them are out of order. We don't get to use them much. They are always being requisitioned by visiting officials from other ministries and then are misused and left out of order.

"For this reason I decided to set up a checkpoint in Niefang." Niefang is in the mountains a little over sixty miles east of Bata at the point where two roads from the interior connect to the one road leading to Bata. "The big smuggling is brought there to sell. So I want to put a checkpoint there to look at all the trucks and vehicles passing, making sure that they are not smugglers."

When I asked whether I could visit this checkpoint and see how it was working, the director readily agreed.

We talked for a while about incentives for customs officials. He said that the lack of rewards and punishments caused inefficiency and corruption. "I have no decision-making power here. Everything has to go to Malabo to the director general of customs and most things from there to the minister." He told a story about his attempt to discipline two officials who had extorted bribes. Their cases had been sent to Malabo where they had sat without action for over a year, while the officials continued on their jobs.

I thanked him and left for the regional office of the Ministry of Public Works. A director general was visiting from Malabo, the huge and amiable architect Miguelín. The minister had told him about our economic rehabilitation project.

"You must see the roads and the port," Miguelín said. "They need repairs. The minister asked me to help you see the roads. You can take a trip tomorrow with one of our road engineers."

He gave me a French study to read. He introduced me to the road engineer, César, who would take me on a tour the next day. César and I arranged to meet at my hotel at eight.

The next morning at quarter to eight, César and a driver arrived in a small Spanish-made copy of a Land Rover pickup. I said I'd be finished with breakfast in ten minutes. The driver said, "Fine, I'll be right back." Forty minutes later he returned. "I had some business at home," he said.

"My wife is sick." We crammed into the tiny front seat. There was space for two, so long as one was a child or a dog. We were, however, three men. I was wedged against the door with my arm around César, who was clammy and fragrant. As we drove to the ministry, I suggested that we didn't need a chauffeur, that César and I could go alone.

"Oh no, that would be impossible!" César exclaimed. "You don't know how bad the roads are here! They are full of holes and very winding! It may rain, too. We need a driver."

Just then our driver made an erratic turn with a slight skid—on, I noted, a good road and at a clearly visible intersection. In a lightning calculation, I reckoned that the discomforts of a couple of hundred kilometers in these cramped quarters were not convincingly outweighed by the likely increment in driving safety due to our chauffeur's apparent talents. I hadn't studied economics for nothing.

When we got to the ministry, I talked with the minister and insisted that César and I go alone. César then said he didn't know how to drive. Fine, I'll drive. The minister asked if I had my driver's license, as we would surely be stopped by police at checkpoints. I said I'd go back to the hotel and get it. Into the Land Rover and off I went.

At the first intersection I made a discovery. The vehicle had no brakes. I made an erratic turn with a slight skid. Pump those brakes. After five pumps a slight slowing. Holy smokes! Right turn, right turn, and back to the ministry I went.

"This vehicle is unsafe, it needs repairs," I explained to the minister, Miguelín, César, and the driver. The driver said no, it was fine. I said it had no brakes. Miguelín arbitrated. He got in, started off, and got to the intersection. He made an erratic turn with a slight skid. A couple of minutes later he was back. A diplomat by nature, Miguelín found a compromise position between mine and the driver's.

"I can see what you mean about the brakes, Roberto," he said. "On the other hand, the driver is used to them."

The minister seemed embarrassed and ordered that the brakes be fixed. Tomorrow we would go. I got a lift back to the hotel. I decided to drive south by motorcycle to Mbini, a town at the mouth of the river of the same name.

A few minutes later I was off. Nearly two miles outside of Bata, the dirt road to Mbini began. The road had holes and huge ruts and almost no traffic. On both sides stood dense walls of jungle whose interwoven trees, vines, bushes, and grasses seemed impenetrable. I passed small clearings in the forest, containing a few houses with wood-plank walls, some painted in faded white, most with thatched roofs. These clearings were clean, even pristine. The soil was the red African dirt of the continent, not Bioko's black volcanic topsoil. Goats and children seemed to be grazing together. The goats scattered at the sound of the motorcycle's engine. The children waved. Whoa, watch the road there. Mud from last night's rain. Slipping and slithering.

After about forty miles came Río Mbini. The river was much wider than I expected. The low concrete bridge must have been over a mile long. The rapids were tremendous. The rainy season's runoffs had swelled the river and created islets of rocks and giant trees, surrounded by rushing cannonades of water.

I arrived at Mbini about an hour later. In colonial times it must have been an important commercial and government center, for abandoned, official-looking buildings were spread over a large area with many empty spaces. But with the ravages of Macías and the economic collapse, it now looked like a ghost town. Mbini had no electricity at all, and the people I spoke with said there were no jobs, either.

A dirt track took me to the beach and then out to the point. The scene was spectacular: the Atlantic Ocean in the distance; the huge brown river flowing slowly by; the dense jungle on the distant other side; above me, craggy trees overhanging the sand; and just behind me to the left, a gorgeous pink house up on the rocks with a hundred-and-eighty-degree view of the water.

On a whim I turned the bike down a narrow, muddy path through the jungle and proceeded motocross-style, fording creeks and climbing stones and the large roots of adjacent trees. I passed several humble huts, whose inhabitants looked with friendly astonishment at the tall white man on a motorcycle. After a while it began to rain. In a nearby hut in the middle of jungle, three men were sitting on a modest porch. They welcomed me to shelter. After they had their fill of questions about me, they told me about themselves. They were content with their lives. This area had plenty of food, they said: fish and fruits were abundant, and they raised ducks and chickens. They would like better roads, some day electricity, but knew that would be a long time. The schools did not have books or paper, they said, and the clinic did not have medicines.

"You can go back this way," one man pointed out when the rain stopped. "It will take you to the beach, and you can follow it back to Mbini."

I proceeded on the new path, and as the jungle thinned a bit I passed cozy dwellings built on stilts. I could look through the open doors and glassless windows into little living areas with tables and chairs and picture calendars on the walls.

The beach route was spectacular, with trees and rocks and views of the sea. Soon I was in Mbini and began the journey home. Storm clouds blew in. Just past the big bridge, the skies opened up. I pulled low the bill of my San Francisco 49ers cap to keep the pelting rain out of my eyes. In minutes the road was covered with water. From the look of the horizon's stacks of cumulonimbus clouds, I didn't think this storm would let up, so on I went, rooster-tailing mile after mile. As I rode past, people would laugh and hoot from their huts. I was laughing, too, challenged by the road and pleasantly soaked to the core.

An hour and a half later, I made it to Bata. It was still pouring at the Hotel Rondo as Modesta and the clan watched my arrival in disbelief. The rain on the tin roof over the dining area sounded like pebbles in a pan.

"Where have you been?" Modesta cried.

I told them.

"Chico! You are a crazy man! You will catch pneumonia! Change your clothes and come into the kitchen and warm up by the stove."

This I did and was soon treated, in a kitchen full of curious people, to hot soup and a lot of teasing.

Into the Interior

The next day I forayed inland.

I stopped first at the Ministry of Public Works. César explained that funds had not been found to repair the Land Rover. I said no problem, I would go by bike.

"You can't!" he cried. "The roads are so bad! And it may rain!"

I persisted, and César didn't argue much; he was probably relieved he wouldn't have to go. Soon I was off, first north a few miles to the Bata crossroads, then east into the bush.

The land was flat for twenty miles and then began to rise. I passed small villages of waving children and the everpresent goats. The houses often had roofs of thatch instead of tin. Most dwellings had unusual walls of dried mud, made by creating a kind of webbing of cane, into whose holes were inserted globs of mud. When the mud dried, the surface looked like brick. This construction was said to be cooler than wood.

The villages surprised me. The areas between houses were spotless, but

121

the houses themselves were filthy and smoky and cluttered inside. Each village had an enclosed area called the house of the word. The roof was thatched, and the woven walls were only about chest high, open all the way around from there to the roof. From here the men could sit and watch all that transpired in the village and on the road.

The road itself was in a deplorable state. It had been asphalted long ago but not maintained. Brush grew to its edge, so that rain would flow over the road and erode the hardtop. The resulting potholes, fissures, and mini-gorges were devastating to vehicular traffic. On the motorcycle it was like driving a slalom. I could avoid tire-tearing ke-thunks far better than a four-wheeled vehicle could. No wonder everyone said trucks didn't last.

Experts on such matters say that Río Muni's forests of tropical hard-woods are the richest in the world. As I climbed into the mountains, I looked out on valleys and cliffsides of towering trees, many over two hundred feet tall, backed by banks of storm clouds. The best scenery came after Niefang. I took the southeast fork onto a road now dirt, then paved, now dirt again. Up I went, surrounded by steep mountains whose exotic shapes and mists recalled old landscape paintings from China. Except here the mountainsides were teeming with trees, big trees, the tallest trees I had ever seen. I stopped at a waterfall and watched the clouds drift by the timber-lined peaks.

For three days I went back to Niefang and its environs. I talked with the customs officials, with Niefang's agricultural extension agents, with people in the market. I visited a rural development project run by the French. In a niche they had carved out in the middle of the mountains with fertile soil and plentiful water, they were testing new plant varieties and horticultural methods. The fields were full of African women; and at the end of the cleared area, up against the wall of the jungle, were three small, concrete dwellings constructed for the French experts. There was a swing set for the two French children and a large cage for the pet deer.

Each night I returned to the Hotel Rondo, and each afternoon on the way storm clouds would blow in and start pumping. On arrival I was always as wet and wrinkled as a freshly soaked prune. Modesta and her crew would shake their heads and laugh and admonish. Little Wendy shadowed her Tío Roberto everywhere.

In the evenings I read about agriculture in Río Muni. Yams, peppers, and plantains were produced; in Spanish times, fruits and vegetables of all kinds had been plentiful. But now there was little market for food, and subsistence farming was the rule. Coffee was once the continent's cash crop, with many small producers, but it had virtually dropped dead under Macías. I saw former coffee plantations abandoned and overgrown, and the marketing infrastructure had almost disappeared.

What remained to export was timber. Many French and Italian firms were coming in. It was said that their methods were exploitative: cut down trees, haul them out, ship them as giant unfinished trunks. Few jobs were thereby created, and few profits remained in the country. About a million dollars a year in tax revenues were generated by timber exports; it was said that bribes kept this sum to a third or a fourth of what it should have been.

The continent had, I thought, great economic potential. The neighbor to the north, Cameroon, had what I guessed was a four times higher per-capita income than Río Muni's. In oil-rich Gabon, which borders on the south and east, the average income was at least eight times higher. In Cameroon and Gabon, prices were high for the food Equatorial Guinea produced.

But the roads that might link Río Muni to these potential export markets were closed in the south, ruptured in the north, and rough to impassable throughout. Despite the UDEAC countries' free-trade policies for food, customs officials on our side and theirs caused delays and often extorted bribes. Under these conditions, macroeconomic reforms will make little difference; you can get the exchange rate right and free up prices, but the magic of the marketplace will remain in the bottle.

On independence day there were great celebrations with bands and dancing troupes and drumbeats in Bata's central plaza. I returned to the Hotel Rondo at about three to find some twenty family members sitting solemnly in the shade. I asked Modesta if anything were wrong. No, she said, but since some of them had to be on hand at the hotel, all of them had stayed instead of joining the festivities. This seemed a waste, so Modesta and I decided to get the music going and the wine flowing and have our own celebration.

I threw for the wine and beer and Modesta provided food. Mónica cranked up the tape deck. Soon everyone was dancing. Little Wendy and I joined in, and one of the great-grandmothers happily taught me an African dance. Each of the children received a ride around the lot on my motorcycle. Later one of the old *abuelas* needed to go home to change. I offered her a ride on the motorcycle. Though she'd never been on one, she was soon gamely sitting sidesaddle on the back of the Yamaha, being subjected to teasing and screaming laughter all around. We took off thunderously, and she was hanging on and laughing as we raced across town to her house. When we arrived at her street, one of her peers was sitting on the porch. She burst out in glee and shouted something at the *abuela* in Fang.

"Nothing, honey," responded the granny. "This is my new boyfriend!"

Our independence day party lasted till about ten that night. The next day I returned to Malabo on the *Trader* with a satchel full of special dishes prepared for the trip by various of my new friends at the Hotel Rondo.

Fitting Strategy to Environment

Soon after returning to Malabo, I began teaching a series of seminars for public managers. This was part of a two-month course organized by a United Nations project on public administration. The students were the first public officials to receive training in Equatorial Guinea in fifteen years.

When the U.N. had returned to Equatorial Guinea in the early 1980s, its experts looked around for things to do. Since no one in the government answered the phones, typed letters or responded to them, or kept track of the abundant paperwork the U.N. passed along, the experts saw what had to be done.

"Let us create a new generation of secretaries and clerks," was their cry.

I had attended the graduation of the first class of secretaries trained under the U.N. project. Invited by the ravishing and redoubtable Ramona, the twenty-one-year-old valedictorian and secretary to the Planning Minister, I chose a seat near the door of the auditorium at the Spanish Cultural Center. The students wore tight skirts and heels, and their parents and friends were decked out in their finest Western garb.

The ceremonial occasion called for rhetoric, and no one has ever accused either the United Nations or Equatoguineans of underdevelopment in that domain. A series of U.N. and government officials spoke. And spoke. And spoke. Their words were grand, their sentences endless. In orotund turns of phrase—indeed, in spiraling helices of phrase; in snarled fishing lines of phrase; in endless small intestines of phrase—the speakers ingeniously explored and invented connections between *qwerty,* alphabetical filing, and socioeconomic advance. After an hour I slipped away sleepy and benumbed, thereby forfeiting (Ramona later told me) a couple of speeches more, the presentation of the diplomas, and a graduation party that featured canned soda pop and Nescafé.

Having begun with secretaries and clerks, the U.N. project was now tackling administrators. The present course was aimed at Guinean officials who, despite fairly senior rank, usually had only a junior high or a high school education. Nonetheless, the course was a highly condensed version of a South American master's degree in public administration—that is, what the course's designers had taught or had taken back home. The course comprised a bunch of six-session instructional modules, including one on sociology, another on economics, a third on statistics. The material was relentlessly academic in the worst sense. Readings from antiquated texts were reproduced by stencil machines and expected to be read and regurgitated. None of the modules contained a single example from Equatorial Guinea.

I had been invited to teach by the doe-eyed number two of the project, an Argentinian with the remarkable nickname of Mambo. This woman was so attractive and so genuinely angelic that you would do anything for her—even listen while she talked about her husband back home in Buenos Aires.

"We'd love it, Roberto, if you could lead six classes on planning," she sighed. Whenever Mambo spoke, it was with her big green eyes locked on yours and in a soft, husky voice I involuntarily associated with intimate communication—in her case as uncontrived as breathing, but nonetheless devastating.

She unlocked her gaze, and retrieved an outline of topics prepared by the project's Chilean number one, a gray-bearded troglodyte who was Beast to her Beauty. The outline had headings like "Definitions of planning." "History of planning." "Alternative models of planning." "Planning and control." I thought of Don Constantino's notion of planning as telling people what to do.

"How about if we talk instead about what it means to have a national or ministerial strategy?" I asked.

"Whatever you would like, Roberto," Mambo smiled winningly.

So I met with the troglodyte. He looked over some of the cases I brought. I talked about the idea of a strategy and how to help government officials think strategically. He was skeptical; this was new material to him. In the end, though, he said, "Do what you think best." I supposed he couldn't sniff at a warm body willing to teach six classes for free.

I have led such seminars with top policy makers around the world. The guiding idea is to show how the choice of economic strategies and organizational structures should depend on the local "environment." This idea is familiar from the business literature. "A strategy should depend on the environment; it should not be determined in the abstract." A business is conducted in an environment of economic and political factors beyond its control: for example, the supply-and-demand conditions in the market for the product and in markets for factors of production like labor, capital, and technology. The environment is, in the short run, a given; the business can't change it with strategy. Research has shown that the best strategy and structure for a firm in a highly competitive, high-risk environment with a few large investments will probably not work for a firm in an oligopolistic, low-risk environment with many small investments. No one business strategy or structure is right for all markets and all circumstances.

The same qualitative lesson holds for countries—and for ministries and sectors. Development *strategies* and institutional *structures* should fit together and both should fit the country's *environment.* What works for one country may not work for another. To institute this idea, looking at real examples is invaluable. Participants examine how countries and ministries changed their strategies and structures to cope with changing environments. I like to use success stories, where countries or ministries turned things around. Nothing motivates like success.

In these six sessions, we began by unpacking the idea of the *environment.* For a country or ministry the term includes demographic and geographical factors, resources, and the state of international markets and industries. It also involves politics. Who will gain and lose from policies in these markets? What external actors are important? If changes are needed, who has to decide and how?

In each of the cases we studied, the students took turns describing the environment. I would write their contributions on the blackboard. Then they considered how the environment had been changing. What demographic or ecological factors, economic conditions, or political variables had shifted? What features of the environment were volatile? With a little practice, the students were good at assessing the environment.

Then we would move to *strategies.* For example, when thinking about a national economic strategy, we started with the government's objectives— growth, distribution, self-sufficiency, and so forth. Then we asked what industries and products could be the motors of future growth. What was needed to crank up those motors? What were the key macroeconomic policy levers? What might be done to make markets work better, improve public investment, overcome bottlenecks, mobilize demand? To answer these questions, we had to look at how well markets were working. We then asked where the government might appropriately intervene—or withdraw—from existing interventions. We asked about the specific services that might be provided, to which clients, and in what sequence. We analyzed the human and financial resources available for implementing various strategies.

Though I had to mix in some lecturing to explain concepts, the cases were good enough to bear most of the pedagogical burden. For example, we studied a country that had switched from a state-controlled to a fairly free-market development strategy—something like Equatorial Guinea's entrance into the UDEAC zone in 1985. We examined a government program to boost nontraditional exports, which involved a government reorganization and several new policies, plus a simultaneous pullback of government controls.

The idea of reorganization introduced the third dimension, *structure.* This term refers to institutions in both the public and private sectors: both bureaucracies and markets. In each case we studied, we began by analyzing public and private structures as they existed, and then asked how well they were suited to the environment and to the various alternative strategies.

In the case of public agencies, we focused on four elements. First was formal organization: for example, the degrees of centralization-decentralization, integration-specialization, and private-mixed-public management.

Second were personnel policies, such as recruitment, promotion, training and, especially, incentives.

Third came systems of information and control. And finally, we examined participation. How did clients, the public, and functionaries participate in the decision making and implementation?

Under each dimension we asked, What structural changes might be considered? In the last case we analyzed all three dimensions: environment, strategy, and structure. Were they consistent? Given changes in the environment, what new strategies and structures should be considered?

Each case was written in two parts. The first part presented the problem faced, but gave no solutions. This was what students prepared before our classroom discussions. The second part showed what the country in question actually did. This they would study after class—after their own analyses of the problems and the alternatives.

The effect was galvanizing. As before in my consulting and teaching, I was fascinated to see how a simple framework could stimulate creative analysis. And the process of working through real cases together kindles both enthusiasm and confidence. It readies people to tackle issues closer to home.

Though we met twice a week, I began to hear stories of the participants staying up till all hours and spending their mealtimes reading and discussing the cases. Their enthusiasm was remarkable. At the end of our last session, there were loud cheers. Several nights later, I had a party for them at my house. Because the new Minister of Planning had also been invited, plainclothes policemen were in attendance. He didn't show, but it was a heady occasion, featuring lots of beer and music and self-congratulation. The policemen drank along with the rest of us and seemed genuinely part of the general glee.

Finally, I thought, something has happened in Equatorial Guinea.

At the end of the two-month course, I was invited back for a three-day exercise, whose goal was to look at a problem in Equatorial Guinea and consider what to do about it. The participants were divided into three groups, one of which was to examine Equatorial Guinea's economic strategy. I told our group that I would be the note taker if they liked, and would answer questions, but the problem and its solution should be their own.

They rose to the occasion. One of the participants, a brilliant man named Saturnino, organized the daily discussions and kept them going when they flagged. He helped everyone join in, and I tended the blackboard.

They analyzed Equatorial Guinea's environment. A small economy historically based on export enclaves—cocoa, timber, and coffee. A small but fairly literate population. A disastrous infrastructure, the description of which led to considerable discussion of Macías's economic and political legacies. A country divided in two parts. The language spoken being Spanish, rather than the French of neighboring countries. Untapped potential in food production, fishing, and mining.

They looked at the major shift in strategies announced in 1985: the private sector was henceforth to be emphasized, and the state to do less in the way of setting prices and running enterprises. But this shift had not been realized. The structures of government and the markets themselves were not yet appropriate for the new strategy. Bureaucratic procedures stifled enterprise and investment. Corruption and tax evasion were widespread. Political influence was used to receive loans—and to avoid repaying them. Some markets were underdeveloped; others, oligopolistic. And the banking system had gone under: in some respects the country was suffering a depression not unlike that of the United States in the 1930s.

The discussions were fascinating. The framework I had taught them helped them organize their thinking. Our discussions in class had also built a healthy spirit of questioning and of arguing about alternatives. By the end of the third day, the group had developed the following summary:

THE SEMINAR'S ECONOMIC STRATEGY FOR EQUATORIAL GUINEA

Problem 1: The Banking System (Lack of Liquidity; Malfunctioning Credit Markets)

Strategies: Infusion of money; better management of banks.

Package of Measures:

(*a*) Policies to make people pay their debts [by this the students really meant "high government officials"], including penalties, incentives, publicity, political support.

(*b*) Better systems for approving loans.

(*c*) Enforcement of reserve requirements in banks.

(*d*) Get capital from Banco Exterior de España for Guinextebank.

(*e*) Foment competition among banks (invite in a French bank like BIAO).

Organizations Responsible: Ministry of Finance, BEAC, Ministry of Justice; help from IMF, Banco Exterior de España, Spanish government.

Problem 2: Lack of Investment

Strategies: Increase investors' confidence in country; improve property rights; streamline rules and bureaucratic procedures for investors.

Package of Measures:

(*a*) Publicity campaign abroad, touting EG's prospects.

(*b*) Penalties for abuses of other people's property [again they meant "by government and particular high officials"].

(*c*) Permit foreigners to own land.

(*d*) Carry out a property survey, including a review of land titles.

(*e*) Simplify the investment code.

(*f*) Consider a one-stop investment promotion office.

Organizations Responsible: Create a new governmental coordinating committee for foreign investment.

Problem 3: Malfunctioning Markets (Internal; External)

Strategies:

(*a*) Foment agricultural cooperatives to reduce exploitation.

(*b*) Improved marketing infrastructure, including market buildings, roads, and communications.

(*c*) Improve quality measuring and pricing policies for exports.

Package of Measures:

(*a*) For cooperatives, provide training, credit, and technical assistance.

(*b*) For infrastructure, invest in roads, market centers, and the provision of market information.

(*c*) For quality, upgrade quality control agents (especially for cocoa and timber) and improve their technological tools; enforce price differentials based on quality.

Organizations Responsible: Ministries of Labor, Public Works, and Agriculture; need foreign aid.

Problem 4: Macroeconomic Disequilibria

Strategies:

(*a*) Reduce imports.

(*b*) Raise exports.

(*c*) Reduce government spending.

(*d*) Increase government revenues.

Package of Measures:

(*a*) To reduce imports, increase food production and move to solve problems 1, 2, and 3; need also unencumbered foreign aid such as my project.

(*b*) To raise exports, liberalize markets and reduce export taxes.

(*c*) To reduce government expenditures, reduce debt payments (via renegotiation), reduce the number of ministries, and cut back on official travel.

(*d*) To raise government revenues, cut back on tax and customs evasion and raise the prices charged for public services like electricity and water.

Organizations Responsible: Finance (need presidential support); Agriculture; foreign aid and Paris Club; ministries of Industry and Commerce and of Public Works for user charges.

In one of the other working groups, there was a flap. One participant thought that some people were "criticizing the government," and complained of this to certain high political figures. A cold chill went through the school. If one criticized, was one a conspirator?

But on behalf of our working group, Saturnino made a superb presentation. His eloquence and ability to respond to questions made me think he was the ablest person I had met in Equatorial Guinea.

To come up with a feasible strategy for Equatorial Guinea would, of course, require much work. But I was pleased. It was the first example I had seen here of people working together and thinking strategically.

Finding Surf

At last, in February 1987, the Toyota Land Cruiser I was to use arrived in Malabo, seven months after I had ordered it. Now, after days of paperwork, I drove it from the port to the Casa Verde. Gleaming white, with chrome wheels that were standard with the oversized tires, it attracted an admiring and congratulatory crowd. The children on the street joined me in festive washing and waxing. Then we took it on a triumphant tour of Malabo. The Land Cruiser had bucket seats for two up front and two small fold-down benches in back, which could hold a couple more adults—or, as I was now learning, a dozen squealing and singing children.

The car meant I could now look for waves around the island of Bioko.

Heretofore, my surf searches had been confined to Luba Bay on the southwest side of the island, where rudimentary transportation was available but waves were not.

No one in Equatorial Guinea knew anything about waves. The only people who evinced any interest in the sport were the guards at roadblocks, who inspected my surfboard as if it were a torpedo. The lack of local surf consciousness was worrying. The anthropologists of yesteryear no doubt could have concocted any number of explanations for this ignorance. They might have labeled it cultural backwardness on the part of the natives, or perhaps a manifestation of international exploitation. Certainly that workhorse "the legacy of colonialism" would be trotted out. I hoped the truth weren't simpler: "No waves here, Malinowski."

In remote parts of the world, surf can be difficult to discover even when it abounds. You can't just ask, "Hey, big waves around here?" Translated into local terms, "big waves" can mean high tides, heavy chop, rocks that waves splash off of, or (what the surfer wants) big rideable sets breaking far from shore.

Once when on a surf-seeking trip around the northern Philippines I was frustrated by my inability to convey to the locals what I was looking for, a Filipino friend had the solution.

"Say 'Hawaii Five-O,' " she suggested. "Everyone's seen the waves at the beginning of the show."

She was right. Even in the poorest parts of rural Luzon, people lit up in recognition. (Actually finding big waves was of course another matter. Luzon's turned out to be more like Hawaii O-Point-Five.)

In Equatorial Guinea, this allusion was useless. TV sets were scarce, and the local station carried no American programs. Consequently, I had to communicate with body language.

"Excuse me, *amigos*. Have you seen anything like this around here?" I would ask, and crank up my arms to mimic a big wave breaking, make noises like crashing surf, and then wait as my astonished African audience would first stand dumbfounded and then erupt into peals of laughter.

Around the globe, surf pilgrims face other chronic difficulties. Big waves don't happen every day. Usually they come in certain seasons; and even when the season is right, a spot may be flat one day and have eight-foot boomers the next. It took me a while to learn that Luba Bay is seasonless and free of quotidian variation. Luba's rule turns out to be "flat one day and one-foot rollers the next." Its sets are null sets. Thank goodness for the Hotel Jones and its grilled fish and chilled Kronenbourg. You can build up a real appetite watching a mirrorlike ocean and sobbing.

Early one morning, I took my dog Chispa and the surfboard to explore one of the two sand beaches on the western side of the island. We drove ten miles from Malabo and turned onto a track right out of Mickey Thompson's Mud Racing Classic. It had been a rainy week, and the big trucks, hitting the beach to fetch sand for construction, had left ruts as deep as three feet. We negotiated about two miles of slipping, sliding, stalling, and sloshing till we reached the mouth of the Río Apú. The Land Cruiser's fat tires and four-wheel finesse survived all tests. We forded the river and looked down a mile of beach. To the right was jungle. And to the left, alongside some rocks in front of the river mouth, surfable waves were tubing.

"Yee-*hooo!*" I hooted, and Chispa, excited by my excitement, began barking and running around the car. I unloaded the board, waxed up, and paddled out about seventy-five yards. Four-foot sets formed off the rocks and then peeled off to the left, permitting a short, fifteen-yard ride. Drop, turn, up, and out: that was it. The takeoff was hairy. You dropped in just to the left of a big exposed rock, and beneath you the water was only two feet deep, with a submerged rock ledge peering up from below.

It was a sign of my deprivation that I was stoked by this set-up.

One of the nice things about surfing in unridden territory is that you get to name the spots you discover. I called this one "Denture Cream." For its potential, thankfully not its achievements.

At the north end of this beach was another break, "Bathing Caps." There on Sundays you would find a busload of Soviet swimmers, most of them sporting ridiculous-looking headgear, bobbing outside what was at best a two- to three-foot shorebreak. Hardly a great surf spot; but for the truly desperate, Bathing Caps offered possibilities for body-surfing, as well as for the promotion of détente.

The Project Commences

The International Monetary Fund returned at the beginning of 1987. So did the loan officer, Horace, the economist Esteban, and the administrative officer, Dominique, of the World Bank. We were not in good shape for their arrival. The economy was traumatized by the liquidity crisis. Since tax collection was way down, the government's budget deficit had grown. The estimated deficit did not include the large but unquantified expenditures made on the UDEAC meetings—these were "extrabudgetary," outside normal procedures and accounts.

Horace and Dominique were preoccupied with the Bank's technical assistance project. They had found evidence not only of mismanagement but of possible corruption on the part of the Guinean administrator, my friend Salvador. An audit was under way, and many bills were missing.

Meanwhile, the IMF was focusing on the banking and budget crises. The IMF recommended that the Banco de Crédito y Desarrollo be closed, that the Guinextebank's situation of bad loans be carefully audited by an international firm, and that the French bank BIAO be allowed to open a branch. The IMF also wanted cuts in public spending, including the payroll. There would be no agreement with the Fund until the expenditures for the UDEAC conference were clarified and the banking crisis resolved.

No IMF agreement. Therefore, Horace said once again, our rehabilitation project would not get its funds either. And once again my counterarguments were useless.

The IMF departed. So did Horace and company. I was despondent.

Suddenly, three days later, Horace and Esteban returned.

"Hello, Bob!" Horace said, appearing at my front door. I would have been only slightly more surprised to see Michelle Pfeiffer. Though much more pleased.

"We are back to make the economic rehabilitation project effective!" Horace said.

All right! So, maybe equally pleased.

What had happened was this. Horace had cabled the Bank about the failure of the negotiations with the Fund. Somebody high up at the Bank had said, "Wait, isn't the economic rehabilitation project supposed to be fast-disbursing? What is holding it up?" After hearing the answer, the decision had been to compromise. Horace and Esteban had been instructed to return and get a letter from the President that promised to close the BCD and "redimension" several controversial items in the public investment program. Upon receipt of this letter, the project would be declared effective and the first installment of what was now, with the declining dollar, a thirteen-million-dollar loan would be put into play.

With Don Bonifacio's intervention, the presidential letter was procured. It then took a couple of months for the Bank to finalize the paperwork and another month to transfer the funds to the BEAC bank. But we knew we would get the money. It was a great relief.

To celebrate, I contracted malaria.

It came on one evening at a friend's house. I was lying on the floor watching a tape of the Super Bowl. At halftime I got up. This took about thirty seconds. I was stiff as a rusted spring. My back felt as if it had recently been beaten with croquet mallets. I was feverish. After the game I went home to bed. Through the night the earth's gravitational field seemed steadily to increase its power. Turning over required a major effort. Even breathing was energy intensive. The utter exhaustion of each muscle and joint was almost sensuous. I wondered what Michelle Pfeiffer would have thought of it.

In the morning my back ached and I was very hot. Invisible fingers had been hooked under my eye sockets and were pressing outward onto my browbone. I was barely able to walk. I saw the doc, and the blood test verified his diagnosis: "cerebral malaria." I took heavy-duty medication against that chloroquine-resistant strain. Then back to bed.

After two days of grogginess and pain came nausea and diarrhea. I could no longer take care of myself and went to stay at the house of some kind friends. My temperature had fallen to 102°. The third night I woke up at one thirty and was unable to sleep the rest of the night because back cramps took over in whatever position I adopted. On day four, things started settling down into simple exhaustion—I hadn't been able to eat more than a couple of bites a day. On day five I had a small meal and by the seventh day I was almost well. I felt thin as a membrane: I had lost sixteen pounds.

But I reckoned that suffering malaria was a rite of passage. Now I could consider myself a fully broken-in Equatoguinean.

Small Initiatives

Our project would not be solvent for months, but I felt we had to make some things happen. So I created a small charitable fund of my own, whose first uses were to tackle cocoa and small business.

A German cocoa expert named Cord Jakobeit, whom I had met when he had a fellowship to Harvard, wrote that he would be visiting Cameroon in February. When I invited him to spend a week working with us at my expense, he agreed and donated his time. Before he came, I met with the Guinean cocoa exporter Aurelio, now president of the Chamber of Agriculture and Forestry, a kind of marketing board for cocoa. Aurelio arranged a seminar hosted by the Chamber, which—remarkably for Malabo—was attended by Guinean heads of cocoa cooperatives, agricultural officials, and cocoa exporters. (No one came from the World Bank cocoa project.)

Cord did not talk about Equatorial Guinea, but contrasted the Ivory Coast's success with cocoa over the last decade with Cameroon's stagnation. What policies, he asked, explained the difference? Pricing policies were roughly the same, he showed. But the Ivory Coast had done much better because of its policies toward transportation, agricultural extension, and marketing.

For an hour after his talk, Cord fielded enthusiastic questions and comments. Aurelio was very pleased.

The second visitor was Marc Lindenberg, the head of the Central American business school INCAE, who I hoped would stimulate interest in "microenterprise," the small-scale businesses that make up what have been called the "informal sector." For many years I have been interested in how the informal sector can be helped to prosper—and in how microentrepreneurs graduate into medium- and larger-scale activities. Fostering the indigenous private sector in Equatorial Guinea, I thought, would be crucial for economic adjustment to work. But how? Under Marc's leadership, INCAE had done pathbreaking work in studying and designing policies toward microenterprise. I hoped he could help us consider the alternatives. We arranged for a visit at my expense, and Marc generously donated his time.

The topic fell under the domain of the Ministry of Industry, Commerce, and Enterprise Promotion. Its minister, Don Camilo, had at last returned from Bata. It was with a heavy heart that I finally met this member of our project's coordinating committee.

Don Camilo had been in charge of the arrangements for the UDEAC conference of heads of state in Bata. Things had gone well at the conference, and the President had granted everyone who had labored hard to prepare it a long leave to begin the new year. Don Camilo's wife and six children had left by plane for Malabo. But just after taking off the plane crashed. All the passengers perished.

The shock went through the whole country. The President was said to have intervened personally to ensure that Camilo would be able to leave his old house, full of memories and ghosts, and move into a new one. After a month's leave, Camilo returned to Malabo and his job.

When we finally met, I offered him my condolences. Then I summarized the status of our project. I explained Marc's forthcoming visit. Camilo agreed that the subject was important, and when Marc came, he was ready.

The Ministry of Industry and Commerce was located a little over a mile out of town, off the airport road, in an abandoned hotel complex. Its modular construction and odd geometry meant that trips from one office to another might lead you outside, inside, outside again, and finally inside to your destination. Since Don Camilo's office was being rebuilt, Marc and I met him in the dank abode of the secretary general.

"We have to create groupings of the microentrepreneurs," Camilo said. "They tend to be too small to be viable. They cannot get credit—they have no access, they don't even know about it, and the banks won't help."

Marc asked about his ministry's activities in this area.

"We worry about the laws affecting small business," Camilo said, "but we are not yet staffed to do any training. We would like to be guided by your experience.

"Our first task is to get statistics about what exists. The situation on the continent is very different from the situation here on the island. Then we should try to group the various enterprises together. Put all the tailors in one place, all the carpenters in another. We would regulate them and provide them services. All of them would have a special identity card.

"Until now there has been no policy regarding small business, no policy of credit and none of technical assistance to them."

I asked about the markets for the products of microenterprises.

"Our job is not to motivate markets," Camilo asserted. "It is to regulate. The marketing is the job of the Chamber."

Marc worked hard during his week in Malabo. At the end he presented his ideas at a Friday evening meeting at my house. Aurelio came, as did the assistant secretary of Industry and Commerce and ten or twelve other government officials and experts. It was the first such get-together I had heard of in the country. After it was over, Marc and I went to our appointment with the minister at his home.

The minister's section of town was without electricity that night. The humidity was palpable; a storm was about to break. Oil lamps flickered along the sidewalk and behind the windows. Marc and I found our way to a stairwell in the back of Camilo's four-story apartment building of concrete. The place smelled of urine and garbage and was so dark we could hardly make our way. At the door of his apartment, a housekeeper met us and took us to an L-shaped living room filled with dark, massive furniture, the walls lined with empty brown bookshelves.

Don Camilo greeted us. "It is good to have you here," he said to Marc. "It is an initiative, it gives us a push. Now we are going to pass a law to help the small businesses."

Camilo wore a white collarless shirt embroidered like a tablecloth. He offered us drinks. Mine was a beer, but Marc's and his were beverages that required ice. Camilo's custom was to freeze tall glasses with an inch and a half of ice in the bottom. The drinks were suspended above and then, in mid-consumption, the partly melted ice would surface in familiar ice-cube fashion.

Marc summarized his impressions. He contrasted our environment in Equatorial Guinea with that of the poor countries of Latin America. We were in a situation of total collapse, whereas they were merely under-developed. The task facing our small businesses was survival in a world without liquidity. Moreover, these enterprises received absolutely no services, not even private ones. Eventually the government's economic reforms would help small business. But additional steps should be considered in the areas of credit, training, marketing, and technical assistance. Marc outlined three alternative policy initiatives—a kind of Baby Bear, Mama Bear, and Papa Bear—and recommended that we do a survey and several case studies to understand the problems and the opportunities better.

Camilo listened attentively. "Here we cannot even call them micro-enterprises," he responded. "The decapitalization of our economy makes it so difficult. Small family enterprises defend themselves via mere subsistence.

"We should discuss these issues with the section chiefs, have a conference on small enterprises. One here and one in Bata."

Marc told of successful workshops involving public and private sectors, diagnosing problems and designing solutions together.

Camilo said he had sponsored a seminar something like that when he was Minister of Education, with the help of a now-departed U.N. adviser. "We had a seminar for several days to consider the strategy of the entire educational sector. We considered what reforms we should make in our organization." Camilo went on to describe it in some detail. Later he gave me a written copy, and I noted the similarities between the approach and the environment-strategy-structure framework.

"Meetings like that give us a better capability to solve problems, to plan, to fix objectives," Camilo continued. "It's not worth a thing that an expert comes and talks and talks and talks and the Guineans take notes.

"We did it like a revolution. It wasn't breaking with the past and leaving it, but studying it and improving the systems."

Marc and he were on the same wavelength. We had another drink. Camilo told us about his brothers: one was a bishop in Río Muni; another, a forestry engineer in Spain; and the third, at the family home in Cogo, a city on the coast at the border with Gabon.

"It is a family tradition to do something," Camilo said. "We are sportsmen. We want to surpass ourselves. I ran the government's sports activities until 1984, and then I became the Minister of Education. I found the ministry to be very passive, demotivated.

"And now I am the Minister of Industry and Commerce. I know nothing of economics. I have asked for an adviser, but nothing has happened. I find this ministry, too, demotivated. I would like to get it going."

I told Camilo about a week-long workshop with forty high officials of the Ministry of Industry and Commerce in Panama. The theme had been recasting the ministry's mission: from controlling and regulating the private sector to fomenting and helping it. We had enjoyed a great success, though recent political events had soured the environment. Marc mentioned one of INCAE's workshops in Costa Rica.

"That is exactly the sort of thing we need," Camilo said. "You both can count on me."

It was time to go. In a moment of exquisite insensitivity, I said I was taking Marc out tonight to celebrate the completion of his week in Equatorial Guinea. Would the Minister like to join us?

"I wish I could come," Camilo said softly, looking down. "I cannot."

He paused and then picked up an album of photographs. He leaned toward us and opened it. Inside were pictures of his beautiful children. The oldest looked about twelve. Camilo flipped the pages slowly. There was a big photo of a shy, smiling, clear-eyed bride.

"I do sports now," Camilo said. "I run in the mornings and play basketball in the afternoons. But I have not gone out anywhere at all. People visit, but I am not . . . ready. I am not ready for people."

He looked up at me. My throat was choking from the inside.

"You know, Mr. Minister," I said softly, "I cannot say because I have never had an experience like yours, but my guess is this . . . you have to let people love you."

There was silence. Then Camilo shared his grief with us. The next minutes were open and deep and raw, like a birth. Camilo gave, and Marc and I received his secrets. Outside, as if in cosmic sympathy, the skies had opened and the rain was cleansing the city.

Finally, there was a pause. I think we were all in tears.

"I cannot imagine a tragedy like yours."

"I cannot either," Camilo said. "I wonder sometimes if it is real."

"This World Is Yours"

Every couple of weeks I saw Madre Josefina and the nuns at Basilé. They still had no news from the Ministry of Education about our proposed international seminar for the kids. I drafted a new letter to the Minister of Education for Madre Josefina signature. It said, in effect, that she was delighted that the ministry had raised no objection to the seminar, which would therefore begin in one month's time. Make them say no instead of waiting for them to say yes: let's use bureaucratic inertia to our advantage.

She laughed. She signed. And we began planning the participation of Malabo's international community in weekly presentations to the students.

I visited possible presenters. The idea, I explained, was to share something about their culture, geography, or history, in any way they liked, but politics and ideology were off limits. People got excited. Visitors agreed to come from Nigeria, Finland, Cuba, Argentina, France, Spain, China, the Soviet Union, the United States (not me), and Germany. The Cameroonians did not respond, the North Koreans were too busy, and the English were unimpressed by the prospect. At the last minute, Madagascar fell through when Ana of the Hotel Jones contracted malaria.

The week before the series at Basilé began, I did a warm-up session for the students. I wanted to tell them what this was all about, how it should be fun and not a chore, that they should ask questions. We met in an old classroom with dark and weathered desks and chairs, some light coming in from the windows, a blackboard, and a podium. The children ranged from twelve to eighteen, and 95 percent were girls (the boys were from Basilé itself; the girls were boarders from all over the island). They sat two to a chair because two classes were combined. They looked down shyly at their folded hands. I introduced myself, made a few jokes, and said we were there to have fun, to get to know each other, and to learn. What did I hope they would learn? A little about three big lessons. First, what seems strange to you is not necessarily bad. Second, though the first thing you may notice is that groups of people differ, the more you know the more you realize that individuals differ much more, so you can never judge someone by what group he or she belongs to. Third, despite all the differences, we all have a lot in common. Like our hopes and laughter and anger and love.

Then we talked about how to ask questions of our guests. At the end I asked whether they had any questions for me.

There followed a long embarrassed silence. I waited. Finally, a girl rose and spoke so softly I could hardly hear her. She repeated, "What is your last name and how do you spell it?"

The next question was how old I was. Then how many brothers and sisters I had. There were questions about America: what kinds of foods we have, how many people there are, what is "abundant" there.

Two questions were particularly touching. One scrawny boy asked, "Do the men all get drunk in your country like they do here?" A girl wanted to know whether I had any children. I explained that in my country people didn't have children unless they were married. This drew expressions of surprise. One girl slapped her thigh and cried, "Chico!"

The next week the ambassador from Nigeria came. He drove up with a small entourage, his black Mercedes at the end of the line risking its high-priced suspension on the atrocious road. Over a hundred students and all the nuns packed into the school's biggest classroom. The ambassador's men unloaded a sound system and a huge map of Nigeria, which they toted into the school. The school's generator was ignited. Soon the classroom was pulsating to Nigerian rock. The show was about to begin.

The ambassador brought staff members from the various regions of Nigeria. He also brought his twelve-year-old daughter, dressed cute as a cutout with her glasses and pigtails and school uniform, who happened to be visiting during her Nigerian school's vacation. The ambassador wore the colorful garb of the Yoruba people, and his staff each wore regional dress from other parts of the country.

The music was lowered. Standing at the microphone his staff had installed, I introduced the ambassador. Thunderous applause. The ambassador spoke through his embassy's interpreter. He told a joke. He turned to the map and went through it in detail. He described Nigeria's different regions and peoples.

"People from Nigeria can wear whatever kind of clothes they want. For example, Stephen over there is dressed in the style of the Hausa. Ibrahim is dressed in the style of an Ibo. And I am wearing the clothes of a Yoruba man. But, as it happens, Stephen is a Yoruba, Ibrahim is a Hausa, and I am an Ibo. We just happen to like the clothes we are wearing!"

Later the ambassador's daughter spoke for a few minutes. The girls were captivated by her and asked her many questions about her school and her friends and how she lived.

The presentation concluded with questions to the ambassador, more music, and great applause. Then Madre Josefina and the nuns led him and his entourage on a tour of the school. His daughter was besieged and stayed behind with the interpreter, her smile like the new moon.

We had some refreshments with the nuns. The ambassador was glowing from his success; the nuns were as happily flustered as the winners of an unexpected prize. The girls had prepared a thank-you card with a drawing of the school on the front. Later in the week the ambassador called me to say it was one of the things he had most enjoyed doing in his four years in Malabo.

The sessions continued late every Wednesday afternoon. Two Argentinian women talked about their country with wonderful humor and style. Different pedagogical techniques were employed. The Finn and the Russian showed slides. The Frenchman played the guitar, whereas the Cuban read off statistics concerning electrification and the miles of roadways .paved since the revolution. The Chinese, embarrassed at the prospect of talking, showed a film. The Spaniard lectured on the history of Spain.

The last week coincided with the end of the school year. We had a celebratory party. I brought up my electric guitar and battery-operated speaker. I sang a couple of songs with big beats, and they banged their desks and sang the choruses. Then I wrote on the blackboard the words to a new song we would all learn, *"Este Mundo Es Tuyo."* Sung to the tune of "This Land Is Your Land," its translation is "This World Is Yours." The chorus went, "This world is yours, this world is mine, no matter if you're Guineano or if you're Chinese; whether you're French or a Spaniard, this world is for you."

It didn't take long to learn. The children sang it louder and louder, happier and happier. Finally I thanked them and closed up the guitar and got ready to leave. They wouldn't hear of it. They stomped, they pounded, they sang *"Este mundo es tuyo . . . ."*

So I played a trick on Madre Josefina, who was standing near the back door. We would do the song one more time, I told the girls, if Madre Josefina would come to the front and lead us.

She burst into laughter and shook her head. But the class pleaded and squealed. Finally, she giggled her way to the front and, standing beside me with that joyous smile, led off loud and strong: *"Este mundo es tuyo, este mundo es mío"* and the girls went wild. We sang the song four more times.

The song stuck. I might be walking down a street in Malabo months later and suddenly come upon schoolgirls singing *"Este Mundo Es Tuyo,"* taught to them by their friends from the school in Basilé.

Innocent Gift

Easter 1987. I missed being home. I thought of Don Milagroso and Don Constantino, who were still in jail. Wasn't there something I could do at this time of joy and renovation to cheer their bleak lives?

They couldn't receive visitors except for their families. Maybe I could send each of them a book. I had a small collection in Spanish that the previous residents had left behind. I found Alvin Toffler's *The Third Wave* for Milagroso, a good-looking novel for Constantino. I signed them innocuously. Inside Milagroso's book I wrote: "Dear Don Milagroso, With best wishes for Easter from your friend, Bob."

I took the book to the Finance Minister's secretary, Yolanda, a friend of Milagroso's wife, and asked her to pass it along.

I didn't think about the matter for several weeks. One day when I was visiting the Finance Minister, Yolanda said, "Roberto, I must talk with you. Please see me after work."

I came by at three. Yolanda took me to a place where we could be alone. I asked her what was the matter.

"Roberto, do you remember the book you gave me to give to the wife of Don Milagroso? Well, I never did, Roberto. You do not know our country. Such a gesture would not be understood. I know you meant well, Roberto, and I did not want to disappoint you or make you think badly of our country, so I took the book home with me.

"Then an unfortunate thing occurred. A visitor to my house saw the book on my table. He picked it up and looked inside the book and saw Don Milagroso's name, and yours. Both are unusual names here, Roberto. He reported it to the police.

"Did you notice I have not been here at work for two days, Roberto? Do you know where I have been? I have been at the police station. They interrogated me for two days."

I could scarcely believe it.

"They asked me over and over about the book. I told them, Roberto, I think it is true, that you were Don Milagroso's friend from a long time back and that you meant the book simply as an Easter present. They did not believe me at first. Finally, they became convinced that it was all innocent, and they let me go, and they will not bother you, Roberto."

I told Yolanda I was sorry for involving her in such trouble.

"I am sorry, Roberto. I am sorry for my country."

What to Buy

Eventually the funds for our project were deposited in the BEAC bank. The project documents had created a coordinating committee made up of Don Bonifacio, the Finance Minister (president); Don Diego, the Minister of Planning; Don Camilo, the Minister of Industry and Commerce; and me (secretary). Don Bonifacio and I had to sign every check and every "withdrawal application" for replenishments from the World Bank.

The coordinating committee was to figure out, within broad limits, how to allocate the project's funds. To do this, it was supposed to come up with a medium-term development strategy for the country.

We had preliminary meetings. I prepared a paper in question-and-answer form about the economic rehabilitation project: what it was, what its objectives were, how it would work, and what the committee's role should be. Then we had a series of seminars to analyze economic and sectoral strategies in other countries, as preparation for our work on Equatorial Guinea.

Our third session took place on a Saturday morning at ten thirty in the BEAC conference room, as air-conditioned and antiseptic as a Nordic air terminal. On the agenda was a short case I had written called "Just the Equipment We Needed." Only two pages long, it briefly recounted three instances of ill-fated imports in a project like ours I had visited in Ghana. I hoped to provoke the ministers into thinking about how we could avoid such mistakes.

In one instance, a Ghanaian minister had declared a piece of equipment was "urgently needed." Based on his entreaty, the equipment had been purchased through the World Bank project. But as the piece arrived in Ghana, so did an identical machine donated by the British government. One was sufficient, so the second turned out to be redundant.

The project had imported another machine that worked for a couple of months but had no spare parts or maintenance system to back it up when it failed. Consequently, it sat unused in a warehouse—as did a third import, a vehicle whose wheels had been stolen soon after it arrived.

I stood beside a flip chart placed at the corner of the long conference table. The three ministers sat on the other side. I began by asking what problems they saw in the case. A real softball.

No response. Diego looked at his folder. Bonifacio had his arms folded and his eyes down. Camilo, at the far right, was looking at me with his hard expression. Last night they had been tired at the end of our evening seminar. The pause continued. Could it be that they had forgotten the two pages already? Finally I asked, "Would you like some time to scan the case again?"

"No," said Camilo, "that's not necessary." Then he added, as if things were simply too simple, "There aren't problems here, just one big problem. That is to say, they didn't take care to import what they needed."

When you get a reductionist answer, your best strategy is to say nothing and wait for the person to say more. I waited. Camilo finally did say more, concluding with: "They didn't do a systematic assessment of their needs."

I wrote this on the flip chart. Bonifacio added a point. There was a pause.

I asked Camilo, "Can we examine your idea of a systematic assessment of needs? In the case, remember, the minister had said that this equipment was very important for the ministry's work. An interministerial committee had agreed. What else would you have them do so that import needs would be systematically assessed?"

Camilo stared at the flip chart, then at me, then at the flip chart. Out of the corner of my eye, I could see Diego looking at the flip chart and then at Camilo. Bonifacio was at attention.

"Let's see," Camilo began, thinking out loud. "We would need a more careful examination than happened in the case of what really were the priorities."

Camilo went on to say that the mere statement of a need, even by a minister, was not sufficient. He described at length the problems of getting priorities straight in Equatorial Guinea. "The Public Works minister may read in a magazine about some piece of equipment and then ask us to buy it. That is not enough to tell us what is needed."

"Or whether the good is really appropriate," added Bonifacio. He then told two remarkable stories of the wrong imports being made. He lambasted donors who solved the problems of their own businesses in trouble by peddling their goods to poor countries. In one case, Equatorial Guinea had received fishing boats that were secondhand, overpriced, and inappropriate. The Spanish firm supposed to help with supplies and maintenance filed for bankruptcy the day after the Spanish government approved the deal.

As he was speaking, I wrote on the flip chart "Look gift horses in the mouth." When he finished his story, Bonifacio said, "You've written about gift horses. You should also write, 'loaned horses.' In these two cases I've been citing, they were loans to us, not gifts." Bonifacio was a good man—a trained economist and a person of passion.

Diego gave a brief example in a humble voice of the same sad phenomenon, and then Camilo launched into an account of how the government got blamed for corruption when the donors gave or loaned goods but did not help get them distributed within the country. "Who pays at the end? The people do, because the country is in debt."

Bonifacio added, "If those fishing boats had been right, and we had had the help from the Spanish firm that was promised, we would have never again needed to import fish. We would have had enough fish for five—say, ten years."

As I listened, I could not help reflecting once again how often these folks had been reamed. By the Spanish, then by Macías, by the Russians in the

1970s, and (they thought and probably sometimes were right) by the very foreign "aid" that has left them indebted and dependent. Statistics showed that Equatorial Guinea's foreign debt tripled from 1980 to 1985. Relative to the gross national product, that debt was one of the highest in the world.

No wonder it was hard in such a country to forge trust. And then there are the undoubted mysteries of the international order: Guinean government officials had not been trained to deal with the complications of overseas markets and economic models and laws and procedures.

By the time Bonifacio and Camilo finished their stories and explanations, with minor observations by Diego, the flip chart was full of problems to be faced when importing goods for a government. Their list was not bad. I asked them how, given these problems, we should structure our project. On a new sheet I reorganized the problems as follows:

WHAT SHOULD OUR PROJECT BUY?
THE MINISTERS' LIST OF ISSUES

The Need

For what, exactly? An import or something else?

The Import

Could we repair what we have instead?
Are other donors likely to provide it or could they?
The right good/specifications
At a fair price

Use of the Import

Do we have the warehousing/storage?
Do we have people trained to operate it?
Do we have a system to maintain it?
Do we have a system to make sure it is not stolen, misused?
If appropriate, do we have a viable system for distributing the good (for example, tools, food, small boats)?

Actually Procuring the Import

Who does the procuring? (central board, and so on)
World Bank procedures
Customs procedures

Ideas flew. Much discussion concerned how to identify a need. One minister said that the ministerial action plans could not be relied upon. "Too many unrealities in them," he judged.

Should we use short-term consultants to help assess what ministries said they needed? Camilo made a little speech for the negative. Its gist was that consultants were expensive and often didn't know the country's situation, and anyway we should try to use national capabilities. As usual, my job was not to argue but to note the contribution on the board and then pass it to others for comment. Later I did add two points. I reminded them that over the past year I had been unsuccessful in motivating the ministries of Public Works and Health to come up with a list of needs linked both to ministerial aims and to their other resources. The ministers responded that with our coordinating committee now functioning, they could put their weight behind these efforts. I would no longer be flying solo.

And I told a couple of stories about ministers in other countries who had used short-term consultants—if they were terrific and did know the kinds of problems the country was facing—not only to give substantive judgments but also to help the ministers catalyze a ministry into action. Camilo liked that idea. He related it to his seminar in the Ministry of Education.

At the end, several big points came through. A wish list of imports was not the answer. Nor could we simply rely on a minister's statement of need and an interministerial committee to evaluate such statements. We would need a process to relate imports to a ministry's action plan/strategy; to take into account the equipment a ministry already had (whether it could be repaired; compatibility); to take into account what other donors might give, and analyze it in advance; and to make appropriate changes in systems of maintenance and control of materials.

Our project's money could be used not only to buy the imports but to help with these other steps. For example, we could obtain technical assistance to help assess needs. Our committee could convene donors to discuss particular ministries. And the committee could support the reform of systems of maintenance and control of materials.

The group was fired up. They wanted two more meetings next week. Camilo said, "I'm getting to really enjoy these encounters."

The Problem of Commitment

The seminars were designed to make a practical difference. There were two parts to that.

One would be working out what our project document called a

"medium-term strategy" for the country: an intellectual task, and a hard one. We had to focus on the foundations of a successful economy that were lacking in Equatorial Guinea—and many other African countries. Clear and stable property rights. Infrastructure, and its maintenance. A well-functioning credit system, especially for small business and agriculture. More competitive markets with plenty of information and low transactions costs. Effective incentives for public- as well as private-sector employees. The control of corruption.

These were delicate topics. But I was convinced that free-market economic reforms would fail without doing something about them. They were the structures and institutions needed to make the new strategy work.

Successful reform also requires political commitment. As in many other African nations, Equatorial Guinea has declared itself for free-market economic reforms. But do the leaders really mean it? Increasingly in Africa, the international community has doubts.

Cynics blame the lack of commitment to economic reform on corruption and self-interest by the man on top, his political cronies, the ministers, and indeed the change-resistant civil service. But this may not be the whole story. Another element is sheer government incompetence. Many African countries suffer from feeble cabinets, paltry systems of policy making, and erratic decision making at the top. They may promise to do something and then not do it simply from incapacity. I had just received a study of another African nation, which said:

> A consistent and timely response to the deepening crisis was impeded by the fragmentation of information and decision-making. All major decisions . . . are visibly concentrated in the person of the Head of State, but many other decisions are taken in a dispersed, haphazard way throughout the administration. . . . What planning has taken place has largely been in a formal bureaucratic sense and rarely linked to what has actually to be done to make what is planned materialize. . . . Economic considerations are relegated to second priority, because first priority is granted to short-term political considerations, often in a disconcertingly erratic manner. . . . In such circumstances, the incentive to enhance the Government's economic policy capabilities tends to be undermined, no matter what the prevailing economic situation calls for.[1]

Ignorance and caution also play a role in explaining the lack of political commitment. Put yourself in the place of an African leader. What can you expect from committing yourself to free-market economic reforms? The truth is that no one really knows. You can certainly find plenty of rhetoric about the magic of the marketplace. But when they are candid, the best economists—even at the World Bank and the IMF—recognize that no one knows for sure how to get out of a crisis like Equatorial Guinea's. Consider this conclusion by one of the leading experts at the Bank:

> This article has shown that the links between policies and objectives are complex, with large gaps in knowledge on both theoretical and empirical grounds. . . . It has to be recognized that the analytical basis for some micro policies in an adjustment program is relatively weak. The theory underlying the effects of eliminating distortions (real and financial) is not well suited to policymaking, as it quickly raises welfare issues. For example, whether removing consumer subsidies will raise overall efficiency and production is still an open question; the same is true of a devaluation.
>
> Even on the macroeconomic front, some serious theoretical and empirical issues are still unresolved. This [the author's] article has shown, for example, that the effects of fiscal policy on demand are ambiguous. . . . Finally, and perhaps most important, there is still much to be learned about what drives growth in developing countries and in particular about the relationship between short-run stabilization policies and long-run growth.[2]

If expert economists confess ignorance, how do you feel as the president of an African country—especially if, like most presidents, you have no training in or feel for economics?

Moreover, as president of an African country, you may lack basic economic information and tools. In Equatorial Guinea, despite its foreign advisers, not even a simple macroeconomic model was available while I was there. So if you were President Obiang, you had to make policy with poor data in the light of an uncertain science in a backwater at the edge of the world. Would your instinct have been "full speed ahead"?

There is a final cause to the lack of commitment to free-market reforms—worry about political dynamite. Often the country undertaking structural adjustment bears the immediate costs of reform, both economic and political, while the short-run benefits redound to the country's international creditors, who are immediately repaid for past debts with the new structural adjustment loans. Another piece of dynamite is capital flight. Since Equatorial Guinea entered the Central African economic zone, capital flight had been severe, and this had helped cause the breakdown of the banking system. New estimates of the gross national product, such as they were, showed negative growth in both years since the big reform. And there were once again rumors of political discontent with President Obiang and his economic program.

So commitment will be hard to come by. But my experience in other countries indicates that seminars and workshops, like the ones the ministers and I were holding, could help. The participants analyze their own economy, maybe for the first time. They work through some of the fundamentals of an economic strategy. They generate and analyze alternative courses of action. In the process, some of the confusion surrounding economics and economic reform is dispelled. The participants are stimulated to rethink and then to do.

I wanted to reach beyond the three ministers of my project's coordinating committee. Would it be possible to hold, as several Guineans had suggested, a series of workshops for all the ministers, for the President's advisers, perhaps for the President himself? My friend Aurelio was the key to such an initiative.

Meeting the President

Aurelio was at his desk in the small office behind his store. It was ten on an April morning and by Malabo standards not hot, but necklaces of sweat adorned his neck and cheeks and forehead. In terms of perspiration, Aurelio was All-World.

"*Amigo* Roberto!" he exclaimed. "How are you? Too much time has passed since we've seen each other."

Aurelio was no glad-hander, and I liked his warm welcome. Several things about him stood out. He was sincere, knew how to say no as well as yes, and had a sense of humor. He was very close to the President. And he was said to be involved in many bad debts in his role as private cocoa financier and exporter. One of his associates put Aurelio's unpaid debts at the astronomical sum of three hundred million *cefas,* or a million dollars. "Aurelio hasn't acknowledged the debts as his, though," this man said.

After Cord's visit, Aurelio and I had been meeting informally to talk about cocoa and the role of the Chamber of Agriculture and Forestry, of which Aurelio was president. In colonial times, the Chamber was the sole importer of all the things needed for cocoa and coffee growing and the sole exporter of the finished products. But since independence it had grown weaker, sapped by granting credits that were never repaid. Now technically bankrupt, it was limping along in its grand old building on the main avenue only thanks to the World Bank's cocoa rehabilitation project. Through this project, the Chamber supplied about a fifth of the inputs needed for cocoa growing, graded cocoa, carried out some agronomical studies, and signed export documents.

My conversations with Aurelio had ranged across Equatorial Guinea's many problems. Neither of us thought the ministers were doing a good job of tackling the tasks at hand. As in many countries, the ministers were political appointees who often had no experience in the substance of their ministries or in running large organizations. I had told Aurelio about the success in other countries of workshops designed to help top officials formulate effective strategies. He had liked the idea, and we'd agreed to talk about it again.

So I raised it once more that day in April 1987.

"I'm in favor of it. We need it. Thank you for the description you sent me of possible workshops for the ministers. I think they would be very useful. Why don't you write up a longer version, and I'll take it to the President and let him look at it?"

I did so later that week and gave it to Aurelio. Weeks went by, and I didn't hear anything. When I stopped in to see Aurelio in May, we talked again about cocoa. The President had formed an emergency commission, composed entirely of Guineans except for one representative of Casa Mota, to make recommendations in three weeks about what to do about cocoa. Aurelio talked to me about the commission and what it might accomplish.

"I fear for the future of cocoa in this country," Aurelio said. "The trees are getting old, and the production costs are higher than our neighbors', and the price of cocoa keeps dropping. No one is investing in cocoa here. I just don't know."

The long-term issues Aurelio described boiled down to the viability of cocoa in the country, a problem requiring study. Neither of us had confidence in the judgment on this matter of the foreign experts on cocoa, who were focused on their project's loan repayment rates or the correct application of fungicides. What we needed was an analysis of the underlying economics of supply and demand, nationally and internationally. For example, we might bring Cord back for a couple of months to carry out such a study. I suggested that the commission recommend a follow-up committee, which would include the private sector, government officials, and foreign experts. This committee would take a deeper look and make recommendations by the end of 1987, in time for the following season.

And then we discussed the workshop idea. "I talked with the President about it and he's interested," said Aurelio. So, I asked, what will happen? "The President will be in touch."

A month later, we met again about cocoa. Aurelio brought up the workshops.

"The write-up you prepared for the President was kind of rough," he said. "The President wants something more formal. A letter. A description of exactly what would happen in the course. Who should participate. When. Where."

I thought the President himself should decide who and when and where.

"No, you should lay it all out for him. If he wants to change it, he can. But do it formally."

I left Aurelio's office shaking my head. Back to the same strokes. Should I think of this as another "investment in trust"? Or another fruitless initiative? Well, why not keep trying? The President was virtually inaccessible—sealed off, some said, by his cronies and advisers. Aurelio was my only chance. That evening, laptop computer at hand, I produced what Aurelio had recommended. A letter with appendices. What would be learned (I hoped). An outline of each case study, the questions to be addressed, the lessons to be learned. A one-page biography of the instructor, which included an informal concluding paragraph about why I had wanted to come to Equatorial Guinea ("because I like the country, to help as much as might be possible, and to learn firsthand about the problems of Africa"). The next day I gave it all to Aurelio in a manila folder.

"*This* is what is needed," he said. "I'll take it to the President tomorrow and let you know."

The following Thursday afternoon in early August, Aurelio stopped by the house.

"Roberto, I gave the President your material, and he has read it carefully. I just finished seeing him and he wanted to get you to the palace right now. But since it's late he decided tomorrow morning would be better. He gave the order to protocol. They'll call you first thing tomorrow at the Ministry of Finance."

The next day was a scorcher. Even early in the morning, I could feel that clamminess on my palms and the adhesive feeling of shirt on ribcage. Usually I wore a shirt and tie to work—short sleeves, tie loosened—and had a blazer on hand for ministerial audiences. Today I suited up. I had a nine o'clock with the Minister of Finance, a nine thirty at a warehouse that was storing the project's office furniture, and a ten o'clock with the Minister of Information and Tourism, who was trying to take away my house for the use of his secretary general (he later relented). No call from the President at nine. I checked back in before ten. There had been a call to confirm my last name. I left word with a woman who was sitting in for the minister's secretary, Yolanda, while she was momentarily out of the

151

office, that I'd be at Information and Tourism. Nothing came there. But when I came back by Finance at about eleven thirty, Yolanda was frantic out on the street.

"The *jefe* is waiting!" she cried. "Go over there!"

I was off. Down the waterfront road, right at the plaza, by the church and the Palace of the People, straight ahead a long block and there were the gates to the presidential area. The sun was roasting. Two armed soldiers were sitting in an unimpressive guardhouse. I said I had an appointment with the President. They checked a list. I wasn't on it. Just then a car pulled up behind me.

It was Don Jesús of protocol. "Follow me," he said, and we went through the gates.

The presidential area behind the gates was off limits and had been since Macías created what one writer called "a presidential ghetto surrounded by high walls topped with electric wire." *Ghetto* is an apt word. Despite its presidential affiliation and the fact that only the President's confidants and their families lived behind the gates, the houses and streets were run down. Colonial houses with battered old shutters and peeling paint. Concrete dwellings with walls once whitewashed but now stained by the runoffs of countless rainstorms. Laundry hanging on lines from balconies. Half-naked children in the noonday sun. Like the rest of Malabo, a slum with charm. But an enclosed and exclusive slum, and therefore a ghetto.

We went several blocks ahead, turned left beside a particularly dilapidated building, and drove toward the harbor. A row of palms stretched off to the right above a low white wall backed by a fringe of grass, and the sun-graced sea far below. We took another left and immediately saw two guardhouses with Moroccans, a parking lot, and the palace. Extending from the five arches in the palace's façade, curved green plastic overhangs created a welcome shade but had overtones of a drive-in restaurant. I followed Jesús underneath them.

Just in front of us was a huge room like an assembly hall in front of which were standing several elegantly dressed Guineans. I greeted Don Vladimir, the presidential adviser. Behind Jesús, I entered a reception room. Black soldiers were seated in various uniforms ranging from combat fatigues (a sleeping fellow) to full dress. Jesús and I proceeded through a door at the back and up two flights of tightly angled stairs. At the top we entered an elegantly furnished small room. There sat three Moroccans in suits. One was an older fellow with scars or birthmarks that made his face look like a map. I had seen him at all the important presidential events.

The two younger ones looked relaxed. The Moroccans were the defenders of the inner sanctum. Above them on both sides of a large door was the national shield of Equatorial Guinea.

Jesús took me down a corridor on the left into a small room.

"Wait here, please. The *jefe* will be with you in just a minute."

I sat in the room's first available chair, one of four around a card table. I looked around. The room evoked an English spinster. The card table was dainty, asymmetrically octagonal, with four brass ashtrays built into the wood border and black leather in the middle, decorated with gold embossing. The matching chairs seemed too small for adults. Next to me was a small bureau with a marble top. Toward the window were two green couches with antimacassars. A couple of old-fashioned lamps. Above the bureau a print depicted an English navy ship. The walls and ceilings didn't match: they were of the modern sort that can be moved or replaced section by section. What they did have in common with the rest of the room was that nothing reflected any aspect of Guinea old or new.

I went to the window and looked through the venetian blinds onto the sunblasted street. The telephone lines cast stark shadows. Across the way was a white concrete fence with handsome green ironwork on top. A garden with an exotic V-shaped palm. And then the nicest colonial house I'd seen: the home of the chief of state.

Clean and restored, the house had a friendly, rambling aspect: three stories high with a kind of tower and a huge, handsome wood balcony, green shutters contrasting crisply with white walls, real tile on the roof. My line of sight went past that balcony right into a large open window on the second floor, where a statuesque woman dressed in white was holding a baby in her arms. Two other children clad in white lolled by her feet. They were still, as if in a dream. Behind them was a large painting in tones of brown and gold. The scene was framed by the house's white walls, the trees behind the house and, through the trees, the blue of the sea beyond the Point of African Unity.

I returned to the card table, and soon a young official in a gaudy suit came to tell me the President was ready.

I walked down the corridor, past the three Moroccans, and into the anteroom. A cluster of smartly dressed Moroccan and Guinean soldiers looked me over. One of them had a walkie-talkie. He spotted the lump from the sunglasses in the pocket of my coat and stopped me.

"What's that?"

I told him.

"Let me see." I showed him. And then he let me pass. I turned right, the door opened, and there were the President and the Minister of Foreign Affairs.

They stood and stepped forward from a tufted leather couch and chair. They were smiling. The minister being closest, I shook his hand and said "Don Ignacio," and then shook the President's hand with a "Your Excellency." The President motioned me to an empty chair, greeting me warmly. Which was welcome, since the air-conditioning system seemed to have been designed for the Astrodome. The temperature in the small, den-like corner room was about 60°.

The President thanked me for the material I had sent, and talked about training the ministers.

"We do not know many things we need to know. This is an opportunity to learn. We should never let pass an opportunity to learn." He looked at Don Ignacio, who smiled at me. Not many smiles in officialdom here.

The President spoke earnestly. He was leaning forward on the couch, his hands folded on his lap. He wore a dark suit with unusually fine lapels, a dark tie, a white shirt, and glasses. He looked older than his pictures, thicker below the jaw.

The President went on about the proposed workshops. "It sounds like an excellent idea, something we need." He spoke briefly and bluntly about the incompetence of high-level officials. Training, he thought, might be part of the answer. "Before we get it started, I wanted to hear from you in detail."

I told him about the complicated job of a government minister. He or she has to be politician, policy maker, and manager, all at once. Yet in many countries, many ministers have little preparation for this difficult job. In Equatorial Guinea, I thought the problem to be one of confidence as much as anything else. It was not that ministers were not capable or hardworking. They just had not had much practice at formulating strategies and making them happen. This short seminar would give them some practice and a few concepts. I added that it might help a problem found in most countries: the fact that ministers do not work well together as a cabinet. By working through real cases together, the ministers might develop a sort of team spirit.

The President reiterated the problems of making the cabinet work. "This sort of training is of the highest priority," he concluded. "I want to support it, and I want to attend."

I asked whether his presence might inhibit the ministers' participation.

If he wanted to work through the materials, perhaps we could have some private sessions together.

"All right, I see what you mean. But the first session should be one I inaugurate. We can have it here. Then we could have subsequent sessions here or——"

"At the Foreign Ministry," Don Ignacio put in.

"Or at the Foreign Ministry," the President echoed. He then talked about the need for strategic thinking and careful management given "the crisis"—a label he used several times about the current situation. After telling Don Ignacio to get the Prime Minister to name who should attend, the President turned on the charm.

"What is very welcome about this initiative of yours is that it is an initiative. This is very rare here. Many advisers are happy just to sit back and relax. But you are trying to help us. You have identified a problem and have proposed a way to deal with it. This makes me very pleased."

After a little more talk, we said goodbye. More smiles, warm hand-shakes. I went out through the soldiers and the suit-clad Moroccans, down the stairs, past the roomful of soldiers (the man in fatigues now awake), and out into the steamy afternoon. I took a breath of warm air, took off my jacket, and walked over to the car. I had finally met the President. As I drove away from the palace and past the presidential ghetto's weary poverty, I wondered what this would all come to.

6

Technical Assistance

ONE sunny afternoon a friend and I took a trip around Bioko. At kilometer 32 on the southeastern side, for no particular reason except random adventuring, we took a left at the village of Bososo. We made a steep and scenic half-mile or so descent to the village. At the end of the village, an overgrown track led into the jungle. We decided to see where it went.

We pounded down a rock 'em-sock 'em trail through overhanging jungle. I'm talking four-wheelers only, hang on to the dashboard, and watch out for the branches hammering your windshield. Butterflies abounded. The grass on the track was often higher than the hood, and we couldn't see the sky for the forest. But after a couple of miles, we made it to the shore and continued along for about a hundred yards, where a fallen tree blocked the path. We got out and walked down a trail to the sea.

The setting was awesome. Rugged coves of lava rock were backed by dense, dark green forest and, high above, the mountains and the mists. A narrow lava point directly in front of us hooked out thirty yards to the right, forming a little bay within the larger bay. On the left the water reached back into a lagoon. The sun was shining, and the sea was translucent.

Right in the middle of the hooked point in front of us was a natural bathing pool, crystal clear, which resembled a custom-installed, large, tranquil spa. At high tide, the waves would fill and refresh this pool. I christened the spot "La Piscina," "the swimming pool."

Off the tip of the hook about ten yards was a large rock. Between hook and rock, thick four-foot waves were cresting.

We could only body-surf that day, but were back with the boards on Sunday.Taking off between the hook and the submerged rock, it was possible to go left or right. The takeoff was hairy as the wave would bunch and throw out over the rock. Surviving the turbulent section created by the rock, you could skate left about twenty yards across the cove. Or you could angle right on a steep shoulder and head into the protected mouth of the hook. When it was big, the right was excellent for body-surfing.

The rock later earned its own name, "Dagmar's Folly," after an Austrian friend. One day as Dagmar was swimming innocently nearby, suddenly up loomed a gnarly six-foot set. Her unfortunate instinct was to go to the rock and try to hang on. The wave pitched up and blew her off the rock like a volleyball. Luckily, apart from seeing her whole life flash before her eyes, she suffered no consequences.

La Piscina could get big and at low tide would break top to bottom. When the waves were high, another surf spot was visible about three hundred yards to the north. Thick eight-foot walls would explode about thirty yards off a rocky beach. From La Piscina it looked rideable. I paddled over and during a lull checked out the rocks inside the break. The waves turned out to be breaking in about three feet of water on a dangerous lava shelf. And when the walls returned, I noticed that they feathered from both sides inward. There was no place to escape. This spot earned the name "Plaster of Paris"—and remained unridden.

I began to visit La Piscina regularly and brought friends. We could camp gloriously above the little point and sleep to the waves crashing on both sides below. The sunrises could be spectacular.

But a greater discovery awaited: "Punta Sorpresa," "Point Surprise". To understand the circumstances of the initial encounter, a climatological digression is in order.

Among its many unique attributes, the island of Bioko has great storms. My favorites were the short-lived and remarkably violent outbursts called, misleadingly, "tornados." No funnel clouds here: rather, a sudden upswing in the winds, which would go from zero to fifty and up to eighty miles an hour in a matter of minutes. Then fabulous downpours ensued, at a rate of two or more inches an hour. In the gusts the rain whipped horizontally through windows and even across rooms. You had to batten down everything. During a good tornado, my three-story dwelling shook like a 5.5 on the Richter scale; and around town, invariably a few roofs would be blown off. And then the tornado would end, only an hour or two after it commenced.

One night at about ten a spectacular tornado blew in. The old house began to rock in the violent wind. Our zone of the city was without electricity, so all around was dark. But the skies were beginning to perform, and I went out to the large, soft hammock that looked over the sea and watched the show.

Three gigantic armies of clouds—one west, one north, one northeast—were in electrical communication. One would flash, another would respond, then the third would turn on as well. Total darkness would turn to bright light, then darkness, then light, like a kind of cosmic camera. The big tree toward the sea would be transformed from dark outline to giant X ray back to dark outline. The windchimes serenaded overhead.

The cloud banks approached quickly, and the storm grew intense. Big bolts of lightning began to alternate with the flashes. High-pitched cracks punctuated the deep rumblings that spread stereophonically from one rim of the sky to the other. It began to blow harder and harder. Then came the rain, huge isolated drops at first and then a downpour. The tin roof boomed, the chimes went crazy.

Lightning bolts as long and tentacled as veins began to go on, go off, go on again. Then lightning as bright and fragile as the filaments of a hundred-watt bulb. Then another trick: lightning bolts started to shoot horizontally from one cloud to another, shimmying across the night like a school of frightened minnows. Suddenly in the lot next door came the crash of a small tree blowing down. I swayed back and forth in the hammock and watched the palm tree by the sea be suddenly silhouetted as if against the sun, then disappear.

The monsoon blew in. The rain came in horizontal sheets. I had to escape to the bedroom. I dozed off surrounded by the sounds of the thunder and the shakings of the wind.

The next morning, I went with some friends in two four-wheelers to La Piscina. The track from Bososo to the sea was littered with fallen branches and two small trees, which we had to stop and clear away. The tide was out but huge waves were rolling all the way up and into the natural pool. The sets off Dagmar's Folly were a solid six feet. Off to the left, Plaster of Paris looked like "Bioko Five-O." I paddled over there just to admire the giant tubes. And as I sat on the board in a safe spot to the left of Plaster of Paris, off in the distance I saw what I thought was a gigantic wave go by and then disappear beyond the point about two hundred yards farther north.

Five minutes later, it happened again. A small mountain of water came from far out at sea, then walled up, and cruised past that point.

I paddled over—and found the dream of a lifetime.

Ten-foot walls were peeling off the point, open to the right, with a good sixty-plus yards of never-before-ridden face.

During a lull, I paddled inside to check out the lava and possible submerged rocks. The very inside section was over about four feet of water, but otherwise there were no problems. The takeoff looked pretty easy.

So I paddled out and waited for a set. One of those mountains loomed on the horizon. In it came. I lined it up, began to paddle. The wave raised me up and up, and I began to move with it, stood up, and whooshed down the big drop. I made a big bottom turn. There is no sight in the world quite as wonderful as looking down a long, open wall of water way over your head. I headed for the lip, dropped down again, made another turn, drew a long line down the wall, and then, before the inside section, exited flying over the top of the wave.

I hooted at the top of my lungs. It was one of the most exhilarating moments of my life.

Strategic Dialogue

It was a Friday about noon at the Ministry of Industry and Commerce on the outskirts of Malabo. Rain was cascading through the trees and the reeds. In the office of Don Timoteo, the secretary general, large drops occasionally fell from the ceiling onto the corner of his desk, splashing like aquatic mortar shells. His office, without electricity and open only to the courtyard, was as dark as a dungeon.

Timoteo and I were working over the details of a series of seminars. At last our work on the coordinating committee had fired up Don Camilo, the minister. He was pondering how to transform his "moribund" ministry into a promoter of small business and exports, instead of being just a regulator. He wanted me to organize some workshops for senior employees to help them rethink the ministry's mission.

A young employee slunk into Don Timoteo's doorless office and cowered before the secretary general. In Equatorial Guinea, subordinates stoop their shoulders, avert their eyes, speak in whispers. A secretary general in turn assumes this manner before a minister. Probably a minister does the same before the President. I pondered the effects of this behavior. Wouldn't the hierarch's perception and judgment eventually atrophy? Surrounded by flatterers and sycophants, excluded from real contact with real people, might he not lose contact with reality?

The young employee spoke so mousily that he could not be heard. Don Timoteo asked him to repeat.

"The minister just called from the presidency," he said. Friday was the day of cabinet meetings. "He and the President are going to Bata this afternoon and want señor Klitgaard to come on Monday. Señor Klitgaard should talk to the Minister of Finance for details."

Why Bata? The young man said he had received no reason for this highly unusual instruction. I wondered what could have provoked it. Could this have to do with nontraditional exports, our case study on the cocoyam (*malanga*?) Or was it something with the President on the proposed seminar for ministers? Or could it be the banking crisis?

The next day, Saturday, I saw the French financial advisers, Guy and Jean. They were despondent. Guy had prepared a memo for the President about the country's unfulfilled promises to the International Monetary Fund. There was still no agreement with the IMF—and would not be unless the government's promises came true. In a couple of weeks, the Minister of Finance and Guy would be going to Washington for the annual joint meeting of the Fund and the World Bank. It would be nice if beforehand Equatorial Guinea could take concrete actions to turn promise into reality. Cabinet decisions had been made about such things as reducing the public payroll and closing an embassy and a consulate, but nothing had actually happened. More ominously, a cabinet decision taken three months before to follow the Fund's advice and close the bankrupt Banco de Crédito y Desarrollo was wavering. There was talk that the government wanted to reopen the BCD. To do so, they needed money—about as much money as our economic rehabilitation project had in unrestricted funds.

Guy was also going to Bata on Monday. I mentioned my mysterious invitation. Jean suspected something.

"Aha! I told you before that they wanted to use your project's money to refloat the BCD, didn't I? What are you and the World Bank going to think about *that*?"

I tried to find out from Don Bonifacio, the Finance Minister, Sunday evening when he showed up at my house. He entered without ringing, and Chispa's barking alerted me. I went out and greeted him at the top of the steps.

Bonifacio was not his usual dapper self. Gone was his customary necktie. His shirt's large, diagonal plaid clashed in color and pattern with his plaid pants. I noted the hint of a paunch. Bonifacio's eyes were glassy, and his posture a little bowed.

"We both have to go to Bata tomorrow," he announced. "The President and the Minister of Industry left by boat on Friday."

I asked what we were going for.

"We have to continue our work on the coordinating committee and we cannot do it here, since the Minister of Industry will be gone. So we will meet over there.

"You should make all the arrangements for us both to fly," he said. "All right?"

Did he mean I should buy him a ticket, too? Yes. With what money?

"The project's money," he said.

The project's money?

"Yes, the airline will no longer accept the ministry's chits. So will you make all the arrangements?"

Monday was sunny and scorching. Guy was at the airport when I arrived at eleven.

"The plane is still in Bata," he said. "It's had a flat tire. No one knows when it will get here."

Air travel was precarious here. Not only, of course, the tragedy of Camilo's family, but a month before the only aircraft of the local airline had a brake failure upon landing in Malabo. The plane, unable to stop, kept on taxiing—right into the VIP Lounge next to the terminal and through its concrete wall.

Guy and I had a cold drink at the airport bar. He showed me the memo he had written for the President at the Minister of Finance's request. Inexpertly translated from the French and including odd accents and verbs and prepositions, it recounted what had been promised and not yet done, but didn't say why the promises were important or what the President could do to make them happen. But it was remarkable that Guy would see the President, and anything this blunt and implicitly critical would have an impact.

"The country can't go on promising and promising with no action," Guy said.

We talked about the banking situation. The limits on credit expansion had not been observed. The BCD and Guinextebank, both technically bankrupt, had nevertheless been receiving more credit from BEAC, the equivalent of the central bank. The new bank BIAO, jointly owned with the French and solvent, had been opened but was not getting the credit from the BEAC that it needed. Consequently, the private sector was stifled for lack of loans.

The banking problem had political dimensions. The BCD was a Guinean bank. Guinextebank was Spanish and Guinean. Some people were probably worried about having only one bank, a French bank at that— particularly the Guineans and the Spaniards who had benefited from BCD and Guinextebank loans. BIAO was adopting a stringent, conservative policy toward loans. Surely many people feared being excluded from future loans. The person said to owe the largest amount to Guinextebank was the President himself. Other top officials were also on the list of debtors.

Eventually our plane arrived, and we flew to Bata. Soon I was warmly welcomed by massive Modesta and ensconced in the Hotel Rondo.

There was no electricity and no water. Thus, Bata in the dry season. But the next day it rained. Within hours, we had both water and electricity.

That first evening at seven Don Bonifacio came by, and we drove over to where Don Camilo was staying, an apartment above the regional office of the Ministry of Industry and Commerce. We had to use flashlights and kerosene lamps. We sat at a table facing the street. The shutters were open, but there was no cross-ventilation. Soon my shirt front was drenched.

"We are here to continue our work on the economic rehabilitation project," Don Bonifacio said.

We spent the next two hours reviewing our committee's progress and our agenda, and we agreed to meet the next night to discuss the case study of malanga exports (see pages 168–71).

I spent the next day at Public Works, trying again to nail down road repair plans and equipment needs. At seven we met at Don Camilo's abode, this time with electricity but still without air movement.

We dug in on the malanga case. As usual, getting started was hard. But eventually the two ministers did a terrific job of analyzing the many barriers to nontraditional exports in Equatorial Guinea:

You need an export license, which takes a lot of steps and a lot of time.

You have to pay a 25-percent export tax.

You get hassled by customs officials, people from the presidency, policemen, and people from Don Camilo's ministry.

There is no credit available.

The Chamber of Commerce only deals with cocoa and coffee and offers no services to the little guy exporting things like malanga.

Transport is problematic.

Few middlemen exist, so economies of scale are not exploited.

Then we went on to strategies to deal with the problems. Don Bonifacio pushed Don Camilo. "Your ministry is the key here. You have the job of fomenting international commerce."

To my surprise, Don Camilo wouldn't have it.

"The problem is production, and that's the business of the Ministry of Agriculture. The question of taxes is in your ministry, Finance. Much of the marketing should be done through the Chamber of Agriculture. I can't take the lead on an issue like this."

We went back to the successful case of Colombia we had studied a couple of months before. The government there had undertaken a series of measures to stimulate nontraditional exports, such as cut flowers. It had devalued the currency and controlled inflation, and had set up a special agency called Pro-Export, which did things like provide credit. If you produced a nontraditional export, you could get a rebate on the imported inputs you used. And the government helped with tax incentives, technical assistance, and the encouragement of private trade associations.

Did Equatorial Guinea need something like Pro-Export?

The discussion became less contentious. We brainstormed. We tried to figure out what facts we needed to know to address that question. Before we knew it, it was ten o'clock. I was famished and asked if we could continue the discussion the next day. My colleagues showed mercy and said yes. We headed down the stairs and into the night. The temperature outside was ten degrees cooler than in the stillness of Don Camilo's sitting room.

Don Camilo drove me to the hotel and on the way offered to buy me a drink. We entered the bar owned by a relative of Don Camilo's who treated him royally. All ministers here, whether relative or not, had something of that effect—or if not royalty, then something akin to feudal nobility.

After she brought our drinks, he turned to me. "You know what's amazing about these meetings we're having? We have a dialogue."

I asked him what he meant.

"A dialogue, an exchange of ideas. You can ask me questions, and I can ask you. We can try to estimate things we don't know. It is very constructive."

The mystery of the summons to Bata was solved. No mention of the banking crisis, no meeting with the President. Simply Don Camilo's desire, shared by Don Bonifacio, to continue our analysis of economic strategy. We didn't have answers yet, but I felt optimistic about the process.

"The Market Comes First"

What was needed to help nontraditional exports like food? In Malabo, I had visited the Minister of Agriculture. As usual he was dapper and smiling, indirect and modest, a small man in a big job who was surprisingly open about some of his puzzlement about what to do.

"I would like your comments on something. We have been working on a national program for food production. Here it is." He fetched from his desk a twelve-page mimeo. He acknowledged the central contribution of a Chilean adviser, who had formerly worked with the Sandinista government.

"It will be our highest priority. We have to do more to help the vast majority of our people, who work in subsistence agriculture. We can feed ourselves better and we can export food into Gabon and Cameroon.

"Our problem is that our people are not *organized,*" he continued. "We want to organize our farmers in each town and village into groupings. We want to begin with a nationwide program, in every district at once."

The minister avoided the word *cooperative*—probably, I thought, to avoid equating these "groupings" with the failed coops of the past. People working in agriculture had told me that the farmers distrusted coops because previous efforts had resulted in rip-offs. In each village a big man would be named president of the coop and then would simply appropriate the lion's share of any inputs ordered or loans received or profits generated. This sort of cooperation had had the effect of lining a few people's pockets. The peasants had concluded that organizing them meant exploiting them. But to the minister, "groupings" were the first step.

I expressed some worries. Shouldn't the market for the product come first? Was it wise to begin a new program in every district at once?

"We cannot sell what we do not produce," he replied, "so worrying about the market comes later. There is no danger about doing all the districts at once. An individual working alone is not as profitable as work done communally—this is the consciousness the program wishes to create. The important thing is to begin."

I took the paper home and read it. The strategy had two fundamentals. Farmers would be organized. Government extension agents would "supervise and control" the procurement of inputs. It was not clear how the extension agents would do this, what funds would be used to buy the inputs, or what would be done about marketing them. The project focused on the continent and would commence immediately in every district. The need for foreign aid was vaguely mentioned. Mentioned, too, in a few general words was the need to improve transportation and customs clearances at the border with Cameroon and Gabon. Marketing of the produce was barely noted.

A few days later, I spoke with Kurt, director for three years of the U.S.-sponsored cooperatives and transportation project, who was about to leave for good.

"I've never been in a country that could fall back so readily on subsistence and barter," he said. "Three years ago when we started this project, almost no food was available in any market. Even government officials had to have their own source of food. They would take off on Fridays and go into the countryside to get plantains and malanga and bananas and bush meat."

The production of foodstuffs on Bioko had soared since his project began to provide transportation to markets. "Now we've already reached the point on the island where the food markets are saturated with those staples. What's interesting is that no wholesale markets have evolved, no middlemen, no food cooperatives. Each woman—remember that women produce food in this country as they do in much of Africa—comes to market herself, with her own goods, an average of three sacks of food. She stays in the market, sleeps there, until she sells them. As the markets have filled up with food, prices have dropped. Our ridership has stayed constant—lots of individual growers."

The reluctance to take advantage of economies of scale in growing and marketing—which ostensibly is what "groupings" and cooperatives are all about—stems from the distrust of the government bred by the last regime. Some said that on the island there was also an ethnic dimension, since the government people were mostly Fangs and the farmers mostly Bubis. But even on the continent, few coops have actually worked.

Kurt said, "I guess we've visited every legally constituted cooperative in the country—one in horticulture, four or five in coffee and cocoa combined, eight or ten in cocoa. They all talk about two main problems—the lack of a market for their products and the lack of an assured supply of agricultural inputs like hand tools, wheelbarrows, coffee production equipment. Food production is in the hands of the women, and they are sort of organized in women's groups. But these groups are more like clubs. They have none of the traditional functions of a cooperative.

"In nineteen eighty a consultant came here and recommended that coops be formed, and he brought in legal statutes that are evidently from the West. You know, democratic principles, open-door policies, and so forth—great statutes. The government then tried to organize these groups, just how is unclear. There were a bunch of subsistence farmers, just survivors, and someone suddenly says you're a coop. It didn't work.

"Really they are still in a pre-cooperative stage, despite the legislation. When coops evolve naturally, farmers are established and markets exist and coops form to overcome market obstacles. Here the farmers aren't established as farmers and the markets don't yet exist."

I asked Kurt what the government could do to make the markets for products and inputs work better. He mentioned transportation. He didn't think marketing centers were needed, as in many towns the marketing infrastructure from colonial days was not even used.

"We have to study what can be marketed in Cameroon and Gabon, and what can be sold in Bata and Malabo, the two big domestic markets. If there is a demand and we can produce the product at a reasonable cost, then our evidence is that people produce. Once the market opens up, they get their machetes out and come up with the production. I don't think that in traditional food production there are any impediments in production techniques or in organizing the producers, and only a few in inputs. So the market comes first."

The Human Factor

I consulted Vladimir, the President's adviser on social affairs. A bearded lawyer who had studied in Spain, Vladimir was interested in organizing peasant farmers into groups. I had taken him a copy of our work on small businesses, and he came over for lunch to talk about it.

After eating, as we sipped coffee at the corner of the Casa Verde overlooking the volcano, the conversation turned to transportation and other factors in economic development.

"I agree that roads are important," Vladimir said, "but here in Equatorial Guinea they aren't all important. On the continent there are stretches of very bad roads where nonetheless taxi services go. I think we need more credit available to small operators to buy taxis and spares. One of the sad things about this country is how poorly the banking system works. We really don't have a concept of a bank. People get loans depending on who they are, not how worthy their project is."

I hypothesized that favoritism wouldn't be so bad if there were mechanisms to make people repay. That led to talk about corruption and how to stop it, and eventually to Vladimir's ideas about the human factor in development.

"I have often thought that it's a shame that we in black Africa have to

move so many centuries so quickly," he said. "We have to go from here
. . . to here . . . to here . . . to here, right now. We were only really colonized
at the end of the last century, you know. My grandparents never saw an
airplane or a television. And now we as a people are starting way ahead
of where we should be."

Every one of us, I replied, was once a four-year-old. One of the things
I had always liked about being a teacher was watching how fast people
learn. A person can go from high-school senior to world-class physicist in
seven or eight years. Cultures learn and change much more slowly, but
can't people undergo remarkable growth if they have access to people who
care and information and knowledge?

"In the nineteen sixties, you know, we were ahead of the rest of Africa,"
Vladimir said. "Now everyone has the attitude here that you have to get
rich overnight. That's the mentality here and in many African countries.
Politics are such that you become a someone suddenly, overnight, and then
you have to get rich.

"I was in Spain for many years—I couldn't return here for political
reasons—and one of my best friends, his father was a multimillionaire.
You know, a Rolls Royce and everything. Yet the kid was given a Seat six
hundred [the smallest Spanish car] and a hundred pesetas a week for gas.
He had to work for everything. All my friends were like that—you worked
hard and gained little by little. First a six hundred, then a one twenty-seven
[a slightly more luxurious car], later maybe a Citroën. But here we don't
want that. Without having even a bicycle, we want a Mercedes.

"This has various consequences. You do not value what you have. You
do not maintain things. The spirit of conservation is impossible. You do
not add to the total of things, you snatch things away." Vladimir's Spanish
was elegant: *No sumas, sino restas.*

"What I've said is true of most of Africa. When they've had money, it
has gone to Switzerland, now to any place in Europe. In black Africa there
aren't rules of property. What you have can always be taken away, and
I think it is more for political than economic reasons."

I told Vladimir that, despite all its problems, Equatorial Guinea seemed
a more promising place for growth than Bolivia or Nicaragua. When Vladimir asked me about Nicaragua, I told him about the inflation, the scarce
goods, the economic mistakes, the influence of the war, the support of the
typical person nonetheless.

"Well, I must say," Vladimir mused, "that although I do not precisely
support Reagan's policies in Nicaragua, I appreciate them. Take black
Africa. In the nineteen sixties there was a current flowing through Africa,

a current of independence. Not because it was wise, but because it was like a weight on us." Here Vladimir hit the sides of his head with both palms. "Spanish rule was as if you could not buy a drink in a bar in your own land. I am not saying we cannot innately govern ourselves, only that we were ill prepared, and as a result you see all of Africa improvising policies, with consequences that are hardly good."

I mentioned that the world economic environment had not been strong this past decade, which also contributed to Africa's policy problems.

"Yes, that, too," he said. "Let me tell you about my visit to São Tomé." This was a small island republic to the south, a former Portuguese colony. "Well, it's a beautiful island, exuberant vegetation, but very poor, three or four times as poor as Equatorial Guinea. You see nothing in the shops, six things in a store maybe, except for one place where you can only buy things with foreign exchange—it has plenty, but only for the magnates. Compared to São Tomé in this respect, we are like the U.S.A. The currency there is worthless, so the economy suffers.

"But they have electricity and water all the time in São Tomé. They scrub the streets once a week. The hospital is immaculate, like this." Vladimir gestured okay. "Their roads are good. They are poor but, you see, São Tomé has this human advantage. Why? I don't know. We have a material advantage now, but if they ever get a leader who gives them a convertible currency, they will be way ahead of us, because of that human factor.

"As far as that human factor goes, here in Equatorial Guinea we have little." Vladimir's voice had dropped to almost a whisper. "I would say none at all."

We were both quiet. Then Vladimir excused himself and left.

The Case of Malanga

The ministers had asked me to do a case study of one of Equatorial Guinea's food crops. I had chosen cocoyam, the turniplike tuber known locally as malanga. What was holding back malanga production? Could malanga be a lucrative export crop?

I began by consulting Norberto, an agricultural extension agent trained in Cuba. A wonderful young man, smart, smiling, and full of idealism and willingness to work, he shared his Cuban and Soviet books with me, and I found others in the Ministry of Agriculture's uncatalogued "library." Malanga was one of the first plants cultivated by man. More nutritious than the yam or the *yuca,* it is also easily digested and therefore good for children. Eighty percent of the world's production is estimated to be in the region of central west and southwest Africa. It is a good crop for the midlands of Bioko: it does not require much sunlight, likes about seven or eight feet of rain a year, and in soils like ours does not require fertilizer.

And, in fact, Bioko's cocoyam is famous in the region. Cameroonian and Nigerian products are smaller and contain more water; they also do not taste as good. Whether Equatorial Guinea has a competitive advantage cost-wise depends on many calculations of costs, yields, marketing, and so forth. I tried to summarize what was known by reading studies, interviewing experts and extensionists, and visiting villages to consult the women who grew and marketed malanga. The answers differed widely.

Just to give one example: What is the average cost of farming one hectare (2.471 acres) of malanga on the island? One study by a foreign cooperative project said 87,000 *cefas,* or about $300. Another study by a United Nations volunteer came up with 664,500 *cefas,* or roughly $2,300. Same island, same crop, same year. And so it went for estimates of yields per hectare and costs per kilo. And if you asked how local market prices compared with prices in neighboring countries, the answer was that no one knew. The agricultural expert with the World Bank's technical assistance project had proposed a simple and inexpensive market survey of Cameroon and Gabon. The idea had sat in the Planning Ministry without action for nine months, despite many proddings. No one knew why.

Women are the key to food production in Africa. I met many women who grew and sold malanga. In the village of Bososo, near my surf spot of Punta Sorpresa, I was by now well known. I interviewed the women to whom I gave rides to the market. I went to the market itself and spoke with vendors. The following composite picture emerged.

The women spend hours every day tending this and other food crops. The men clear the land, but the women do the rest of the work. When the malangas are harvested after eleven months, they are placed in one hundred eighty-seven pound bags and taken to market. Each woman feels compelled to take her own bag or bags to market.

"I don't trust my neighbor to sell the malanga for me," one woman explained after several of my questions, apparently surprised that I was surprised. "Why? I just do not. She would not give me the correct price or would take the money."

Even a woman in your village, your neighbor?

"Yes, I do not trust them."

Consequently each woman for each bag pays not only the bag's transportation but her own, and has to defray the cost of living for six days in the market—the time it takes to sell the one hundred eighty-seven pounds in small, retail batches. The women may benefit from spending six days in the market, but most of them say they would welcome a way to stay back in the village with their children. The marketing costs paid by the women come to about two thirds of the sale price of twenty-five to thirty dollars a bag—or more than twice the cost of production.

Teodora used to be in charge of women's activities for southern Bioko. She showed me a report by a women's delegation in 1986, which documented abundant actual and potential production of malanga. But the delegation also, said the report,

> described the problem that the women of the villages face with difficulties of selling their products and obtaining benefits, because on the one side there exists a stock of food in the markets and on the other side the high prices applied to them with regard to transport and the municipal taxes; all of which cause a loss of will among the women of the villages to try to increase production.

"Taxes" turned out to refer to illegal as well as legal charges. In the Malabo market, women are tapped by municipal officials and policemen for taxes and bribes that come to 15 to 20 percent of the Malabo market price, or about half the cost of production. I later learned that two thirds of the city's official revenues came from taxes on vendors and market stalls.

The domestic market is sometimes saturated: Why not export? Because if you want to export malanga, you face an array of permits and hassles. And the Ministry of Industry and Commerce was slapping on a 25-percent export tax—even though free trade in agriculture was supposed to reign within the UDEAC zone.

I asked an official at the ministry about these problems.

"Yes," he mused, "it can be said that exporting is too complicated. Almost all the regulations are from the time of the *ekuele* [the old nonconvertible currency whose black market value had been only a quarter to an eighth of its official value]. For example, the twenty-five percent export tax was there to make sure that the foreign exchange would come to the government, because it was of such value when we had the *ekuele*."

One commercial wholesaler in Malabo elaborated. "The government wanted to stop the export of bananas and malanga a few years back for fear that the people would not have enough to eat. Before that the Nigerian merchants used to come over here looking for these products and kola nuts and bush pepper."

I talked with several Nigerians in the Malabo market, who imported cloth and electronic equipment and a few other products. Why didn't they export things like malanga in return?

"Look here, I have to see things from the point of view of making money," one man said. "With exports the government imposes so many obstacles. There are many permits and many payments. Sometimes one has to make extra-official payments. Not just Industry and Commerce but other agencies. For example, a week ago I received a formal note from the presidency asking me for documents and telling me to come to a meeting. Surely they will be charging me more money.

"I do not believe that I can make money in exports, and there are many uncertainties."

Other factors, too, have helped squelch the market for malanga—poor transportation, a lack of agricultural credit, few extensionists who know about food crops, and an absence of grades and quality standards. In fact, Equatorial Guinea's experience with malanga displays a syndrome observed around Africa. Big economic reforms have taken place; prices and exchange rates are "got right." But food production has not taken off. Market institutions, government regulations, and economic infrastructure remain deficient.

So as in most of Africa, structural adjustment has made little difference to food producers—or to their husbands.

Women and Children

In many parts of Africa, women constitute over half the labor force. They grow four fifths of the food. Yet they earn only one tenth of the total money income, and own only 1 percent of the assets. We had no such data for Equatorial Guinea, but I guessed the situation was similar. As in the rest of Africa, poverty and malnutrition hit hardest on women and children.

African women usually bear the heaviest burdens but are seldom in positions of official authority. In Equatorial Guinea, rural women carry on their backs wicker baskets the size of garbage cans, loaded with plaintains or yams or firewood. These are balanced by straps around the shoulders or sometimes across the forehead. Even elderly women stagger along roadways and paths with mountainous loads. I gained firsthand experience of their burdens. Going to and from the beach, I would give rides to women and their loads and their children. In helping them get their baskets into the car, I often had trouble deadlifting the weights the women routinely bore.

They also bear children. Population growth in much of Africa approaches 4 percent a year—the fastest growth of a population group anywhere in the world, any time in history. Given that one child in five dies before the age of five and miscarriages are widespread, the pregnancy rates are even higher.

Sex has other correlates. Women are often physically and sexually abused. I heard stories from men and women of frequent beatings—and this in a society where in more than two years I heard of not a single armed robbery, mugging, or murder. Multiple "wives" are widespread, as is the practice of fathering children and then taking no responsibility for them.

In rural Equatorial Guinea, husbands view their wives differently than we do in the industrialized West. The clearest explanation came from Don Camilo's brother Arturo, whom my engineer friend Roger DiJulio and I called on in the remote town of Cogo, in Río Muni. Roger was visiting from the States, and I took him to Río Muni for a week to look at the rural roads in order to give me an idea of the kinds of reconstruction and rehabilitation that might be needed. We challenged the toughest road first—the one from Mbini to Cogo. For the last twenty-two miles, it made the Baja 500 look like the Golden State Freeway. In this extended boglike area, gigantic mudholes thirty yards long and a yard deep would form. We had rented a four-wheel-drive pickup. Our instructions were: you can make it, but stay right on the tire tracks you see on the road. Fine advice, but the road was under water.

We did make it, however, and in the late afternoon arrived by motorboat in magnificent Cogo, at the river border with Gabon. Fronted by two rivers and crowned by a grove of trees, Cogo had been a prosperous port in Spanish times. Now the town had no electricity, and road connections were out because of collapsed bridges. Jobs were scarce. Yet with many beautiful old buildings and its remarkable setting with water all around, Cogo retains a colonial grandeur.

Roger and I joined Don Camilo's brother for a beer at his house. Arturo described his economic activities: a farm outside of town and a bar in town, plus an outboard motorboat. He talked about his grandfather's forty wives and his own foursome. Buoyed by the beer and his friendliness, I asked him whether it was hard to manage romantic affairs with four wives.

"No, I think you do not understand our system," Arturo explained. "For us it is not like a wife in the West. This is not a question of romance. It is more like an economic arrangement.

"I provide for my wives and protect them. They, in turn, provide for me. I have wives for different purposes. The one you have met is good for cooking and entertaining, as tonight. Two others work in the fields, leaving very early in the morning and returning late in the day. Another one I use for errands. You know, errands are not for everyone. You can send a woman to Mbini with something to do or to get and she may stop in a village along the way and talk with her relatives and finally get to Mbini and forget why she was going there. Or she may just return days too late.

"But this wife of mine, she is excellent for errands. She listens, she understands, she goes and does it, and she returns."

We drank some more beer. I decided not to push the management question. Romance in Equatorial Guinea is not as I understand it.

In this country, some astonishing sexual stereotypes turn out to have a basis in fact. Alcohol consumption is prodigious given local incomes, and it is true that many men drink away the earnings from cash crops while many women are guarding for the family the food and scant money garnered from subsistence crops. Men monopolize formal organizations from village councils to government ministries. Men are the forces of control but also of a lack of control, of dissipation. Women are the creators, the sinews of both home and economy. It is the men who are wasting Africa's money on armaments and corruption and luxuries, the women who nurture the young, grow the subsistence crops, tend the houses, and make markets work. It is a provocative exaggeration to say so: Africa's deepest ills are the ills of African males.

Through women I came in contact with a common phenomenon in Africa, the death of children. In Equatorial Guinea, the child killers include malaria, stomach disorders, measles and, once in a while, cholera.

Twice in a single week, my maid Consuelo had arrived in the morning exhausted. Why? Guineans have a custom something like a wake. When someone dies, they stay up all night consoling each other and singing and drinking coffee. Then the next afternoon at four they have the burial. One Tuesday morning, Consuelo came with the news that her four-year-old niece had died of malaria. The next morning, her six-year-old cousin was claimed by the same disease.

"In this country," Consuelo said bitterly, "we die like dogs."

At eleven that morning, I drove to the airport. One of the girls who worked behind the counter did not look well. Her name was Rosa. She greeted me and after responding in kind, I told her she looked as though she had been sick.

"Me ha pasado una desgracia," Rosa said: something terrible has happened. "Three weeks ago my son died."

173

She looked about nineteen; her baby was one and a half. Shocked, I asked how it happened.

"They don't know. I came home from work and made him dinner, and he wouldn't take it. Then a little later that night he breathed badly, like this." She made a choking, wheezing sound. "Finally he got bad. I took him to the hospital. He died on the way, near the telecommunications building."

The airport was empty, as the plane I had hoped to find had left an hour earlier. It was eerily quiet. Rosa's colleague behind the bar had put her head down on her hands on the bartop, as if to rest from the sadness. A couple of yellow birds flew in through the open windows and perched upside down on small beams overhead. They began to screech and sing. The three of us at the bar were silent for a long time.

Rosa finally looked down at the bartop and said, "What can one do?"— not in abject despair but as a statement of fact.

We were silent again. In contrast, the birds' chirpings were surrealistically amplified by the empty space of the terminal shed. One of them was making a nest like a wicker football hanging from the ceiling. I said good-bye to Rosa and her friend, and drove back through that lush stretch of exuberant bush and cocoa and jungle back into town. Animal and plant life abounded here in amazing profusion. But what about human life?

Underway

No news came from the presidency about the workshop for the ministers. At Industry and Commerce, too, there was some sort of delay. But our project's coordinating committee continued to meet. True, sometimes I was the only one who showed up. Bonifacio, the Minister of Finance, had the next highest batting average, about .750. Camilo of Industry and Commerce and Diego of Planning were .400 hitters. Sometimes the absentees had good excuses, like travel or illness; but many times they forgot an appointment or simply overlooked it—a propensity I became all too familiar with.

Our project's procurement officer finally arrived. Harry, an Englishman who had previously run bottling plants in Nigeria, among other things, was about fifty, tended to use "me" for "my," and looked like a thin Jack LaLanne. He came with eleven suitcases as big as desks. Also accompanying him was his bulky supervisor from a British consulting company, who was there to negotiate Harry's contract. Since he did not speak Spanish, I had to be part of all the negotiations. The coordinating committee and

174

the company had already spent four months haggling over Harry's and his company's fee; the total had come down 22 percent, but the company's chunk was still bigger than Harry's: not unusual, sadly, but nonetheless outrageous. Harry had come without a signed contract, and the supervisor was with him to make sure one was to be had before Harry started work.

Since Harry would be working in the Ministry of Industry and Commerce, the coordinating committee deputed the minister, Don Camilo, to sign the contract on the government's behalf. Getting an appointment with Camilo was difficult. Fortunately, he delegated the negotiation of the final contract to his secretary general, Don Timoteo. But unfortunately, after everything was approved by Timoteo—and typed by me in the evenings on my laptop—Camilo wouldn't sign. "Why should we pay for the gasoline for his car?" Camilo complained. He had ten other details to change. And so I ended up wasting a week doing what the supervisor should have done: the supervisor for whom the country was paying the equivalent of 130 percent of Harry's salary.

But at last Harry was in harness. Having worked with maintenance and control before, as well as with procurement, he would be invaluable as our project's spending got under way. We worked together putting into practice the ministers' ideas about how to decide what to buy. We created procedures through which ministries were forced to link import needs to specific strategies. We developed a method for systematically appraising existing systems of maintenance and control. We developed forms for summarizing what other donors were doing in each area.

We also finally got offices—in my case, fourteen months after arriving. We at last had assistants: in my case, a hard-drinking former secretary general of Planning named Raúl; in Harry's, one of my students in the U.N. course. So we began cranking in earnest on the priority areas our coordinating committee had identified. Roads to enable agricultural markets to work—especially, the rehabilitation and maintenance of existing rural roads. Small-scale enterprise. Preventive medicine and public health. Rethinking cocoa as the motor of growth, and maybe diversifying into food production and fishing for export. We were also working with electricity, water supply, machinery maintenance, garbage collection, and preventive medicine.

Within months in six ministries and the cities of Malabo and Bata, we had set up task forces, invited consultants, and begun the process of identifying needs and designing maintenance systems.

These activities fit into a strategy that went beyond structural adjustment. The ministers thought of it as having three parts.

175

First, we needed to improve private sector institutions like banking and credit, private investment and property rights, and marketing.

Second, we needed to streamline and invigorate various public sector institutions, such as the Ministry of Industry and Commerce, agricultural extension, and the regulatory and tax environment for business. We needed to improve incentives in the public sector, which meant linking part of what people earned to the results they achieved. And we needed to control government corruption.

Finally, we had to improve the infrastructure, especially transportation.

Without these advances, our coordinating committee thought that the government's new economic strategy would fail. Stabilization would not work, and liberalization would not invigorate the indigenous private sector. So we were proceeding on many fronts at once, from small questions of ministerial management to high strategy. At last our project was under full throttle.

But the debt crisis was so severe that we would have to use most of our project's funds to repay Equatorial Guinea's international creditors. Don Bonifacio and I signed huge checks to pay the interest on several debts; if we had not done so, projects would have been canceled and interest penalties incurred. Most of the economic rehabilitation money, then, would never even hit our economy. As soon as funds came in from the World Bank, they would shoot back out to our creditors. Many African countries were experiencing a similar phenomenon. In the last few years, net flows of resources from foreign financial institutions had turned negative.

One day came news of a bizarre scandal. One of the Mongomo clan members who worked at the Ministry of Finance had filed a report to the President saying that Don Bonifacio had stolen some of the money our project had paid to international financial institutions. The source for this story said that an investigation had been carried out and had, of course, shown that nothing of the kind had occurred. This episode was another murky sign of the prevailing suspiciousness—perhaps also of the resistance of some parts of the government to Don Bonifacio's attempts to control the public budget and reduce corruption.

Of the two other World Bank-financed projects in Equatorial Guinea, one was the massive cocoa rehabilitation project, whose goals included reclaiming abandoned cocoa farms and making credit available to existing farms. The other was the technical assistance project, which was in disarray.

The idea of the T.A. project, as it was called, was to hire high-level advisers for five key ministries—Planning, Agriculture, Education, Mining and Hydrocarbons, and Forests and Water. There would also be a short-term consultant on debt and money for other consultants as needed. The project included funds for training of Equatoguineans both in country and abroad. The expert in Planning would also serve as the technical coordinator of the project. He would ensure that the sectoral experts' work fed into the national planning system. The Minister of Planning would exercise overall control, and an Equatoguinean administrator located in the Planning Ministry would handle day-to-day matters.

This was the idea. But its execution had been disastrous. The advisers had become alienated and unproductive. None of the training funds had been utilized. The coordinator had not coordinated, the Minister of Planning had remained uninvolved, and recently the World Bank had found evidence that the administrator was corrupt. The five ministers who had advisers from the project were unhappy with its administration. They had proposed to the President that the project's central funds and its management be divided among the various ministries. In desperation, the World Bank and the Minister of Planning, Don Diego, had asked me to take over as economic adviser and technical coordinator, in addition to my other duties, until a full-time person could be found—perhaps six months or a year hence.

It was an intriguing notion. Imagine we could combine the brainpower of five advisers plus consultants with the money we had in our economic rehabilitation project. We could work with the various ministries to design training programs to get their own people up to speed. We could use the T.A. project to invigorate the entire planning system of the country. Don Diego was my colleague on the economic rehabilitation project and a friendly visitor to my house. The World Bank would be supportive. Why not try?

Why not run into a concrete wall?

Take, for example, the "expert" chosen for the Planning Ministry. Supposedly an economist, the chap knew nothing about the subject and instead spent his time trumpeting a flagrant homosexual relationship with a French boyfriend and building a weekend hut up in the mountains. A full year after the government could no longer stomach this clown, it was finally able to get approval from the Bank for his removal, give him and his German company notice, and dismiss him.

Or take the sofa-sized education adviser, Zoila. She was more notable for her bright-flowered dresses and giant earrings than for her attainments in two years at the Ministry of Education. The word was that Zoila had many friends in the Mongomo clan. Her neighbors in the expatriate ghetto said that late some nights the cars of the President himself and his bodyguards could be found parked in front of Zoila's house. This had been translated in true Malabo style into the assurance that Zoila was sleeping with the President. But in Equatorial Guinea rumor made a lot of crazy claims.

Stanley, the mining and hydrocarbons expert, was an aging Canadian with a pronounced Eastern European accent. He lived in Bata. Stanley's workday began at nine thirty and ran to twelve when, contrary to local custom, he went home for lunch. He then returned to the office at one thirty and worked until the local closing time of three—when the indigenous staff would go home for lunch. Stanley would go home, too, and take a nap. That was Stanley's work day. His major endeavor during it was contacting Canadian mining firms to have a look at Equatorial Guinea's prospects for gold. A year and a half after arriving, Stanley had elicited one response of "strong interest." The regional administrator of his ministry told me, "Why do we have an adviser like him? We need someone to train us, to help us do surveys. He works alone and he works very little. He is a lone wolf." Yet the regional administrator felt that Stanley was somehow the World Bank's man—and, anyway, the project was under the control of the Planning Ministry, so Stanley couldn't be controlled or got rid of.

Hugo, the agricultural adviser, lived in Bata. He was interested in food production and thought the right way to increase it was through the formation of cooperatives with supervision by government officials. He had been the brains behind the strategy the Agriculture Minister had asked me about. Hugo was intelligent and dedicated; also frustrated by endless delays stemming from the lack of technical coordination and the Equatoguinean administrator's refusal to make decisions. For example, Hugo's wife had to spend a week in Malabo to persuade Salvador to buy her a ticket home for Christmas—a provision clearly allowed in Hugo's contract.

The adviser for the Ministry of Forests and Water had not been hired. The country was not in the consultant circuit and had few means of finding talented people. So it asked the World Bank for help. But the Bank was reluctant to suggest advisers. Though the Bank loaned money to the government and had to approve advisers and their contracts, it wanted to preserve the fact and appearance that the advisers worked for the government, not for the Bank. As a consequence, despite the importance of timber to the country's economy and ecology, the ministry had no adviser three years after the project had commenced.

Jean was a short-term consultant on the country's debt, who was seconded from the French affiliate of an international accounting firm. Through one extension after another, "short-term" had turned into a year and then two. Jean would bomb back to Paris once every month or so, flying first class from Douala ("It is the company's policy," he said), and he would prepare and participate in negotiations on Equatorial Guinea's behalf with overseas creditors. Jean was in his late twenties, smart and aggressive; also burned out and cynical. He had helped the country by doing a job for it. But he had not fulfilled his contract's provision for training local counterparts so they could take over. This was one reason that his contract for well over two hundred thousand dollars a year kept having to be renewed. Explaining why training was not feasible, Jean said, "The people I am working with cannot even add and divide—not even the so-called economist who has just returned from six years in the Soviet Union."

My friend Salvador was the T.A. project's administrator. Salvador, a very African-looking, round-faced man of about forty-five, was formerly a businessman in Mbini and Bata. During the design of the T.A. project, a World Banker had "discovered" Salvador and suggested to the government that he be the administrator. The concept was interesting: get a successful private-sector administrator instead of an unknown and probably less dynamic career civil servant. Salvador's salary was about nine thousand dollars a year, a paltry sum compared with the expatriate experts' but lavish by local standards. He was the highest-paid Equatoguinean in any foreign aid project, and his salary was more than double that of a minister of government.

Before I accepted the position, Don Diego and I talked at length about the project and the position of technical coordinator. We dwelled on the strategic aspects of the project—how it could fit in with the improvement of the country's planning process and with the economic rehabilitation project. It seemed important to take a participative approach. Get the advisers and administrator together with the minister and me, explain that the minister and the Bank wished to help them do their jobs better, talk about my role as technical coordinator, and ask them to write short analyses of their key problems, opportunities, and needs.

I had hoped that Salvador's situation would be settled before I entered the scene. The Bank wanted Salvador to be fired and a complete audit held. I didn't want to be in a position of seeming either to take his place or to be the person who bounced him. Salvador's situation, however, proved difficult to resolve. He had backing from the Minister of Education, who also happened to be from Mbini and wanted the T.A. project to be divided up among the ministries. Salvador was fighting for his life—his reputation, his power, and his salary. An audit was begun, but he would continue as administrator till it was completed.

Don Diego organized the first meeting of all the advisers. Stanley and Hugo flew in from Bata. Zoila wore a bright blue outfit. Salvador sat at the far edges of the conference table, as far away from the minister as possible, with a mean look on his face.

Diego accentuated the positive. He and I wanted to help the experts achieve their objectives. We needed a careful diagnosis as the first step. He distributed a one-page memo outlining a report he hoped to receive from each of them within two weeks. Then we would meet again to discuss common problems and solutions. In the meantime, Diego said, the technical coordinator would be talking with each of them personally.

Zoila said this was fine but she wanted the chauffeur that her contract called for. She also wanted immediate action on the library for the educational planning cell. Diego said we would study these problems immediately, and instructed me to talk with her about them.

The meeting went well, I thought. It was, Hugo told me afterward, the first meeting in the history of the project. Zoila talked to me in the parking lot. "I hate that man Diego," she said. "He lies, he is spineless, he will not decide. I told myself I would not say anything at any meeting that he attended. But I did. Can we talk about the chauffeur and the library?"

We could, tomorrow morning. I drove away from the Ministry of Planning, feeling good. Maybe this was the beginning of a big turnaround.

Small Businesses

Meanwhile, on the economic rehabilitation project we were studying import needs and strategies in several key sectors.

Small business seemed particularly interesting, having political as well as economic implications. It was not just a question of redistributing wealth to the little guy; it was building for the future. In other countries, private economic activity tends to progress from small-scale commerce to small and medium producers and eventually to local industries. Equatorial Guinea has little small indigenous commerce.

Somewhat surprisingly, credit programs for small businesses have been succeeding in difficult environments like Bangladesh and Burkina Faso. They have a common mechanism, whereby small businesses wishing to receive credit are required to form small groups of about seven, each one in the group guaranteeing the loan of the others. Then a small amount is lent, by the month if possible, so anyone who defaults gets cut off almost immediately from further loans. Later, credit is coupled with technical assistance in the form of business planning.

Credit is crucial. Getting people to repay is a big problem. As in other countries, a loan tends to be regarded as a gift. I had seen a doctoral thesis at the Harvard Business School on agricultural credit programs in developing countries that documented an average loan default rate of 45 percent—clearly not sustainable.

To encourage repayment, incentives are important. There have to be effective penalties for those who do not repay. In many countries this is difficult because politicians are often involved in giving or getting the loans. There have to be positive incentives for bank officers to obtain repayment. And banks have to screen credit recipients carefully without at the same time confining credit to the rich. If banks used standard screening and collateral rules imported from the West, rich people would be the only ones with appropriate credentials of credit-worthiness, and large loans to the rich might be the only ones that could justify the banks' large transactions costs.

What could our economic rehabilitation project do to help microenterprise in Equatorial Guinea? If the BCD had not folded, we would have set up a rotating loan fund directed especially toward small, indigenous workshops and businesses. But the French bank BIAO was not interested in any such endeavor. After Marc Lindenberg's visit, we linked up with the United Nations' deputy representative, who was also interested in small business. He would invite the U.N.'s International Labour Office to come to design a project; in the meantime, we would carry out a survey.

I recruited the four best high-school mathematics students, two girls and two boys, to learn statistics and survey the workshops of Malabo. We met a lot of small-business people, had a lot of fun, and learned something as well.

We confined our attention to indigenous workshops with fewer than fifteen employees that made or repaired a durable product. These were the people, we thought, who might be centrally involved in the country's economic rehabilitation. We included motor mechanics, clothes makers, carpenters, furniture makers, electricians, iron workers, shoe repairers, painters, metal workers, and a maker of cement blocks. We excluded food preparers and vendors, purely commercial enterprises, barbers, and small agroindustries.

The research was time consuming. The students enjoyed the various steps: deciding what we wanted to find out, designing a questionnaire, testing it, defining the universe, administering the survey, tabulating results, and analyzing the data. They had adventures along the way. The owner of a workshop might refuse to participate the first time they visited, maybe even the second, but on the third visit might say, "You are serious, aren't you?" and give the students an hour of his time. At the end we had data from thirty-four workshops on their costs, revenues, employees, and problems faced. Nineteen other workshops could not or would not come up with appropriate information.

These were small enterprises—the median number of paid employees was three, and the median capital investment about $3,500. Many were one-person "firms" with unpaid family members contributing. Total monthly costs averaged about $1,400. Raw materials made up 45 percent of costs, and about three quarters of the raw materials were imported. The average wage was about one and a half times the average wage paid to government officials.

The average firm had losses of 7 percent in the previous year. But this estimate included the implicit cost of their capital investment; if one excluded that component, the typical firm's revenues were about equal to its costs. A few firms made good profits, but we could find no statistical criteria that differentiated successful firms from unsuccessful ones.

The workshop owners and managers told us their major problem was lack of credit. None had received a bank loan in the recent past; only a few had been able to come up with loans from family, friends, or the informal loan market. The other problems they cited were the supply and costs of their imported raw materials and the lack of liquidity in the economy. They did not have many difficulties with labor, transport, production, or processing. None of the firms exported any share of what they produced.

This was grassroots African capitalism, vigorous and hard-working. Though they worked with primitive technologies and few management skills, in the short run these were not their problems. What they needed most were liquidity and demand. They needed access to credit, easier regulations, help in developing export markets. And the government had to get off their backs. Two thirds of the revenues of the cities of Malabo and Bata came from taxes on small businesses, peddlers, and market stalls.

The government had to see small business as something to be freed, not something to be regulated, taxed, and licensed.

The Meeting at My House

Meanwhile, the people on the T.A. project were slow to finish their memoranda on their problems and plans. Hugo of Agriculture was right on time, and Jean's memo came soon thereafter. With a little prodding, Zoila and Stanley produced their pieces. But Salvador, the Guinean administrator, was recalcitrant. I stopped by the Planning Ministry one day and asked him where his memo was.

"I don't work for you, you know, Roberto. I am the administrator of this project. I report to the minister." He was looking down at the floor, as if examining the dirt crusted on the corner tiles.

"Hey, Salvador, relax. This isn't from or for me, it's from the minister. We're all trying to get this project going so you don't face all the problems you've faced in the past."

"Well, I want the request in writing," Salvador said sullenly.

Whew! I thought. I consulted the minister and he asked me to draft him a memo to Salvador, which I did. Three days later, in came Salvador's memo. It complained and complained about the World Bank—not surprisingly perhaps, since Salvador had been accused of corruption by the Bank and would soon be audited by a firm from Cameroon. But it wasn't a bad memo: it had some good ideas about what could be done to make the project work better. I wanted to make sure we could help Salvador, as well as the experts, early on.

So we planned a meeting where everyone would talk over problems and possible solutions. Don Diego and I went over what we hoped the meeting would achieve. A restatement of objectives. A summary of problems. A brainstorm of possible solutions. Since our evening meetings for the economic rehabilitation project had gone well, I suggested to Diego that we meet at night. It would make it friendlier, less formal. We could even have the get-together at my house.

Diego demurred. I argued for forging a more relaxed, collegial attitude. Finally, Diego acceded: my house, next Monday night at seven thirty. Stanley would not be able to attend, and Jean was in Europe; but Zoila, Hugo, and Salvador would be in town.

When I informed Salvador, he did not like the idea.

"At your *house*, Roberto? That is not correct. It should be at the Planning Ministry." He still averted his eyes.

I explained the reasoning behind my house. Salvador was not impressed, but agreed to come.

So we met the next Monday at seven thirty. Celestina and Consuelo stayed late and served refreshments and appetizers. The whiteboard and felt pens from my office were in the center of the living room, balanced on the bookcase, so I could take notes that everyone could see. Don Diego sat in his accustomed spot on one of the two facing couches. Hugo was scrubbed and brushed and eager. Zoila's earrings would have been at home on a Christmas tree. Salvador arrived last, accepted a soft drink, and sat hunched up at the far corner of Diego's couch. He looked as happy as a dental patient.

Don Diego led off, as planned.

"The administrator and the experts have prepared analytical memoranda about the problems encountered and their objectives for the next six to twelve months," he said, "as well as about the concrete steps that should occur for the project to move forward. The purpose of these reports, just as the purpose of our meetings, are not to cast blame on anyone, but to search for ways of resolving problems."

Then Diego asked that we review the project's objectives. I stood by the whiteboard and prepared to write down what people said. There was a pause. Then Salvador said, "To make sure that the experts worked well under the project." I wrote this down.

Hugo said, "Another goal is to strengthen the institutional capacity of the government."

I asked what that would take.

Hugo said training for the Equatoguinean personnel.

"Also methods and administrative models adapted to the Guinean reality," Zoila offered. "And materials and administrative means, like offices, data, planning cells, equipment, and documentation centers."

At least she didn't mention chauffeurs—something she had been badgering me about almost daily. I had told her finally that the first thing we were going to do would *not* be to hire her a chauffeur.

Salvador spoke. "Better follow-up of projects in general, better management."

I asked if there were any further objectives. A long pause. Finally, Diego said: "To formulate medium-term plans of socioeconomic development, at the sectoral and national levels." These were the words of the original project document: the *raison d'être* in the eyes of the project's designers.

We talked about this objective. I made the distinction between plans and strategies, and asked the group whether, given the situation in Equatorial Guinea, a formal "national plan" or educational plan or agricultural plan was desirable. The experts spoke: first Hugo, then Zoila. Their gist was that formal plans involving macroeconomic models, manpower planning, or agricultural input-output models were beyond Equatorial Guinea's capabilities. These required data, sophistication, political understanding, and resources that the country did not yet have. Even if we had those things, I opined, formal plans might not be the best use of the country's resources.

So we talked about strategies instead, in the sense now familiar to Diego from the other project, about a *process* within each ministry and in the government for formulating strategies. We talked about implementing strategies, too.

They discussed various kinds of technical assistance. In the usual brand an expert comes and carries out a task, the classic case being writing a report and then leaving. Much rarer was an expert who worried about implementation, how the report could be used in practice. And rarer still, at least in Equatorial Guinea, was the expert who worked with the Guineans and trained them.

Zoila and Hugo said the latter two categories were what we needed. Don Diego nodded in agreement. So I asked them why these types of technical assistance were not provided well in Equatorial Guinea. Why so little concern for implementation, and why so little collegial work among experts and locals?

The group began to cook. I erased the whiteboard, and quickly they filled it up with a long list.

"Sometimes we agree on a strategy in a ministry, and then in a short while the strategy is forgotten, as if it never existed. We do not have a memory."

"Lack of a dialogue between the technocrats and the politicians."

"The philosophical aims of the politicians are difficult to operationalize."

"Politicians take decisions for short-term political reasons, not for reasons of long-term strategy."

After these factors were on the board, out came the technical limitations: data, models, computers, and so forth. But I was struck by the salience of politics and process.

How could we improve these processes for formulating and implementing strategies in Equatorial Guinea? Again, a burst of ideas.

Training. Seminars for the politicians. Meetings where policies are explained to bureaucrats. Emphasize that many policies are by nature inter-sectoral and not the province of only one ministry. Simplify planning to emphasize the "grand lines of strategy," instead of long, technical documents and lists of projects. Do a better job of coordinating foreign aid.

And, Hugo said, one might use the resources of the T.A. project to "subsidize" better processes of policy formulation and implementation in the ministries.

We had run out of time, so we decided to think more about this *how* question at our next meeting. Each expert would prepare a short memo to the rest of us about how policy formulation and implementation might be improved in his or her ministry. The idea was to reconsider ways that the T.A. project's funds, consultants, training opportunities, and political support could help the experts help their ministries more.

The meeting ended. We talked for a while, and then everyone shook hands and said goodbye. I was pleased. Lots of cooperation, lots of ideas. A little stiff, not yet friendly exactly—but it seemed a good first step.

The next morning I wrote up a summary of the meeting, without naming names. I distributed it to Diego, Salvador, and the experts with a note reminding them of the time of our next get-together.

The President's Answer

A few days later Don Bonifacio beckoned me to his office.

"Roberto, we have to help a colleague of ours," he said in an intimate tone. "The Minister of Planning is in trouble. As you know, he does not get along with Salvador and wants to fire him. But Salvador is tenacious, and he is well connected. The various ministers who participate in the project want to decentralize it so they can control their share of the funds. The Minister of Education has complained to the President about the Minister of Planning. The Minister of Education has defended Salvador. He has criticized the slow central administration of the project."

Like Salvador, the Minister of Education was from Mbini.

"I have been asked to participate in the administration of the T.A. project," Bonifacio went on. "but I do not want to undercut the Minister of Planning. So I wonder if we could design a new administrative structure for the project. A coordinating committee like the one for the economic rehabilitation project."

We had talked about this before. The coordinating committee in this case could include the ministers of Education, Agriculture, Mining and Hydrocarbons, and Forests and Water, as well as of Planning. And now Don Bonifacio of Finance as well. Maybe me, too, as the technical coordinator. Such a committee could have two virtues. It might defuse Diego's immediate political problems and provide a vehicle for interministerial strategy formulation—now almost absent in Equatorial Guinea.

"I am going to talk with the President and with the Minister of Planning about this idea," Bonifacio continued. "Then I will call a meeting later this week of the ministers involved and you. Please prepare me an order of work for it." An order of work was an agenda; all government meetings had to have them. "Be prepared to talk at this meeting about the advantages of a coordinating committee."

I got up to go. Bonifacio had one more thing to say.

"Roberto, let me give you a piece of advice about Doña Zoila, just between you and me. She is very well connected, Roberto, *very* well. Leave her alone, don't cross her."

I returned to my office. A coordinating committee could be a great step for the T.A. project, I thought. It was a way to get the project on track administratively and substantively. I admired Bonifacio's daring, his loyalty to Diego. I prepared a draft order of work and sent it to Bonifacio. The next morning I got it back, approved, unchanged. A little later he telephoned.

"I have called the ministers and we will meet in my office at two o'clock. Please attend."

I passed the day on other chores. A little before two, I arrived at Don Bonifacio's office. His secretary Yolanda was there. But Bonifacio was absent.

"The Minister of Finance has been called to the presidency," Yolanda said grandly, as though announcing the fact to the Organization of African Unity. He had been gone since noon.

I waited on one of the oily couches in the waiting room. I reviewed again the project document, the experts' memoranda. Time passed. Three o'clock came. The ministry was shutting down; everyone had to leave.

I went home to lunch. Later I tried to get in touch with Don Bonifacio to find out what had happened, but he was not home.

The next morning at ten, Bonifacio called my office and told me to come over to his.

"Welcome, Roberto," he said, motioning me to a chair in front of his desk.

"Buenos días, Señor Ministro. What happened yesterday at the presidency?"

Bonifacio paused and smiled.

"Roberto, I have bad news for you. For me, too—for all of us. Yesterday the President convened me, the Minister of Planning, the Minister of Education, and several others. There were many criticisms of the technical assistance project, of its administration. There were also criticisms of you. You had a meeting in your house the other night. The President had a copy of the minutes you prepared, and he had been told that it was a subversive meeting, where criticisms of the government took place, in the private residence of a foreign expert. The Minister of Planning and I defended you strongly, Roberto. We went through the minutes with the President and showed him that the purpose of the meeting had been to analyze the problems we faced, not to criticize the government. At the end, he understood. But others had been telling him, what does this Klitgaard man want? The Minister of Education told the President it was wrong that the World Bank should have you take over another project and dismiss the only Equatoguinean with any responsibility in a foreign aid project—namely Salvador. He tried to make it seem that you were taking Salvador's job. Again, we defended you strongly against this misinterpretation. We told the President that you were doing this because we had requested it, that you would not be earning any additional salary for this, that you were trying to help the country. But the argument was not over, for one of the President's advisers said that Klitgaard was also the man who wanted to teach us. Why should he think he can teach us, it is our country, he said, what does *he* know?

"The President has rejected the idea of a coordinating committee for the T.A. project. When Salvador goes as administrator after the audit goes through, you, too, will have to let go the position of technical coordinator of the T.A. project. And I think for now your idea of the workshop for the ministers and presidential advisers should be set aside.

"Don't be discouraged, Roberto, I beg you. We will continue to move forward with our economic strategy on the economic rehabilitation project. We will work closely together, as we have in the past.

"Roberto, I can see you look discouraged. So am I, Roberto, so am I. This is a sad thing for me to tell you, and I feel ashamed of my country. But Roberto, do not lose heart. How many times have you consoled me when I faced difficulties and defeats? How often have you encouraged me? Many times, Roberto. I could always count on you for a wiser perspective. And now you must count on me and listen to what I tell you. I know my country. I know what you are trying to do, Roberto. And the President will know, too. We have many ignorant people here, Roberto, people who want to hide themselves from the outside world and what is happening there, people who want to cloak themselves in the safety of their own ignorance. That is why we need you, Roberto, that is why you are here."

Later I saw Don Diego. He was shellshocked by the meeting at the presidency. But he had survived.

"It was not good, I can tell you that."

I asked him how the minutes from our meeting had reached the President.

"I wondered this myself," Diego said. "I was sitting by the President's side. He had a photocopy of your minutes. At the top of the photocopy was written, in your hand, the name of Doña Zoila."

7

Rehabilitation

ZOILA denied any knowledge of how the minutes had reached the President. Salvador said he didn't know, either. There was little point in pursuing the matter. My role in the technical assistance project would shrink to helping the experts solve minor problems. The workshops for the ministers and presidential advisers were scuttled. And it was a depressing thought that beneath the placid surface of respect, I had enemies.

When things got bad, there were escapes. Tennis in the afternoons, dancing once in a while at the discothèque, visits to Casa Mota for dominoes. Just to get on the motorcycle and blast off into the jungle was a solace. Once in a while I would visit a cocoa plantation at night and watch the huge, wood-fueled cocoa driers in operation. Under bright lights from a generator, two eight-yard-wide mechanical rakes would proceed slowly down and up the two concrete platforms covered with cocoa beans. The aroma had overtones of bitter chocolate. A giant tin roof protected the driers from rain, and at one end, forming a kind of wall, was a stack of split lumber five yards high and thirty yards long. All day and all night, five or ten Guineans would be tending to things. At night some of the field workers would hang out. There was some drinking, raspy radio music, and aimless conversation and joking.

I often went surfing at Punta Sorpresa. It never got as big as that first morning I discovered it—and even that same day, as the tide came up, the waves dropped considerably. But it was often a solid five feet with bigger sets. Local fishermen said it got enormous during the rainy season, but my visits never coincided with the waves they described as fifteen feet high.

My friend Roger, visiting from L.A., set the Bioko boogie board record for biggest wave. We had camped one night just above La Piscina. At dawn we drove to Punta Sorpresa and found a good swell. I had a close look at his big ride. I was paddling out and saw Roger drop in on an eight-foot monster. Roger weighed two hundred and thirty pounds, but that wave shot him down the face like a stone skipping on a stream. He angled right and blasted forty yards before exiting over the top of the wave. I paddled over to him and asked him how the ride was. His smile was in the Madre Josefina category.

Maybe we should have called the spot "The Grin."

Music was also a good escape. My French friend Pierre and I would get together and play electric guitar, sometimes with another French guitarist, sometimes with members of Besosso's band, sometimes just the two of us.

Friends helped, too. I saw Madre Josefina often. She had moved from the school at Basilé to be the head of the orphanage in town, so she would often stop by the house for a cold drink and a conversation. Teodora and Musto would invite me over, and I them. The robust cocoa grower and exporter Aurelio and his wife, Ofelia, were becoming my best Guinean friends. He would take me into the bush to visit a pineapple plantation, now almost out of business; or we would have a beer together down at the port and talk of agriculture and Africa.

But the Spanish cocoa exporter Guillermo and his wife, Marisol, had suddenly left Malabo. Word was that they'd gone for good. Guillermo's business had suffered greatly with the decline in world cocoa prices. Rumor had it that he was in trouble over unpaid debts at the BCD and the Guinextebank; one story said that he had been expelled from the country and given seventy-two hours to clear out. But Guillermo's house was being tended by one of his young Spanish cronies. His things were still there. Was he gone forever or just for a while? You never really knew anything in Equatorial Guinea.

What about women? My beloved was in the United States. I wanted to be true to that love, so between visits by her or by me, my sex life was to a normal sex life as Equatorial Guinea's economy was to a normal economy: wretchedly impoverished, with lots of potential supply and demand but no equilibrium, and in desperate need of overseas aid. I was experiencing underdevelopment in ways I hadn't imagined.

It was possible, though unusual, to enjoy a social life in Malabo without sacrificing fidelity. Since there were only about a half-dozen white bachelors in Malabo and our incomes were at least fifty times the local average, even Willard Scott could have had his pick of the town's panoply of young lovelies. Several women were particularly notable.

Ravishing Ramona was the secretary to the Minister of Planning. She had bright eyes and skin as lustrous as polished wood. She understood about my girlfriend back home, and we had a lot of fun together.

Elke had recently returned from Spain, where she was a model and on TV. I had first heard about her from Horace, the aging World Banker.

"Bob, you would not believe it!" he said dramatically upon entering my house one morning. I did not know if he was talking about the banking system, the mosquitoes in his hotel, or the obtuseness of one or another Equatoguinean official. It turned out the source of this particular outburst of disbelief was Elke. "This girl is simply the most beautiful, the most alive." Eventually his flood of adjectives abated and Horace summed up. "If I were a young man I would marry that girl!" He then quaffed a glass of water.

Elke was three-quarters white. She was a little older and more sophisticated in European ways than Ramona. The natural position of her mouth had the lips slightly apart in the middle, as if ready to kiss. She had long flawless legs and a big, charismatic smile. She had had a boyfriend in Malabo but had broken up with him. At the time I think I was the only foreign bachelor in Malabo not suffering from malaria, dysentery, or old age. So Elke turned her eye on me and launched a campaign.

But before getting to that, I must mention Serafina, the daughter of Teodora and Musto, returned from Spain. Serafina was twenty and bursting her buttons with female hormones, energy, and aspiration. She had Teodora's smile but not the bulk, and she possessed that outrageous innate confidence beautiful women sometimes attain. Soon she was doing evening newscasts and became, because of her looks and poise, a local star. She had been spoiled by her conservative parents, who wished her to come back and settle down. But after her romance with Elke's brother, the TV newscaster, broke up, Serafina was everywhere looking for companionship. She would stop by my house for a drink, she would visit Sal, a young bachelor at the U.N., to talk, and she would go to parties or the newly opened discothèque till late in the night.

Now Elke knew both that I had a girlfriend back home and that I was friends with Serafina and especially Ramona. She also knew that she herself was the foxiest thing on two continents and knew, or thought she did, that she was irresistible.

REHABILITATION

The boyfriend of Elke's sister Tili was my guitar-playing friend, Pierre. Along with a small crowd of regulars and spectators, Pierre and I used to play tennis in the late afternoons at one of the two courts in town. When Elke decided to go on the warpath in my direction, she began to come watch me play tennis. Her eyes were always glued on me; her smile was always dazzling. One Sunday she came along with Tili and Pierre to La Piscina. She and I drove home together.

We arrived back in Malabo and agreed to meet later at my house for dinner. Elke showed up alone. Tili and Pierre had to stay home, she said. Her lips were glossy, and her short shorts very tight. We ate and we drank and we smiled a lot. Later we sat on the couch and listened to music.

"Bob, I think we should do this," Elke declared. For some reason the girls loved the name *Bob,* pronounced with a long *o* to rhyme with "robe." "I know you have a *novia* back in America, Bob. I, too, do not wish to get involved. Why don't we have a relationship with no strings attached, no promises, no regrets?"

She elaborated.

If my sex life was akin to Equatorial Guinea's economy, Elke's offer was an economic rehabilitation project.

But I demurred. I explained myself to Elke. She explained herself to me. Elke was a very good explainer. But I won out.

She was disappointed but did not give up. If I were an impoverished economy, she was an aid donor wishing to induce structural adjustment. We went dancing once in a while, went to the beach with other people, saw a movie at someone's house. She took pains to be inspiring. I took lots of cold showers and wrote particularly passionate love letters home.

Elke tried one more tactic: witchcraft.

I had gone to Douala to buy some things for our project. When I returned a few days later, one of the people working at the airport asked me about the fight. What fight?

"Over you, man, over you!"

The scandal had the town abuzz. Ramona and Elke had duked it out, screaming my name and abuse at each other, in front of twenty people at afternoon tennis.

As everything else did in Malabo, the story had four, or forty, versions. Ramona blamed Elke, and Elke blamed Ramona; Serafina had also been involved. The way things happened seemed to be this.

Elke decided to cast a spell on the women blocking her from me—the one back home and, she perceived, Ramona in Malabo. So with Tili and Serafina in tow, she consulted a witch doctor in Malabo's poorest barrio.

She explained the situation. He said he could help. They should return the next afternoon with a chicken and a fertilized egg.

Elke procured both. The next day the three women journeyed back to the witch doctor. He killed the chicken and broke the egg, pronounced some imprecations, touched Elke, and declared the problem solved.

He had not foreseen Serafina's mouth.

A week later Serafina decided to tell Ramona what had occurred. Ramona was outraged—and frightened. She believed in witchcraft. She wanted to get the spell removed, quickly. So in anger and anxiety she went with one of her girlfriends looking for Elke.

As it happened, that afternoon Elke and Tili were at the tennis court watching Pierre in action. Ramona and friend found them there. Upon seeing Elke, Ramona lost it.

"You witch! You whore!" she screamed. She attacked Elke and suddenly the two of them were clawing and pulling hair and punching. Tili tried to pull Ramona off her sister, and so Ramona's friend attacked Tili. And so it happened that four of Malabo's most dashing women hit the turf, screaming and biting and flailing away, in front of twenty amazed onlookers.

For Malabo's expatriate community, where a head cold is headline news, this was the juiciest, most salacious item of the year. The story rocketed around town, followed hourly and then daily with later additions, in the manner of feature stories, which elaborated Ramona's reasons, Elke's aspirations, and Serafina's tattling. It was all the richer for my absence, for people could laugh in anticipation of my reaction when I returned.

That first night home, I must have had ten visitors to the house.

"Hey, Bob, how *are* ya?" they'd ask, with grander grins than I had ever seen on their faces. "What's new?"

If Malabo's *Gossip News* had carried a retrospective story two months later, it would have included this upshot: Elke went back to Spain. Serafina no longer came over for drinks. Ramona and I remained friends. And neither Ramona nor my girlfriend were harmed by the hex.

Serafina had better luck causing trouble for Sal. One afternoon Sal came to the house. Though we were acquaintances, he seldom visited.

"Can I come in, Bob? I need your help."

Sal was in disarray. He was in his twenties, tall, and handsome. He worked for the United Nations as a junior administrator. I led him to the corner table overlooking the volcano and brought him a beer.

"You won't believe this," Sal said. "I know that you know Serafina's mother, Teodora well, so I'm coming to you. Today at the U.N. offices Teodora came after me. She was hysterical, man, absolutely crazy. 'You have been taking advantage of my daughter,' she said. 'Now you've got to take her with you to Canada.'"

Sal would be leaving Equatorial Guinea for good in a month.

"I swear, Bob, I never even *touched* that girl. Yes, she'd come over to my apartment and we'd watch videos and talk, but I never did *anything* to her. Honest."

It was possible. Serafina used to visit my house, too, with no effort at seduction. Flirting and being with Westerners were simply more attractive to her than staying at home. The fact was that Serafina didn't have enough to do. Her TV job was only a few nights a week, and her days were free. I had tried to get her interested in doing interviews journalist-style with small business people in Malabo. She piddled around with the idea, but she never got down to it.

"Teodora said she would *kill* me, Bob" Sal said. "She said if I saw her daughter again she'd take a knife and go *whoomp.*" Sal made the motion of an uppercut. He was as serious as a medic in an emergency room.

I sipped beer to squelch my amusement. The vision of Teodora blasting through the U.N. offices yelling threats at Sal was rich indeed. Sal's alarm, though real, was somehow absurd.

"Can you help me, Bob? Can you talk to Teodora? She wants me to come to their house tonight to talk with the father and the uncle. I'm afraid to go."

We talked for a while. I suggested that Sal write Teodora a letter—calm, humble, forthright, saying what he'd just told me. Then I'd take it to her and calm her down. Sal agreed. We worked on the letter. He went home, still shaking. After lunch I got on the bike and went to Teodora and Musto's. No one home. I went again that evening. Everyone was out. So I left the letter and a short note of my own saying that I'd like to see her.

Next afternoon, Sal was again at the door. Hysteria this time.

"Bob, Bob, do something," he cried. "Serafina's tried to commit suicide. She's at the hospital with her family. I can't go there or they'll kill me. Please go."

I was there in a flash. A few inquiries led me to the ward on the second floor. Serafina was lying in a dilapidated cot with an IV in the top of her hand, her parents and a cousin on one side, and a wan smile on her face.

"Hi, Bob," she said.

Teodora and Musto were glad to see me. I sat down with them beside

195

Serafina's bed. Serafina was fine, no danger, not even very sick. Seeing how well she looked, I risked asking her what the devil she thought she was doing when people loved her so much. She smiled. Musto was understandably distraught; his anxiety bent him like a fishing pole. Teodora, on the other hand, was fired up with worry, a cauldron of nervous energy. Later I went outside with Teodora and asked about the story about her and Sal and the threats.

"It's true, Bob, I was desperate. This is my only child. You know how these men are. They take the women and then they leave them. I told him if he was with her, then he should take her with him to Canada. He denied it all, said he wouldn't. So I told him I'd kill him."

We were standing alone on the dirt road in front of the ward. In the distance the sun was doing its late afternoon magic on the volcano. The forest looked like velvet. I could not believe what I was hearing. This was Teodora, my feminist and activist friend, a woman whose character I had long admired. Now she sounded foolish. I expressed my disappointment in her words and actions.

"Well, it is true, Bob. All right, I lost my head. That's true. It was not the right thing to do, that's true too. But I am an African, Bob. Beneath it all I am an African. The savage comes through me. This is my baby and I must protect her."

We had a long talk. At the end Teodora agreed to write Sal an apology.

A couple of days later, she came to the house with the letter in hand.

"I wanted you to read it first," she said.

It was a very nice letter. Civilized. Apologetic. On the other hand, if I were Sal I wouldn't think that stopping by Teodora's house was a great idea.

A few days later Serafina herself came to the house. We had a long talk, too. I was beginning to feel like a parish priest. Chastity, confessionals, and cold beer.

"You know something, Bob," Serafina said toward the end. "I did not really take the pills I said I took. I was faking it. There was no suicide attempt. I only wanted my mother to stop doing so many silly things to interfere with my life."

Serafina was my friend, but I had a lot of trouble with that. We talked for a while more and I guess it boiled down to the lying. I told her she should never lie when she didn't have to.

Make that chastity, confessionals, *preaching,* and cold beer. All I needed now was permission from the Pope.

Don't think any of it was much help, though. True, Sal departed for

Canada on schedule and unstabbed. Thanks to her parents' scrimping for the plane ticket, Serafina returned to Spain a few months later. And months after that, I was at Teodora and Musto's for dinner. She showed me some photos Serafina had sent, apparently taken in some modeling situation. Her hair was streaked with blonde and spiked like Tina Turner's, and the clothes were tarty. Teodora said they had only heard from Serafina once; they did not know where she was or what she was doing.

Were Elke and Serafina victims of the clash of black and white, African and European, poor and rich? Was I?

It was hard in Equatorial Guinea to keep things in perspective. On the one hand, I was humbled daily by my ignorance of the local economy and of local politics. My heart was continually torn in sympathy and disbelief at the poverty and disease and depravity. I was frustrated to the point of despair by all the things that could go wrong. In Equatorial Guinea Murphy's Law would be a legal encyclopedia.

On the other hand, as a Westerner working on a foreign aid project, I was a kind of local superstar.

A German visitor named Ursula provided a useful perspective. Few tourists go to Equatorial Guinea. There had been two American ones in 1987, and the U.S. ambassador took the trouble to meet them and find out what had brought them there. But Ursula was an intrepid soul; and after several weeks kicking around Cameroon, she happened on to the *Trader* and made the trip over to Malabo. The *Trader*'s engineer arranged for her to stay with two bachelors working on a foreign aid project. She spent a week in Malabo, making the expatriate rounds, eating at the Beiruth, going to the new discothèque. She flew out to Douala on the same plane I was on, and we sat together and chatted.

Ursula was between jobs—this trip was a kind of reward before she took a position on the German equivalent of National Public Radio. She was blonde, in her late twenties, with a nice upturned nose. She had once taught school in Africa for a couple of years, and this was her return voyage. Ursula was attractive in a nuclear-power-plant-protester kind of way but, despite her soft voice, she had a hard socialist edge.

I asked about her impressions of Equatorial Guinea.

"Contradictions," she said. "So many contradictions." She went on to talk in Marxist terms about the economy and the government and the international order. Finally she said, "I don't know if I could live here like you guys do."

Thinking this was a kind of compliment, I took a humble tack. Hey, you get used to the insects, lack of electricity, lousy food, humidity, absence of intellectual stimulation, and frustrations of being unable to do what's needed. Shucks, ma'am, it's nothing.

"No, that's not what I mean exactly," Ursula said. "I mean the contradictions in the way you live. You guys have so much more money than they do. All the women want you because you have money and status and access to culture and fun and things that are just impossible for them to get otherwise. You have your projects with your offices and you have your trips back home. It's like a different world. You have too much power. I don't think emotionally I could handle the contradictions."

Fighting depression was an occasional problem in Equatorial Guinea; keeping healthy, a perennial one. I contracted amoebic dysentery and couldn't shake it. The medicine to fight it had powerful side effects—making you weak and dizzy and nauseous—and a few days after seeming to go away, the dysentery would return. After six weeks of this, on a trip to Douala I saw a specialist. He said that the amoebas were gone but, not atypical for long-term cases, my insides had been ravaged.

"You have holes in your intestines now. Any irritation can cause you to be sick again. Take this medicine to coat your digestive system before every meal, for three weeks. That should give things time to heal."

He turned out to be right. I was impressed by the professionalism; our medical services in Malabo were abysmal, and many medicines simply unavailable. So, when my maid Consuelo's chronic stomach trouble worsened, I offered to send her to Douala to spend some time in the clinic.

Consuelo was thrilled at the idea. But getting the necessary paperwork proved difficult. For her exit permit, Equatoguinean law required written permission from her soldier husband, written permission from her husband's commanding officer, written permission from the official in charge of her part of town, and written permission from the police. Days turned to weeks, weeks to a month. Finally, she had her exit permit in hand. I took her down to the *Trader,* and my friends on board promised to look after her. We arranged for someone to take her to a hotel and to the clinic. Four days later, Consuelo returned. She already felt better. Within two months she gained ten pounds and was much stronger. Her perennial diarrhea was gone.

I was never as sick as Consuelo, but other ailments plagued me. When the harmattan dust returned in November, I contracted eye infections. First one eye closed completely, then the other; for a day, both were closed tight;

but after a week, I was fine. I caught malaria again, this time a mild case that laid me low for three days.

I also got maggots in my back.

Equatorial Guinea's insect life includes what in pidgin English is called the bush fly. This unpleasant animal enjoys laying its eggs in wet clothing hanging on the line. The United States embassy regrets this practice. In official literature prepared for those coming to Equatorial Guinea, the embassy sternly advises that all clothing be ironed, "including underwear and socks," in order that bush-fly eggs be killed. Without ironing, the eggs move from the clothing to your skin, and then grow into larvae. The larvae—or maggots—nourish themselves by eating away at your muscles. The maggots develop into boils. The locals say that you have to wait till they get big enough to pop out, like pimentos from oversized olives.

So Consuelo routinely ironed all items of clothing. Who knows how many overcooked bush-fly omelets I unwittingly wore in my well-pressed wardrobe? But once, apparently, one of my shirts contained survivors. I got some pimples on my right latissimus dorsi. The pimples grew. I didn't diagnose my problem until one night in bed when I rolled over, one of them protested. I felt a burrowing deep in the muscle. I rolled again; and again, there was an annoyed tweak from within.

Next morning, I hustled over to a Guinean doctor's. She asked me to take off my shirt. She looked at my back and said, "Oh, you poor man!" The next ten minutes were spent with fingernails and tweezers poking, squeezing, and eventually pulling out the invaders, four of them in all. For the next couple of months, my back had holes like small craters.

But I got well.

Progress and Incentives

Despite the setbacks with the T.A. project, our economic rehabilitation project rolled forward. Our coordinating committee met regularly. Harry was digging in on the nuts and bolts of import needs, equipment maintenance, and competitive bidding. Our project was working with many ministries and with the cities of Malabo and Bata. We had hired local professionals on the project. One of them was the remarkably gifted Saturnino, the star of the U.N.-sponsored seminar discussed in chapter 5.

Saturnino had been fired from his previous job. He and another man had been instructed to carry out an audit of the Minister of Territorial Administration, a powerful and allegedly evil man whose turf included the cities and towns and control of the police. The audit had uncovered corruption.

In a well-known ploy, the minister responded by accusing Saturnino of corruption. He was able to get Saturnino fired. The word was that the Minister of Territorial Administration was also after Don Bonifacio.

Still there were always rumors. Meanwhile, our project was active on what seemed like a hundred fronts.

We worked with the Ministry of Public Works on the repair and maintenance of roads.

With the cities of Malabo and Bata, we undertook emergency repairs of the water supply system.

With the French—in many ways, against them—and the two city governments, we worked on systems of garbage collection.

We invited Chinese consultants to help the Ministry of Public Health develop a strategy for preventive medicine. We ordered medicines for emergency distribution—controlling as carefully as possible how they would be distributed.

We helped the electricity company develop a pricing policy and techniques for collecting bills.

With the International Labour Office and the United Nations, we worked on a project to encourage small businesses.

In agriculture we sponsored an experiment giving more equipment and better incentives to agricultural extension agents. The agents' success, and the experiment's, would be determined by measurable outcomes that the agents themselves had defined.

We helped the government and two international agencies assess the possibilities for and obstacles to food exports.

We sponsored studies of property rights, the cocoa industry, the fishing sector, repairs and maintenance in the transport sector, and incentives in the public sector.

Our *modus operandi* was similar in each sector. Work with the officials to develop a strategy. Link the strategy to a plan of work and the plan of work to needed resources. Assess systems of maintenance and control. Check what other donors were doing. Finally, import the needed equipment and materials.

And as our work in each sector progressed, similar themes stood out.

Participation was important. Involving the people from each ministry and the cities could take months or even a year, as in the case of the ministries of Health and of Public Works. But without their participation, we were likely to come up with the wrong answers and, even if we got the right ones, official resistance to change.

We learned that government officials had few incentives to work hard and make things happen. Salaries were meager. The average government salary, even if spent entirely on food, would not cover the estimated cost of a basic basket of food for a family of four in Malabo and in Bata.

Moreover, what one earned did not depend on what one accomplished. Public sector pay was not linked to performance. Promotions were based on seniority and patronage. So our project sponsored four experiments where pay bonuses were contingent on meeting performance objectives. All four worked. In water supply, collecting electricity bills, agricultural extension, and road maintenance, people produced more when they could earn more by producing. No surprise there—except that so many economists and aid agencies had overlooked incentives in the public sector even as they insisted on better incentives in the private sector.

Since the government lacked strategies and plans of work, when we moved to develop them—for example, in the city of Malabo—we were usually welcomed, even if the pace of work was agonizingly slow and halting. On the other hand, we sometimes met resistance from foreign aid agencies. In public health, for example, the World Health Organization did not welcome our Chinese consultants. Their message: this field is our field, not yours. The Germans and French felt this way about electricity; the European Community, about water supply; and the Soviet Union, about the maintenance and repair of transportation equipment.

Sometimes resistance came from other projects of the World Bank. Our project invited back Cord Jakobeit, the German economist who had studied cocoa in other African countries. He stayed two months and carried out the first full-scale economic analysis of the cocoa industry. But when Cord arrived, Everton of the World Bank cocoa project told him he could not look at any of that project's data.

"It is confidential," Everton declared. "To get any data from our project, you will need a letter signed by the ministers of Agriculture and Finance and the head of the BCD."

Pure baloney, but I drafted the letter and got it signed with Don Bonifacio's help. Everton then had no choice. Cord got the data.

Maybe Everton had anticipated the study's results and feared their implications for his project. Cord showed that Equatorial Guinea was not competitive as a cocoa producer. Further expansion was not economically warranted. Instead, the country should concentrate on a "quality niche"— producing excellent chocolate on the farms that were economical.

Our coordinating committee translated these results into a redirection of agricultural policy. Instead of emphasizing the rehabilitation of uneconomical cocoa farms—at state expense, meanwhile strengthening the monopolistic Chamber of Agriculture and, incidentally, benefiting the fat cats who had seized cocoa farms—we proposed supporting agricultural diversification, marketing, and land reform. Eventually this approach took root. The World Bank reoriented the next phase of the cocoa project and designed an agricultural development project along our lines.

We complemented this emphasis with five million dollars for equipment and technical assistance for road rehabilitation. Rural roads would be crucial for the development of agricultural marketing and exports. And we fortified the agricultural extension agents with an experiment.

The latter came about in a touching way. I had gone into the interior of Río Muni to meet with agricultural extension agents and learn of their problems and opportunities. One night in the village of Evinayong, we met in a lantern-lit room with seven extension agents. The most senior was near sixty, with a wonderful wise face lined and lined again by work and smiling. He spoke with rough eloquence of their problems.

"We have villages that need us, which we can simply not reach. Juan over there, he must walk forty kilometers [25 miles] from village to village. No transport, no money for transport.

"Then we get there, we have little to give the farmers. For example, a disease is now attacking the green chilis that the farmers can sell amply across the border to Gabon. We do not know the proper treatment for this disease, so we cannot advise the farmers. We have no way of finding out what the solution is for them.

"As a result we feel ourselves to be without a function. We are told to help the farmers form groupings, but how can we advise them to do this when we have no ability to help them produce more?"

They talked for two hours. Finally the old man said, "Don Roberto, this has been an educational conversation for all of us. Now I have a question for you. This is not the first time that someone, a foreigner, has come and asked us about our problems. About nine months ago some Germans came through. They promised us help, Don Roberto, but we have seen nothing. This has been our experience—many promises, no reality. So what I would like to ask you now, Don Roberto, is what do you think will come of this evening?"

I was properly modest about what could happen. But four months later, we had under way a small, experimental project that provided some tools, transportation money, and financial incentives for the agents based on the results their farmers achieved. And it was a great pleasure to visit Evinayong two months after that, meet again with the extension agents, and see in their faces the satisfaction that something had happened and good results were already evident.

Another theme in our project was the importance of property rights.

Now in his middle fifties, Luis was a principal figure in Casa Mota, working alongside the owner and patriarch Don Julio Mota, who was perhaps ten years older. Luis spoke beautiful Spanish but without oratory or affectation. He was thin with a full head of hair barely graying. He wore tan work shirts and, clipped to his belt loop, two balls of keys big enough to serve as weapons.

Once Don Julio was describing how difficult it was and had been to do business in Equatorial Guinea.

"You talk to the French who have been all over Africa, Bob, and they will tell you that this is one of the most hostile countries. People do not trust foreigners, and they do not trust each other. It is very difficult to make friends here. I could tell you many stories, especially in the past, about having to do the most extraordinary things, bribes and so forth, just to get shipping documents signed.

"These people are suspicious by nature. Take the case of Luis, for example. It is sad. He has been here since he was two or three years old, and you know how nice he is. He does not have a single friend among the Guineans."

One day when Luis and I were talking about cocoa, he described the cultural context within which property rights were conceived by many Equatoguineans.

"You have to understand the traditional system of property here, especially among the Fang but also with the Bubis here on the island. The colonial period was short and, despite being acquainted with Roman law, the Guineans still calibrate property rights in their traditional fashion.

"They were hunters more than cultivators, and even the cultivators were nomads. Land was not stable, it would be used and then abandoned. When the tribe moved to a new area, the chief would assign the land to the tribal notables, the closest land to the new settlement to the biggest of them, further out to the rest of the people.

"In colonial times there was something called the *Patronato Colonial de Indígenas.* The law treated all indigenous people as juveniles. Natives would be judged more leniently for any crime they might commit. And they could not sign any contracts by themselves. All contracts had to be signed by the Patronato, in order to protect the indigenous people from exploitation by foreigners. This *Quixotismo* that Spain always had about its colonies also meant that land was never sold to the colonists but leased for ninety-nine years. This would, it was thought, protect the native inhabitants. In the last years of colonial rule, the period of autonomy in the nineteen sixties, there were what were called 'concessions' of land to foreigners.

"So the idea remains—land is not yours, it is of the state. The traditional idea is also that land is given by the chief to the notables of the tribe."

In these regards, Equatorial Guinea was not unlike many other parts of Africa. That property rights and contracts were violable bred a private sector that has oscillated between opportunism and apathy.

Despite all the problems our project encountered, we were seeing progress. Not everywhere, not fast enough, not without molar-grinding frustrations, but progress. Rural roads were being rehabilitated. The streets of Malabo and Bata were being maintained. Water was more available. More electricity bills were being paid.

Even more important than rehabilitating the country's infrastructure was reworking policies and procedures. Though rural roads constrained agricultural exports, the Ministry of Industry and Commerce did so even more. Public health was a problem less of medicines than of management and maintenance. The reason the country's banks were broke was not because the vaults were deficient. Our project was active in all these areas.

The banking situation was crucial. Led by Don Bonifacio, our coordinating committee devised a strategy for the insolvent Banco de Crédito y Desarrollo. The bank's problems were threefold.

Its objectives were too ambitious. The BCD tried simultaneously to be a development bank—meaning long-term lending for economic growth—and a commercial bank.

Its management was deficient. Criteria for lending were poor. The administration of accounts was weak. Government "oversight" tended to become government "interference"—in particular, the granting of loans to politicos and their pals. The central bank BEAC did not observe credit limits.

Third, the BCD was in financial disequilibrium. Bluntly, it was broke.

In response to these problems, our committee proposed solutions.

The BCD would close; and a new bank, the Banco Nacional de Desarrollo, or National Development Bank, would be formed. The new BND would abandon commercial objectives, leaving them to the new French bank, BIAO.

We spent a lot of time on solutions to the administrative problems.

World Bank consultants would draft criteria and practices for loans. A foreign subdirector with decision-making power would be recruited. Accounts would be computerized. Training would be offered. Incentives at all levels of management would reward making good loans and getting them repaid.

Don Bonifacio devised a strategy for getting the current portfolio of bad debts repaid. A calendar of action was set up for debtors. An automatic 20-percent payroll deduction was introduced for government employees who owed money to the bank. Embargoes and seizures of property were introduced, in coordination with the Ministry of Justice. In a short time, over CFAF 100 million was collected (over $340,000).

Statutes regarding BEAC limits were changed, including "better control of the use by the BEAC Director of individualized attributions"—that is, of political influence on credit.

Foreign financial participation was foreseen. Half of the new bank's assets would come from the International Finance Corporation of the World Bank, the African Development Bank, and two regional banks. Plus assets would enter the new bank from various foreign aid projects, including the World Bank's cocoa project and my project.

Don Bonifacio sold this strategy to the President. The next task was to convince the International Monetary Fund and the World Bank, both of which had wanted the BCD closed.

Meanwhile, the Guinextebank was also insolvent and causing trouble. Guinean politicians wanted to keep it open; Spaniards wanted it closed only if they could free themselves of financial liability in case of bankruptcy; the World Bank and the International Monetary Fund wanted it closed, period.

Small Business Failures

We had learned that small business was constrained by credit and a hostile regulatory and tax environment. The United Nations had money earmarked for small business, so our project deferred to the U.N. and the International Labour Office, which sent in a team to study small business and devise a project.

It was a two-person team. One was a senior Chilean with a fondness for fluffy sideburns, the cap of a yachting captain, and word after word after word. The other was a Colombian whose institution provided training in management and accounting for small businesses. Their second day in country they met with me. They opined that a project was needed that

205

would provide training in management and accounting for small businesses. I pointed them to the credit problem and the need to transform the Ministry of Industry and Commerce.

They wanted to tour the country and they did, for more than half their time. They wanted to carry out a survey of small businesses in Malabo, Bata, and two towns in Río Muni. They did, haphazardly. But they could not assemble the data before leaving, so their project design lacked the benefit of numbers.

They proposed a large project, which would emphasize training in management and accounting for small businesses. Five sixths of its funds would go to foreign advisers, office equipment, housing, and cars. One twelfth would go to credit. None would go to the Ministry of Industry and Commerce.

The Chilean even had a recommendation about who the two resident experts on the proposed projects should be: two departing Latin American employees of the U.N. in Malabo, who had guided the Chilean on his tour. True, neither had any training in small business. But one had worked in the Ministry of Industry and Commerce and "had an interest in the subject"—this was the voluble Gracián (see chapter 4). And the other? Well, he could be provided training in management and accounting for small businesses—at the Colombian's institution. The cost would be only sixteen thousand dollars, to be taken from the project itself—a project supposed to support and train the people of Equatorial Guinea.

It was not hard to quash this preposterous project. But the consultancy had cost about eighty thousand dollars, and that was gone. The U.N. could not move forward with an alternative project for at least six months, until this one had been thoroughly digested in New York and Geneva and, in the end, spit out.

Meanwhile, nothing was happening to help small business. At least, I thought, we could get the Ministry of Industry and Commerce mobilized in its behalf. At long last the workshop for the ministry's staff was initiated.

We met twice a week at two in the afternoon, just before the end of the workday. Don Camilo was out of the country, so Don Timoteo, the secretary general, did the introduction for the first session. About twenty-five employees attended, including all the female secretaries out of curiosity. Only five of those present had read the case we were to discuss.

I proceeded and was encouraging. For the second session, I pleaded, please read in advance. The second session contained fifteen employees, including all the women. Of the men, two were completely drunk.

We had a discussion. One of the drunks started to shout. He was hushed, with laughter, by his peers. More discussion. Finally, a question by the other drunk.

"Professor, you know we are not policy makers or even administrators. We are just functionaries who do what we are told. How can we think about what the ministry should be doing?"

Not a bad question. It turned out to be the one I remembered from this failed endeavor, which, after three more sessions, petered out for lack of interest. Camilo was furious upon his return, but I told him it didn't seem worthwhile to try again with this group.

Banks on the Ropes

Though the coordinating committee was pulled in many fascinating directions, I tried to keep them focused on the biggest task: putting together a medium-term strategy for the country. If it was good, we could use it as the basis for the elusive and crucially important agreement with the IMF. Maybe, too, for a full-fledged structural adjustment program with the World Bank.

In its attitude toward Equatorial Guinea, the Bank was coming around. A very senior World Bank economic adviser had visited in November 1987 and been impressed. The ministers of our coordinating committee had prepared carefully and spent two evenings with the visitor. Before leaving, he told me, "In forty years at the Bank this was as open and impressive a discussion of economic strategy as I have heard." He saw the progress our project was making in the various sectors. He went home and told his colleagues.

In early 1988, we were descended upon by two World Bank missions. The term *mission* now seemed to me curiously appropriate. One of its definitions evokes pilots over enemy terrain, flying in close formation, dropping their loads, and returning home. Another meaning has to do with missionaries, aliens who promise salvation to the natives if only certain, shall we say, structural adjustments are made. World Bank missions partake of both. Disciplined groups parachute in, carry out hectic sorties, advocate and even insist upon changed behavior and belief, and leave.

This visit meant work for me and my colleagues in the government. Data had to be mustered. Papers had to be prepared. The government's act had to be gotten together—sometimes without scripting, casting, or rehearsal. There were many nights of work till eleven.

Preparation was not customary in Equatorial Guinea. Six weeks in advance, late in November 1987, the ministers and I had made plans, allocated tasks, even drawn up a flow chart of needed work. When I had returned from Christmas vacation—a stunning change in climates from my last day in Boston's record −55° windchill to Malabo's sticky 80's—Don Bonifacio of Finance and Don Camilo of Industry and Commerce were out of town. When they returned, we had a meeting but it didn't last long. To my consternation, while I was away they had carried forward none of the preparations we had agreed upon.

The Bank guys were good. Horace had retired, and the able Esteban and Dominique had taken up the slack. They were now like old friends, and whenever they came, they stayed at my house instead of a hotel. The third member of the mission was the Bank's operational head for nine African countries, an Englishman named Albert, whom I had met in Washington before Christmas. At the time he had not wanted to go to Equatorial Guinea, having heard it was dinky and corrupt compared with the rest of his countries. I had persuaded him to give us a try, however. I told him that the country had the resources to make it, that it was a laboratory of underdevelopment, that we were making progress on tricky and exciting issues. He asked me for lunch the next day. We talked some more about Equatorial Guinea. By the end of lunch he had decided to visit, and in the event, he stayed a whole week and loved it.

Albert was dynamic, full of ideas and concrete examples, prodigious in memory, excellent in discussions with ministers. He pressed us on big points of strategy and small points of expenditures. He shared what had worked and failed in other countries. Apart from money, I thought, that was what the World Bank ought to be about: funneling information and ideas and experience into backward countries that lack precisely those things.

Albert quizzed the Minister of Finance closely about the negotiations taking place that week over the closure and liquidation of the Guinextebank. Don Bonifacio assured him that the bank was closed. Yes, Albert could have that in writing. The only issue was compensation from the Spaniards.

"It makes me angry," Don Bonifacio told me at dinner on Thursday. "The Spaniards are to blame for the bank's failure more than we are. Yet they want to leave through a golden door, paying us something and absolving themselves from all the bank's obligations." The bankrupt bank owed over four million dollars to depositors and perhaps twice as much to the central bank. The Spanish had offered to cover the former sum in exchange for washing their hands of the latter. Don Bonifacio had stood firm on two fronts: that the bank should be closed, and that the Spanish should retain legal obligations to be decided in court or in arbitration. That the Guinextebank had not yet been liquidated was the foremost obstacle to an agreement with the IMF. But shutting down the bank was not popular in some circles of the government or with some Spanish business interests. Both groups worried that without Guinextebank they wouldn't be able to get loans from the French bank BIAO. Getting loans from Guinextebank and not repaying them had been a principal source of income for powerful figures, and the prime cause of the bank's failure.

Albert departed with a new surf shirt I had had made for him of outrageous African material, a host of facts and figures, and the feeling that things were moving in Equatorial Guinea.

Esteban and Dominique had to stay on to complete the *aide-memoire* the mission would leave behind. It had to be ready by Monday morning for the government's comments before it could be finalized. The two of them were up till four thirty Monday morning completing the work. They managed to do it despite the raucous revelry of the giant fruit bats that lived at the top of the palm trees across the street. At dusk the bats would come out for a fly-around, scores of them. They were tan and had wingspans of more than three feet, making them some of the biggest bats in the world. During certain times of year, at three in the morning—apparently the time for either high romance or else the fruit bat equivalent of drive-by shootings—they would commence their rounds of debauched wheezing and cawing.

The next morning there was no electricity, and Don Bonifacio stood us up for an eight-thirty meeting. I worked all day. At seven I returned to my electricityless home with a visiting road expert, Frank, in tow. The evening was oppressive. Clouds had been boiling overhead all day. A few measly drops fell at about six but failed to relieve the extreme humidity. I felt like a flat tire that had just been pried inexpertly off its rim.

Frank was at the house to have a quick dinner and then go with me to the U.S. ambassador's residence to see a newly arrived tape of the Super Bowl. I showered quickly, and as I was drying off, someone knocked at the front door. In a minute I went downstairs with my flashlight. Don Bonifacio's driver was standing in the darkness.

"The minister wishes to see you," he said in a soft voice.

I was caught in a bad spot. Don Bonifacio would be leaving the next day, and I had some things for him to sign. I could get them signed at the airport tomorrow. Dominique and Esteban, who had just themselves come in the door from the Planning Ministry, would talk with the minister tonight about the *aide-mémoire*. They didn't need me, I thought. I contemplated the Super Bowl. Its showing was the Equatoguinean entertainment equivalent of a visit by Bob Hope and Kim Basinger to a bomber base in Greenland.

"Please tell the minister I have a guest for dinner and am going to the American ambassador's house. I will go to the airport tomorrow to get the papers signed."

The driver departed into the shadows. I dressed and joined Frank at the dinner table. Vapor clouds seemed to coalesce around the candles, as they did these nights around the moon. Celestina had stayed late to help and was putting down some cold soup. We had to eat and take her home in twenty minutes. I was ravenous. Just as I got the soupspoon in my hand, someone knocked again at the front door. Flashlight in hand, I went to see who it was.

It was the driver again. "The minister says just for a few minutes."

A command performance. I got the car and drove to the Finance Ministry. It was dark as an abandoned fort. Large cockroaches scurried on the stairway. The minister's office, however, enjoyed electricity at every hour, the only spot so blessed in the ministry. His secretary, Yolanda, was perspiring in the outer office. Two sullen whites sat on couches in the unilluminated, airless waiting room, looking as though they had been there for days. Yolanda said Don Bonifacio was in a meeting. I paced the sauna-like corridor.

I wondered what came after the cold soup. It was about kickoff time for the Super Bowl.

Finally Yolanda called me. Ignoring a hostile look from the two waiting whites, I went into Don Bonifacio's office. The light and the air-conditioning seemed from another world.

Don Bonifacio sat behind his desk in a rumpled golf shirt. He didn't look up but continued signing papers. Then he welcomed me and had me sit down. I asked how his recent case of malaria was doing, and he asked about the last day of the mission. I told him I thought the *aide-mémoire* was flattering to us and that the only problem could be certain parts of the public investment program. He was solicitous about my invitation to the ambassador's. We talked about signing some papers. He wanted to do it tonight instead of at the airport.

"I come late to the airport, you know, after I'm informed that the plane is ready. Then there are mountains of people asking me for things and bothering me. There wouldn't be an occasion to sign. Why don't you bring them to the house when you finish at the ambassador's?"

I said that was fine. Figuring that was my exit line, I rose.

Don Bonifacio looked down for a moment.

"Roberto, I have a personal problem to consult you on."

I nodded and sat down.

"You know that I will be flying to Madrid tomorrow. This is a very important trip for me. It has to do with the Guinextebank."

He paused and looked down again. His malaria had abated, but his face looked puffy and strained.

"There are forces that want to keep the Guinextebank open," he continued. "I am going to Madrid to negotiate this point."

He was having trouble finding words.

I thought that the closure was settled, that only the amount of the compensation was at issue.

"Yes, that is what I thought. Now it is not so clear. Tell me as a friend and as an adviser, do you think the bank should remain open?"

I had never studied the Guinextebank situation, as Bonifacio knew. Though we had worked together on a strategy for the Banco de Crédito y Desarrollo, I was not privy to the Guinextebank's financial secrets. He then summarized some of the economic issues: the bank's horrible financial position, the Spaniards' unwillingness to assume responsibility, the size of the settlement they had offered. He was cogent, organized, and impressive.

For the past year or so, Bonifacio had staked his position clearly on the bank: it should close, and the Spaniards should assume their full share of all obligations. Bonifacio was a banking expert. This was his baby, and that was his stand. Why, I asked, should the issue of its remaining open still be alive? What were the arguments for it?

Bonifacio looked down, then looked up and smiled sadly.

"Politics, Roberto."

He told me of an hour and a half's frank discussion that morning with the President. They had gone through all the issues. Bonifacio had told him that, in his opinion, the bank could not be viable without the Spaniards. But the Spaniards wanted out. Bonifacio told the President that the IMF had made the closure of Guinextebank the sticking point in its negotiations with Equatorial Guinea.

"I thought the President was with me, that he agreed. But then later today I learned that he has been spoken to by others."

Why do the others want the bank to remain open?

Bonifacio shrugged his shoulders.

Was it because of Spanish economic interests? No. It was internal to Equatorial Guinea. Were the arguments economic? If so, could we not get some neutral authority to come and help make the decision?

"No, Roberto, these people know nothing of economics." He shook his head. "That is way beside the point."

He spoke a bit more and then paused. It was clear that his trip tomorrow to Madrid would be decisive. It was not clear whether he had the President's support on the most important issue he had staked out as his own in his two and a half years as finance minister.

Finally he looked at me intently and asked, "What would *you* advise me to do?"

" 'Requiem for a Bank,' eh?" I said with a smile. Last fall Bonifacio had told me lightly that when he left his job as finance minister he'd like to write a book of that title. The book would detail the problems of Guinextebank, the subterfuges by the Spaniards, the whole story in which he had invested so much, in his view, on behalf of the country.

I said I would give him my impressions of his situation, without being able to offer judgments on Guinextebank.

I said he might consider resigning. Or threatening to.

Bonifacio watched me at full attention.

He had told Albert the bank would be closed. He had told the IMF the bank would be closed, and they were due here next month. If they came again and the negotiations failed, it would be a long time before they would return. The donors' conference so often postponed—the one to be sponsored by the United Nations in Geneva, where the donors would together discuss a five-year package of aid to Equatorial Guinea—was dependent on a successful agreement with the IMF. The credibility he had sought so intently over the past year would crumble if, after all this, the Guinextebank would remain open.

I told him he stood for his country, that his personal credibility was now an important aspect of his country's credibility. I told him how, after first meeting him in my electricityless living room at eleven at night two Sundays back, Albert had said, "What an impressive man! You can see a future president there." Our coordinating committee had analyzed credibility as the country's key problem in attracting more aid, investment, and loans. Don Bonifacio himself had staked out a courageous and, in his mind, necessary position regarding Guinextebank. If now, at the last minute of the negotiations, obscure political forces could overturn all his work and all his promises, he would be finished.

At some point he might have to play hardball against the political forces that opposed him. That point may have arrived now. The President knew from every visitor that his finance minister was admired and valued. Would the President turn back his opponents if Bonifacio made clear that the decision could involve his resignation?

Then I explored another alternative. Suppose the bank had to remain open. Suppose Bonifacio's task were then to do the best he could for his country. Then it was important to change the face of the issue as perceived by the IMF, the Spanish press, and the other people who would be watching. The one-line summary couldn't be, "Finance minister backs down in disastrous economic decisions because of political forces." It would have to be something like, "Equatorial Guinea and the Banco Exterior de España take drastic steps to clean up the Guinextebank."

To do that, he would need to announce some dramatic measures. For example, the firing of Spanish and Guinean Guinextebank officials. Heads rolling. Calling in new expatriate managers with the power of decision. Involving foreigners on the board of the bank. Inviting consultants of the World Bank to help restructure the bank's management and promising to reopen Guinextebank or its successor only after their recommendations were implemented.

He would need allies in Madrid with whom to talk frankly about the substance and the publicizing of such steps.

Even if he could do all this, he might later decide to resign—after doing his best for the country to make an unpalatable decision have the best effects it could.

Bonifacio talked about the bank's lack of viability, especially when the country was taking many expensive and difficult steps to relaunch the Banco de Crédito y Desarrollo. He drifted back over the arguments. He paused.

"This is very difficult, Roberto." Another pause. "Thank you for your help." He gave me one of the deepest looks I have ever received.

I stood up, and he smiled benevolently.

"This will be very difficult for me, Roberto."

We shook hands, and I left. Yolanda was slumped at her desk. On the couch the outlines of the two whites had sunk a couple of inches lower. I emerged into the darkness, wondering what Bonifacio would do in Madrid.

Frank was waiting at the house. Esteban's driver had taken Celestina home. Frank and I went to the ambassador's with a bag full of Guinness stout. He had held the kick-off for my arrival.

Ministerial Inaction

Why was the Equatoguinean government so inefficient? Why did its ministers seem never to make decisions? The classic answer is that government officials don't care. "If they don't get something out of it," grumped one frustrated aid official, "they won't move."

I didn't like that answer. It was too blunt an instrument. It did not fit many officials I knew, who did care. So I was mildly but undeniably pleased by a surprising example of inaction that clearly contravened the classic answer.

The case involved one of the most infamous procrastinators—Don Diego, the Minister of Planning. It concerned incentives for the ministers who worked on my project.

For months I tried to get them monetary incentives to compensate them for many nights of work on the project. After much hemming, the World Bank finally refused to let us use money from the project account for such purposes, on the grounds that it looked too much like corruption. Far from it, as I saw it: incentive payments would be more like insurance against corruption.

So we had to try to get money from the government's own account, which meant permission from the head of state. Finally, the President agreed. Each minister would be allowed an incentive payment of CFAF 100,000 per month (about $360)—beginning that month; it wouldn't be retroactive.

Bonifacio told me to pay the others first and then him. So I left word with the other two ministers that I had money for them. Don Camilo sent his secretary to my house to escort me to his office with his payment. I went. Typically officious, Don Camilo did not receive me, preferring to sign a receipt delivered through his secretary.

When I went to Don Diego's office, he was out. I left word. I called him the next day. He was busy. I called him later. He said fine. But he made no time to see me. In the meantime I paid Don Bonifacio.

Several days later Don Diego came by the house on an informal visit. We talked about the economy and other matters. I brought out the money, but he said he didn't want it just then because he was going on several other calls.

Another week passed. Our coordinating committee met one evening, and Don Diego didn't mention the subject to me. The next day I spoke with him on the phone and at the end kidded him, Don't you want your money? He laughed and said, Of course.

But days later there was still no word, no action. Here was the infamous "Equatoguinean inaction." Yet here the impoverished Don Diego had everything to gain.

A Mixed Get-together

In the spring of 1988, we enjoyed a long streak of gorgeous weather: bright sunshine and brilliant views of our volcano and of Mt. Cameroon on the African continent, followed by spectacular storms and soothing rains, then sunshine again. The evenings were cool and good for sleeping. Malabo experimented with twenty-four-hour-a-day electricity for a whole month, so you were never sweltering, there was always a fan: it seemed luxurious.

For me things finally seemed to be opening up. After a year and a half, trust was starting to take hold. One example involved Don Leonardo, a famous sculptor who was Minister of Information, Culture, and Tourism. His ministry had taken official control of my house, whose ground floor was eventually to become a museum. Since they had assumed command, friends and relatives of ministerial employees had been installed downstairs in what used to be storerooms and were now four dwellings. Don Leonardo had allowed me to stay when I offered to put the rent money in a special museum rehabilitation fund.

Don Leonardo had been a guest at my house several times. On one excellent occasion, the guests included Besosso, the rock star, and his wife; Aurelio and Ofelia; and the new U.S. ambassador and his wife. Don Leonardo had been shy about attending a party at a white man's house.

"I told the President's brother Armengol, who is the chief of police, about the invitation," Don Leonardo told me later. "He said it was all right to come."

Some weeks later, Don Leonardo stopped by the house in the afternoon, accompanied by the director general of his ministry. As usual his conversation was as bright and rapid as a strobe light. After fifteen minutes he focused. The government wanted to have a big celebration for the twentieth anniversary of its independence, 12 October. The U.S. government might give a satellite dish to receive foreign television transmissions; maybe other governments might be asked to donate something for the celebration.

"What do you think, Roberto? This is just an idea, we are now thinking and talking and I wanted to talk with you."

We worked through some of the obvious questions. Was there a theme to the anniversary? What sort of budget did it have? What did Leonardo want to result from the celebration?

After a half-hour we had some ideas on the table. The celebration needed a theme. The government should not make the embassies and aid agencies think it was just an excuse for more asking. The celebration could serve as a focal point for government action.

We thought of a theme—"Equatorial Guinea, open to the world." The country could both trumpet the economic opening symbolized by its new economic strategy, and also use the occasion to emphasize the political, cultural, and informational dimensions of "opening up." The American satellite dish would fit into that theme well.

Leonardo said he was going to see the President the next day about this, so I promised to bring him an outline of what we had said. First thing the next morning, I went to see Leonardo with a two-pager that organized our ideas.

Leonardo began talking and laughing before I could make it from his office door to the chair.

"You'll laugh when I tell you," he began, and then flashed to six other topics before I had the remotest idea of what might merit even a chuckle. Then he got to the source of his amusement. "I saw the President last night and told him about our meeting."

I didn't laugh but gave him the outline. He proceeded to read it aloud, with eloquent nods of affirmation. Leonardo loved it. He couldn't believe it: here were his ideas rendered via computer into a logical outline.

"You are an artist like me!" he cried. "I told you so when I saw the wind chimes at your house."

He made some changes in the outline, and I went home and revised it. Half an hour later, he had a fresh copy.

That night we chanced upon each other at a new, informal restaurant near the Russian embassy. Leonardo came over to my table, smiling broadly. He poured forth his ideas as rapidly as a tumbler emptying water.

"I saw the President and gave him the outline. All day I have been at the ministry talking about these ideas with the staff, and everyone is excited. The President knew about you, of course, and was very pleased. Also I had a meeting with the American ambassador today and, though I did not talk to him about all of this, I did say that his satellite dish could be the beginning of an opening up of Guinea. Ah yes, the opening of Equatorial Guinea, the President liked that, he's a Bohemian, you know, I'm the longest-serving minister and he supports me always. Also, I saw Aurelio today and we were talking about you. This is really a big step, do you think we should have a kind of conference? People from each embassy could talk about their countries twenty years after independence and how things were then. We could also have the traditional dancers and television . . ."

Leonardo was wired. Through his charming barrage, I smiled and nodded. It was clear, he went on, that we had to do more to open up Equatorial Guinea; we needed more get-togethers, also more trust and confidence.

The next afternoon Aurelio came by my office, perspiring as usual, as though he had just jogged in from the airport.

"Roberto, I want to invite you to a party at my house. You know, I have been thinking about something we talked about. You are right that we have to have more informal contacts with foreigners. So I thought I would do something along those lines. It is Ofelia's birthday Wednesday and Linda's on Thursday"—Linda was their daughter—"so we are going to have a combined party on Thursday night. With things to drink and nibble. Do you think the American ambassador will come? Whom else do you think I should invite?"

Yes, he will come. How about the new U.N. representative as well? Aurelio went over the rest of the invitation list. He was excited.

Thursday night came, and I arrived at Aurelio's and Ofelia's to find the second-floor living room and patio full of guests. Blacks and whites: a rarity in Equatorial Guinea. The U.S. ambassador and his wife were there, as was the U.N. representative; also, many whites from the cocoa industry, a variety of blacks from business, and a few government officials of less-than-ministerial rank. People seemed slightly nervous at being in this integrated setting of people who did not know each other well. But I thought it stimulated a certain garrulousness, with wholesome results. Aurelio and Ofelia were exuberant; and later, before I left, Aurelio collared me by the doorway.

"What did you think, Roberto? Did everyone have a good time?"

"I know I did. I know the American ambassador did because he told me so. I think it was a great success, Aurelio."

"So do I. Did you see how Linda and the children mixed in, too? Here, stay for one more beer with me. We can sit on the patio together."

One beer turned to three, and I was the last guest to leave.

Don Bonifacio and His Colleagues

My relationships with the three ministers on the economic rehabilitation project combined distance and intimacy, but in different ways. Don

Diego had been my acquaintance before he became minister. He was shy by nature, untrained in economics and planning, cautious to a fault; but he was also keen to learn, desirous of moving forward, interested in developing his country. He had been to my house, and I to his, not for social occasions but to consult or to deliver a message. We could speak frankly. But he always had kept a distance and formality to our relationship; and since the debacle with the President over the technical assistance project, he had to be particularly careful of being seen as too close with a foreigner.

Don Camilo, the Minister of Industry and Commerce, was a martinet by nature and a teacher by profession. The subject matter of the ministry he led was to him a mystery. At times he would open up with me—once sharing his grief over the loss of his family, an afternoon talking about racism, a morning meeting of just the two of us where he spoke at length about his year of imprisonment, for no crime at all, under Macías. But for the most part, Camilo stood away from everyone, even his old friend Bonifacio; and perhaps particularly away from me, when I crossed some boundary of intimacy in his mind. After returning from Christmas vacation, we had a meeting of the coordinating committee in Don Camilo's office. I entered and greeted the three ministers with a flourish: "Distinguished colleagues, Happy New Year!" Bonifacio smiled warmly, and Diego took my hand; but Camilo said, " 'Colleagues'? How can you be our colleague? We are ministers of government."

Don Bonifacio, the brightest of the three, was the only one trained in a discipline related to our work (economics, a degree from Spain). He had a great appetite for hard labor. As in most countries I have known that have experienced economic crises, the Minister of Finance was caught in the middle. To creditors and aid givers he represented the government and was therefore the breakwater for waves of criticism and conditionality. On the other hand, inside the government he had to report and to some extent represent what the creditors and aid givers insisted upon. He bore bad news to both sides and could easily be seen by both as the embodiment of the enemy. This had been Bonifacio's fate as well, and the seemingly endless crisis of Equatorial Guinea's banks had added to his crunch.

One Friday night I met with Don Bonifacio at his office. He often put in late nights there. I told him I needed his signature. Malabo had been short of water for more than a week. Despite the beginning of the rains, the situation was actually much worse than at the peak of the dry season. Water was available for only an hour in the early morning, and the water pressure was so weak it wasn't available everywhere. Every morning men, women, and children traversed the streets with buckets and pans of water on their heads. Down in the old port, water flowed from the place where the city water system emptied into the sea. So during these weeks people would walk across town, down the hill to the port, and back, all for a bucket of water.

For several months our project had been helping the city of Malabo carry out urgent repairs to the water system. But this time the leaks were away from the city, where streams fed a small reservoir part way up the volcano and in the large pipes from there down to the city. Harry and several plumbers had investigated. They returned with bad news and good news. The bad: about 80 percent of the water was not reaching the city because of three ruptures. The good: the purchase of a few large rubber seals and clamps, plus one section of plastic pipe, would take care of things.

So I asked Don Bonifacio to co-sign a check for a little over four thousand dollars. He agreed, enjoining me, unnecessarily, to retain all the receipts.

Changing the subject, he asked how the economic statistics were looking. The U.N.-sponsored advisers in the Ministry of Planning had come up with new estimates on the gross domestic product and the balance of payments.

"Yes, I've seen the tables," Don Bonifacio said. "The Minister of Planning gave them to me yesterday after the cabinet meeting. Here they are."

I explained how we hoped to check and refine these tables. On their face, many of the data seemed bogus.

Don Bonifacio asked for an example.

Gross domestic product, for one. According to the table, GDP had grown by 12 percent last year. This would be close to a record-breaking achievement, I said. When I queried the number to one of the U.N. experts, he said the data had not been adjusted for inflation. So we asked one of the other experts at the table, the man in charge of inflation data, to fill us in. The only information was based on the cost of living in Malabo, and here the index had *deflated* by 13 percent last year. Did the experts really believe what these figures implied, that the economy had grown in real terms by more than 12 percent last year? There was much scratching of heads. "Well, no . . . ."

There were other suspect figures. "Public administration" had jumped from 1986 to 1987 by about CFAF 2,000 million, over $6 million—an extraordinary 30-percent increase. Alone, this jump accounted for 5 percent of the 12-percent increase in GDP. When pushed, the expert had said, "A lot of that is foreign aid." But when I looked at the numbers, the 1986 figure turned out to be about CFAF 2,000 million *smaller* than in 1985. Did

219

they really believe that the figures had flip-flopped this much? Was it not possible that something was wrong with the 1986 number?

We were investigating other anomalies. The statisticians said that private consumption was up 7.7 percent while elsewhere that prices deflated by 13 percent and imports for consumption were down by 6 percent. How could that happen?

But apart from unpacking anomalies, we were trying to analyze what the data said about the economic situation. I underlined a few key facts for Don Bonifacio. Traditional exports of coffee and cocoa were way down. Coffee earnings had plummeted because of the lack of credit to local buyers—and because stupid and perhaps corrupt marketing by the Bata branch of the Chamber of Agriculture had driven foreign buyers away. Cocoa earnings were down, despite increased production, because of falling world prices.

Meanwhile, wood exports were buoyant. The increase in wood exports alone accounted for a 1.3 percent gain in GDP. This was good news. So was the growth in local industry and in the category "transportation and communication." From admittedly tiny bases, these had increased by over 30 percent and 50 percent, respectively—about as fast as such areas can grow.

The sad part was that the statisticians had been so busy with details and compilation that they had not begun to analyze the significance of or reasons for these shifts. What did they mean for future policies? For example, take cocoa: prices had fallen in 1988 by another 20 percent, and we were trying to determine what this might mean not only for the balance of payments but also for the country's economic strategy. The World Bank's projections and Cord's report were pessimistic about the price's rebounding.

Bonifacio watched all of this intently, participating with questions and comments. Now he looked troubled. He peered down at his papers, then back at the tables, then up at me.

"The cocoa situation is disastrous for us, Roberto." He paused. "Last night I couldn't sleep, thinking about it. You know what kept driving me? I'll tell you because with you I can always be frank. There are all these technical experts, here and in the World Bank, and I asked myself if I really believed that they didn't know that the price of cocoa was going to drop. They have encouraged us to rehabilitate cocoa. The big cocoa project of sixteen million dollars. And what do we get, a disaster.

"You can see why people think that these foreign organizations are trying to sink us. I kept asking myself, Isn't that what has happened?"

He went on a bit more. There was a pause. I said one reason our project had asked Cord to take a long-range look at cocoa's viability was because we wanted to make sure we didn't leave the sector to the resident cocoa experts. Before I came to Equatorial Guinea, I asked the Bank for studies about cocoa. A report written in the late 1970s said cocoa was in oversupply and the Bank would not finance cocoa projects unless the product represented some very large share of a country's exports—that is, unless it had no real alternative. Equatorial Guinea qualified on that ground, but nobody was confident that prices would go up. The recent large decline to prices lower than any since the Second World War had been anticipated by no one.

Bonifacio listened carefully. I went on. I said that our task was to prepare a strategy ourselves for troubled sectors like cocoa and now coffee. We had Cord's excellent report and model to guide us. Now we had to organize the policies.

Bonifacio said we had to get organized to do so. We talked about who might participate, and reviewed some of the main issues. I said I would get some people together to get started while he was away. He said that would be great.

Another pause.

"Roberto, we are going to miss you when you leave. You are the only one who really seems to understand and to be on our side. Nothing would make me happier than to have you stay for another year."

I demurred. I said that if my girlfriend came in June as she planned, I might be prepared to stay a few extra months.

"A few months? Oh, no, Roberto," Bonifacio smiled. "Longer!"

He was laying it on, but I was glad to see a little energy back in his system. The talk about cocoa and conspiracies had drained him.

An Equatoguinean Curiosity

Malabo had elections, the first in many years; so did towns around the country. It was gratifying in visits to villages in Bioko and Río Muni to see vigorous town meetings dedicated to naming local candidates. More than one, though there was only one party; and the winner in Malabo had been the city's last mayor before independence.

As it happened, the new mayor had a special significance. He had helped audit the powerful and nefarious Minister of Territorial Administration and found evidence of corruption. The new mayor now worked directly under the minister whose probity his audit had assaulted.

A series of strange events ensued. One day my friend Aurelio came by the house. As usual, his face looked as if he had just rinsed it but had forgotten the towel.

"Come, Roberto, there is someone I want you to meet—the Minister of Territorial Administration. I have told him much about you, and he wants to learn of your project firsthand."

We went to the minister's office and were ushered in a private door. The minister was a slight man who, like Aurelio and the President, hailed from Mongomo, the home of the ruling clan. He wore glasses and a calm, inscrutable expression. He was cordial enough. He asked about our activities with the city of Malabo. I briefed him on the project and told him about the equipment and parts we had purchased to repair the water supply system and the roads. He thanked me, and I left with Aurelio.

A few weeks later, on a Saturday afternoon, the new mayor showed up at my house with one of the presidential advisers, also a new city councilman.

"Roberto, can you come? The Minister of Territorial Administration wants to talk with you. He wants a summary of the money spent so far on the city of Malabo by your project."

I went along. We drove to the presidential ghetto. The minister turned out also to be the deputy prime minister. He wasn't home. We drove out of the ghetto and looked for him. Soon the driver spotted his car approaching. The two cars stopped. The minister saluted me briefly and then spoke a torrent of Fang to the others. It sounded like orders.

"Roberto, the minister would like you to write down a brief summary of the amounts and discuss it with him next week."

Fine, I said, I'll have it by Monday.

"No, Roberto. He wants you to prepare it right now, then talk with him next week."

I went home and typed out a one-pager from memory, indicating that the amounts were approximate.

Didn't hear from the minister the next week. But I did hear from Don Bonifacio, early Tuesday morning. His driver came to the house.

"Roberto, come quickly. The minister needs you at his house."

We drove there immediately. Don Bonifacio was sitting on a chair in his small enclosed patio. He looked as though someone close to him had died.

"Good morning, Roberto," he said, motioning me to a chair. "Roberto, did you send a letter to the President?"

"No," I said, surprised.

"Well, I have been asked to come to the presidency in one hour to defend myself against charges of corruption connected with purchases made for the city of Malabo by the economic rehabilitation project."

I told Bonifacio about the minister's request and went home for a copy of the typed memo. By noon we could have copies of all the receipts and a thorough list of everything spent and procured. He said to prepare them. With Harry's help, I did so, and we met Bonifacio at noon.

"Roberto, it will surprise you how our country works," Bonifacio said. "The Minister of Territorial Administration has accused me of stealing eighty thousand dollars from the economic rehabilitation project and taking it to Spain. He said, for example, that we had not purchased the compressor you said we had, that it was a fiction, and that I had put the money in my pocket."

"But, Señor Ministro, the compressor is in the warehouse at the city hall." I found it impossible to believe that the minister could make that stupid an accusation.

"Let us go see it."

Harry, Saturnino, and I took Bonifacio to the warehouse. The compressor was there—as were all the other things we had purchased. Harry had carefully installed an inventory control system and had boxes that catalogued all the receipts. Bonifacio could have kissed him.

"Fine," Bonifacio said. "Then this is what we shall do. We shall invite the Prime Minister and the Minister of Territorial Administration here at two thirty to inspect the warehouse. Meanwhile, I want you to make photocopies of every single receipt, even if you have to use not only our machine but the one at the United Nations. We will give everything to them at that time."

We did as we were told. We returned at two thirty, papers in hand. Also present were Don Camilo and Don Diego, the other members of the coordinating committee. Solidarity in the face of the enemy.

But the Prime Minister didn't show, and neither did the Minister of Territorial Administration. At three o'clock we gave up waiting.

"I will try to rearrange it for tomorrow at ten," Bonifacio said. "Meanwhile, give me the copies of the receipts and I will have them delivered to the President."

The next day at ten, we were all there. Again, no one showed. The minister's accusation was so patently preposterous, I thought, that he must have had a change of heart. So I catalogued the episode in my large mental file called "Equatoguinean Curiosities." I gave the matter no more thought.

One day, suddenly, the news came. The Guinextebank had been definitively closed. The Spanish government had made an ample financial settlement. A commission had been set up to settle the bad debts one by one.

After a long struggle, Don Bonifacio had succeeded. How he did it was, like many important events in Equatorial Guinea, a mystery to me.

Environment of Emergencies

It was the morning of 29 June 1988. The coordinating committee met in our now usual daytime spot, Don Camilo's office. When I arrived, Camilo and Bonifacio were sitting around the former's desk. They were laughing about something, but as I sat down at one of the lounge chairs I could tell it was ironic laughter. When they came over and sat down, still grinning but shaking their heads, Bonifacio looked at me and said, "Roberto, don't let our sadness rub off on you. Keep up that attitude." Puzzled, I let it go.

Camilo said he had two matters for urgent attention. One was the eighty thousand dollar repair on the Bikomo road on the continent—the road to the electric power plant. We had already met on this issue and, after visiting the site and specifying the work and carrying out competitive bidding, approved it. The road was hopelessly dilapidated and virtually closed. The Chinese technicians were refusing to go to work there unless it was repaired immediately. The Chinese economic counselor had told me, "We have to buy a new vehicle every year because of that road. They never fix it. The technicians now have to walk the last four kilometers. So we have to tell the government we are going to stop work."

The threat was becoming real. Camilo read from a handwritten letter from someone important saying that soon Bata would have no power. He asked me when the work would begin. I said that the problem was setting up controls over the money, and that our expert on roads would be back next week to take care of it.

Camilo shook his head in disgust. Though the tone was friendly, the undercurrent was pure frustration. He switched topics. What about his other proposal? He had asked the coordinating committee a couple of weeks ago for help in repairing rural electric stations. What about it? I offered my opinion. The committee had to ask the same questions we did for all our expenditures. In particular, we had to understand why the old equipment had broken down. What were the systems of maintenance and control? How would the operating costs be met in the future? These questions would require study; and, in my opinion, emergency action seemed unlikely.

Don Camilo looked down at his papers and muttered that these were important questions. But, he said, some things were urgent. He returned to the Bikomo road. He waved the letter and talked about the city being blacked out. The road needed repairing now.

"I don't know, Roberto, with all respect. Here we have something urgent, and we have all these procedures and so forth. Sometimes we have urgent things."

He expanded on this theme. There was another urgent matter, one he had officially referred to Don Bonifacio last week but without result. The electricity company was testing some new generators in Bata. French technicians were on the scene, but the ministry needed an additional allotment of diesel. To get this without paying taxes, authorization from the Finance Minister was needed. This Camilo had sought in an "urgent" letter to Don Bonifacio last week. Speaking formally to his former high school chum, Camilo berated *"el señor Ministro"* for his inaction.

"Señor Ministro," replied Don Bonifacio with a bemused smile, "we cannot do everything in this country on an emergency basis. We have to plan ahead. As with the rehabilitation project, we have a strategy, and our actions have to follow those strategies. If not, then your one emergency today becomes five emergencies next week, and the country faces a concatenation of urgencies."

"Excuse me, Señor Ministro, for cutting you off. You know something that our materials tell us well"—Camilo pointed to his binder full of coordinating committee documents—"that a strategy has to fit its environment. You can't do it the other way around. I told Roberto the other day that he can't understand it, being from a country where the infrastructure is all in place and even maintained, that here we have a country without maintenance and where the infrastructure is very antique—you understand me, no?—and things can simply fall apart and stop. In this environment we have urgent needs. We could be working on a road repair, and suddenly the Senje bridge would break. We would have to fix the bridge. Our environment is one of emergencies, and we have to respond to them." Camilo turned to me. "Roberto can leave the country in twenty-four hours and that's that. I cannot. I am here to suffer the consequences, or worse." He waved the letter again.

"Señor Ministro," Bonifacio responded gently, not rising to Camilo's emotional or rhetorical level, "you remember your reaction to the road repairs we were forced to fund on an emergency basis, the road from Bata to Ebebiyin? Remember? There was a lot of pressure, and we agreed to fund it even though we could not assess the plan and did not have anyone to supervise the work. And now what? As you yourself have complained, the work is finished but is poorly done and will wash away after the first rainy season. I agree with what you say about our environment. It is because I understand what you say that we have to plan what we do as well as we can."

"Señor Ministro, what you say is fine in theory, it is perfect. But let me bring you down to the reality of these cases." Whereupon with high emotion and considerable eloquence, Camilo repeated the details of the Bikomo road problem and the need for the diesel fuel to test the generators.

Though Bonifacio changed tactics, his voice remained soothing. "Señor Ministro, your people knew last year when they purchased the motors that they would be tested now. They knew they would need diesel fuel to do so. This should have been planned for and then we could budget the amount and not treat the case as an emergency. Do you know how high my desk is stacked with emergencies requiring urgent funds? In our country, everything is urgent."

Camilo retreated but, in the manner of a body puncher, came right back in.

"I confess that I may have misunderstood what is necessary to get approval here. Perhaps some procedure should have been followed that was not. But now the situation is an emergency. We have French technicians in Bata waiting. True, not at our expense, but it looks very bad that the entire operation is held up for lack of some diesel fuel. Now when a minister of the government comes to you, I don't know, Señor Ministro, it seems that your response shows a lack of confidence in the system of this ministry and in the minister himself."

Bonifacio, smiling painfully, said, "No, no."

Camilo went right on. He was upset, though still under control. "It shows a lack of confidence when my people tell me, and I have implicit confidence in them, that they need so many liters of diesel fuel, and then I pass this along to Your Excellency and you say no, how many liters does this motor take, if it's a smaller motor than Malabo how can it use more fuel, and then my engineers explain that it has a higher number of revolutions or some such, Your Excellency and I are not engineers, and this is my ministry."

Apparently in an earlier and prolonged negotiation over the removal of

226

the fuel tax on the energy company's purchases, Bonifacio had questioned the relative sizes of the Malabo and Bata fuel allotments.

Bonifacio again shook his head. His own frustrations were showing through in his cracked voice.

"Señor Ministro, do you know that last Friday we received your request in the Finance Ministry, and before I went to France on Saturday I was up till twelve thirty working on your problem and others, that I am at the limit of my capabilities to serve." He slowed down. "Last Friday night I signed in the margin of your letter 'approved, urgently.' This has been done, Señor Ministro."

"What do you mean 'done'? We have not seen any action. Today is Wednesday. This is urgent."

Bonifacio looked hurt. "It is *done* as far as I can do, Señor Ministro. I can only do so much, and those beneath me must carry out the orders."

"It is not done, then."

"Señor Ministro, you have to understand that I cannot act immediately on the basis of every request for funds marked urgent. Do you remember how long we worked on the matter of removing the fuel tax from this year's allotment for the energy company? We worked for weeks on it, and now you have a solution. If I should leave and a new Finance Minister come in tomorrow, you would still have an answer that would stand up. You know that this tax on fuel is virtually the country's only source of revenue now. I cannot sign an ad-hoc authorization for the energy company to be exempt for any amount of fuel beyond what we have already agreed. Lamentably there is another feature of our environment which is negative and which I need not explain, but we cannot permit any person who happens to have the evening shift at the energy company to buy diesel tax free. You and I both know what would happen."

"Señor Ministro," Camilo responded, "if you think that when we say we need let's say five thousand liters for this experiment that someone is going to turn around and sell say three thousand of it, well, I don't know, Señor Ministro."

"If you tell me exactly how much you need, then I can authorize exactly that amount. That is what I need. Then I can tell the petroleum company to sell this much and not more free of tax. Otherwise, in our environment, the situation is out of control."

Camilo had been hunched forward in his chair, not looking Bonifacio in the eyes. Now his medical condition was acting up. For months he had been suffering stomach problems, and he would be leaving on Saturday for medical attention overseas. He excused himself and departed for the bathroom.

Bonifacio leaned back against the couch as if finally relieved from pressing his body against an onslaught. He turned to me and shook his head.

"You know, I do not think he understands what I am saying to him. He simply doesn't understand."

I reminded Bonifacio of Camilo's infamous putdown of the Vice Minister of Health at a cabinet meeting—an event that had scandalized her. She had complained that emergency stocks of medicines her ministry had requested of our project had not yet been purchased. Camilo had rebuked her. He told her that, despite many requests, our coordinating committee had not received from the Ministry of Health its strategy or an analysis of its system for distribution and control. The committee, Camilo had said, could not make purchases without such information.

Bonifacio was unimpressed.

"I don't know, Roberto. I don't think he and the others *really* understand that. Maybe they should replace me with another Finance Minister who would be a cashier for their requests for money. 'Here, here, here is your check.' *I* cannot do this."

But then the budget would be spent by August.

"August? By January."

Camilo came back. He apologized for his absence. "When I get worked up, my stomach just cannot take it."

The meeting broke up soon afterward. I said I would find out from the technicians about the Bikomo road effort and report back at our meeting this evening. I would meet with officials from the energy company to plan the needed steps on the rural electricity proposal. I repeated that the repairs were likely not doable by August. Camilo nodded.

Emergency versus strategy. Speed versus deliberation. Action versus planning. Operational versus financial. You versus me. Classic questions. This round was over.

That evening at eight we met again at the Minister of Finance's office. Remarkably, Camilo arrived right on time. He walked quickly up the stairs with barely a greeting. We entered Don Bonifacio's office. Diego wasn't there.

Camilo and Bonifacio exchanged banter about some subject alien to me. Camilo asked about Diego. Bonifacio said he hadn't got in touch with him. Camilo asked me, then said it was my job as secretary of the committee to inform members of meetings. This had not been our convention for half a year, but I let it go.

Bonifacio asked his secretary to call Diego, who said he'd be right over. She told Bonifacio. But Camilo and Bonifacio demurred. "No, let's postpone the meeting till tomorrow, that's all right," Camilo said. "We have that convocation at eleven, we can begin right at nine and kill the two hours."

That was the decision. Frustrated, I left them talking.

Six Ideas for Change

The next morning, we met again. As usual, Diego was quiet; Bonifacio resigned but somehow noble; Camilo hot and cold, laughing then bullying, at once formal and rude.

Last Saturday in Bonifacio's absence we had discussed six new ideas for a structural adjustment program, ideas the government might put forward to the IMF and the Bank.

One was to recast the institutions dealing with commerce. Camilo's Ministry of Industry and Commerce should emphasize promoting business instead of controlling it. The Chamber of Agriculture should get out of the import-export business and certainly not aspire to be a marketing board; instead, it should become an autonomous body serving the private sector and functioning as its voice vis-à-vis the government. To carry out these changes both the ministry and the Chamber would need technical assistance, which could be provided under the structural adjustment program.

A second idea was to form a ministerial committee to oversee the structural adjustment program and address the issue of aid coordination, where so little had been accomplished. The goal would be to institutionalize an expanded version of our coordinating committee, something the World Bank had recommended.

A third category was reform in public administration. The government would launch a campaign to deal with corruption, loan repayment, and domestic arrears. There would be further experiments with performance-based incentives. Redundant government workers would be assisted in finding their ways to the private sector.

Fourth was technical and financial assistance in the area of defining and administering property rights. One possibility was an experiment in land reform with a failed nationalized cocoa project.

The fifth idea had to do with providing credit to small enterprises and agriculturalists.

The sixth was to give much more emphasis to maintenance. We talked about the idea of "endowing the maintenance." When Harvard University is given a building by a rich donor, the university asks that at the same time the maintenance of the building be endowed. Why shouldn't we do the same? Equatorial Guinea might ask for fewer roads, buildings, and vehicles but insist that donors deposit in earmarked bank accounts enough money so that the interest payments would cover the maintenance.

These reforms were central. The country could shift strategies, it could close the Guinextebank, it could cut government spending even more. But without changes in these areas it was hard to see how we could move forward. This had been the driving lesson of all our work on economic strategy.

On these points last Saturday's conversation had been energetic and productive. Camilo had probed and battered but also contributed many constructive suggestions, and so had Diego. They had taken notes, added subcategories, inquired about workable examples, and so forth. We had agreed then that we should discuss each reform in detail, and in Don Bonifacio's presence. So today's first item of business was for me to review the six quickly.

This I did. But the group was tired. Bonifacio was exhausted and hardly responded. Camilo closed his eyes and seemed to nod off. I finished. Diego made a remark. So did the now awakened Camilo. Since I especially wanted Bonifacio's reactions, I asked him where he thought we ought to begin.

"It is difficult for me to comment. Many of these areas are beyond my purview as Finance Minister. Take the reform of the Chamber. You get into problems when you start getting into someone else's area. How would it be done? And then there's the possibility that one would begin a reform and things would unravel and one would end up worse off than one started."

This distant and unfamiliar response was not unreasonable, but it was disappointing. It somehow undercut our purpose. Our committee had been designed to look into strategic issues that were by definition outside the purview of any one ministry. Yes, reform could fail. We needed to talk about how to succeed. How to involve the various players in defining the problems and their solutions. How to mobilize the political will from on high. Then how to get the World Bank and other donors to help through a structural adjustment loan. That was why we were meeting so often these days, to prepare the government's strategy for the negotiations with the Bank.

But Diego expressed sympathy with Bonifacio's remark about the Chamber. Camilo disagreed, his virtually automatic first response to whatever was said. He rocked forward on the chair and punched out his argument like a bantam rooster.

Asserting that the Chamber had to change, Camilo proposed that our committee—I thought, "Roberto"—write up the plan for changing it and then give the plan to the Chamber and the chief of state for their comments and action.

This seemed to me too intrusive. I asked whether it might not be better to have a meeting or two with Aurelio and the new head of the Chamber in Bata and the Minister of Agriculture.

When I posed a point to Camilo those days, it was like throwing a thin strip of bacon on a red-hot pan. Sizzle, crackle, spit.

"I don't understand you," he replied. "You can't expect people to meet and discuss things. Not everyone is as patient as the members of this committee, myself perhaps excluded. You yourself have said that Aurelio is interested in the idea of changing the Chamber's mission. We should just decide how to do it and tell him."

I explained the importance of participation. You'd get a better plan. And you'd avoid the resistance that comes from having your turf invaded.

Camilo spurned the danger. Just do the paper. They can read it and make comments after it's presented to them.

Diego agreed with Camilo, but addressed my concerns.

"We would not present the paper as a final plan but as something that responded to Aurelio's expressed desire, something for discussion and comment. We work better here with a written document to base our thinking upon."

Okay.

We went on to the idea of an interministerial committee to manage structural adjustment. On Saturday, Camilo had thought it not a good idea, and Diego had agreed. Committees waste time, and if they are too large, they are unworkable. Still, some form of high-level oversight was needed.

Now Camilo said to Bonifacio, "What do you think of my idea that we do not need an interministerial committee but simply a strengthening of the Finance Ministry as the oversight body?"

Bonifacio said that it would be easier and more attractive to add this oversight function to the new committee that had been formed to make decisions about investment projects. The job of overseeing structural adjustment was not really Finance's. It fit better under the Planning Ministry. The best thing that could be done to strengthen the Finance Ministry would be to strengthen the ministries of Planning and of Industry and Commerce.

Let it go, I thought. Move on to administrative reform. The idea of better incentives got Diego's endorsement. He repeated the argument that without better incentives for public employees, we would never have competence in government.

"Let's go on to the liberalization issue," said Camilo.

He had asked me to prepare a short paper on the subject, which I had done a week ago. We got out the paper. Bonifacio didn't have his copy. I asked whether he had read it. He said he hadn't. Diego said, "I must admit I haven't either." Camilo said he'd looked at parts of it.

Frustrated, I joked that it was hard to discuss these issues when we hadn't read the background materials.

Camilo was miffed by my remark.

"This is almost an insult to figures of the government. I have read parts of it. Here, look where I have marked the margin."

He showed me a diagram on the second page. Trying to prove he knew its content, he then proceeded to misidentify it. "Right?" he said.

I paused. I didn't want to contradict him. I went on to provide a little summary.

Diego said, "Don't be discouraged. There are various readings one gives a document. There is the first reading, where one glances through it. A second reading. A third reading."

Camilo was reading through the part he had read, and deciphering a marginal note. He quickly intruded a question.

"You say here that structural adjustment involves liberalization. But how is that? Isn't liberalization to do with trade and commerce? You then list all these parts here about structural changes. Why?"

My point was that liberalization was a part of structural adjustment as conceived by many countries, but liberalization by itself was not enough. It needed complementary changes to work, changes in what our committee had been calling "structures."

"But not all structural change requires liberalization," Camilo said.

Strictly speaking, no. You could change structures in all sorts of ways.

Bonifacio said to Camilo, "Yes, you could have structural adjustment away from liberalization."

I nodded. Then Bonifacio said, "I think this is an important subject, as we have said before, and I want to read this document carefully before discussing it. This is a key issue for us and for me personally. So let us meet this evening and talk it over in detail."

232

Camilo continued fumbling through the paper. Diego quickly agreed with Bonifacio's proposal. So did I. The meeting adjourned till evening.

A Strategy for Equatorial Guinea

And so it went, day after day. The ministers were busy, and we crow-barred meetings in when we could. Some sessions were vigorous and filled us with energy. Other meetings seemed to stall. Don Bonifacio was the key man. Without him, Camilo's negativism might have gone unchecked, and Diego might have been content simply to wait.

To transform our deliberations into detailed policies, Bonifacio created a technical committee on structural adjustment. It included directors general from several ministries and me. We had an outline based on successful structural adjustment programs in other African countries:

1. The productive sectors: agriculture, wood, mining, and fishing.
2. Property rights.
3. Investment.
4. Fiscal policy.
5. Pricing policy.
6. Reforms in public enterprise.
7. Reforms in the banking sector.
8. Monetary and credit policies.
9. Foreign debt and arrears.

Under each heading, we needed to come up with detailed recommendations. *Who, what, when.* We also needed to create a two-page "statement of development strategy" for the country. This all took us weeks, night after night. I kept bringing the results to the coordinating committee for their feedback.

At the same time, Don Bonifacio began discussing the issues with the President and the cabinet. Sensitizing them.

The idea was to create a program to present to the Fund—one already debated and approved by the government. For the first time it would be Equatorial Guinea's strategy, not one drafted by the IMF.

The technical committee went through three drafts. Then Bonifacio, Camilo, and Diego presented the third draft to the cabinet in an extraordinary two-day session.

The day before, Bonifacio came to my office.

"Roberto, I need your help," he said. "Some of the ministers do not

233

understand what the International Monetary Fund is. Or what the World Bank is. Would you please draft an outline? Include something about structural adjustment and liberalization. Explain where we are, how far we have come, and why this agreement is important."

I did so, in a question-and answer-format. Bonifacio made some changes and I produced copies via computer.

The next day he began his presentation to the cabinet by going through the questions and answers with the ministers.

Then, step by step, hour by hour, the cabinet debated each point of the draft strategy. By the end of the second day, the cabinet had recrafted and approved what looked to me like a realistic strategy of economic reform.

The IMF Returns

But would the IMF buy it? They were due to arrive a week later, in late July.

We had two things going for us. The Guinextebank had, after all the politicking and delay, been shut down. And Don Bonifacio presented the IMF mission with a fifteen-page outline of the government's three-year program of structural adjustment.

On the negative side, the numbers still did not look good. With the continued decline in cocoa, our tax revenues had fallen still further short of target. Despite Don Bonifacio's efforts to reign in spending, off-budget expenses were still significant. The government payroll was still too large. Consequently, the budget deficit was huge. And though the IMF would be happy about the closure of the Guinextebank and the BCD—and would accept the eventual relaunching of a Banco Nacional de Desarrollo—the government's plans to expand credit over the next year were, in the Fund's eyes, too ambitious.

The Fund's mission was led by a Latin American named Gonzalo. His wavy gray hair was brushed straight back and seemed as stiff as papier-mâché. He had blue eyes and olive skin and a jaw like an open drawer. He was a senior fund official, too senior for such a small and unimportant country. Gonzalo's presence on this trip and the one in the spring meant that in the Fund's eyes this was it. Get an agreement with this country or let it rest.

Once again the negotiations convened in the monstrous BEAC conference room. The conference table was nearly as long as a bowling lane. During the daytime meetings, which were of a technical nature, the table contained many BEAC functionaries and assorted Latin American *expertos* from the ministries of Planning and Agriculture. It was the cool place to be, if you had to be working. But the negotiating was done in the evenings, when Don Bonifacio and Don Diego were present. Most of the experts bailed out at night, though.

Gonzalo and his team, as well as the members of our technical committee, attended religiously—that is, fourteen hours a day. Every clause of the government's draft strategy was pored over. Every date was explored, every task unpacked. There were changes in the draft, also strident defenses of it. We crawled through the document.

Meanwhile, the IMF team had a model into which were inserted the data of each day. Some of the data were facts and figures: trade, banking statistics, the latest budget numbers. Some of these "facts" were as squishy as a baby bush fly. The IMF would pound away at the numbers with the government's technicians and advisers, trying to make them consistent and compatible.

Others of the data being inserted into the IMF model were the results of the crawling negotiations. The government promises to do X next year; what effect will X have on the data? Okay, suppose the government promises Y. What effect will that have? But then, can the government actually achieve Y? Will it?

The IMF team couldn't get the totals to come out right. Gonzalo would have to defend any agreement back in Washington. It had to be shown that the Fund's assistance would close the budget gap and the balance of payments gap—not completely, but enough. It had to be shown that the government's monetary policy was responsible. But in the IMF's model, the gaps and the credit limits kept turning out to be too large.

As negotiations and data hammering proceeded, some members of the IMF team were continually reworking their model. The main numbers man was an American who looked like a middle-aged model in a Lacoste ad.

"You know how this is," he confided to me on the penultimate night at ten o'clock, after I had wandered over to the far side of the conference room where he was cranking away on a laptop computer. "The gaps have got to be manageable. And they still aren't. They aren't yet, I should say. Who knows what they will be before we're through?"

Later he said, "I think Gonzalo wants it, wants an agreement. He's a softie, you know, underneath all the toughness. A sucker for a really poor country like this one."

But the last day came, and still there was no breakthrough. After an arduous day we broke at about six thirty and agreed to begin again at eight. The next morning the Fund team would depart.

The last meeting began coldly. Gonzalo summarized the situation. He praised the government's program. He lamented the condition of the balance of payments. He noted the key questions still to resolve. Credit limits. Tax collection. The public payroll.

Don Bonifacio responded. He took an upbeat line. He thanked the Fund for all its hard work. He said he had discussed the changes negotiated so far in the government's draft strategy with the President, and the President had agreed with each one. The government of the Republic of Equatorial Guinea, he declared, was prepared on the basis of this strategy to reach an agreement with the Fund.

Their give and take continued. But what about the numbers? Lacoste and the gang were still cranking. Lacoste brought Gonzalo a printout. Gonzalo asked Don Bonifacio for a five-minute break. Gonzalo had his calculator out. Then he gave a long set of instructions to Lacoste. Lacoste asked some questions. Gonzalo answered them. Lacoste went off to the computer.

I wandered over. Lacoste was redoing the tables, punching in new numbers furiously.

"A breakthrough?" I asked.

"Hey, you know, you can always fiddle with this category here, it's kind of a catch-all category. If things don't add up elsewhere, play with the catch-all."

He crunched away. He printed out. He took the results to Gonzalo. There was some discussion among the entire IMF team. Then Gonzalo reinitiated the meeting.

"Mr. Minister, members of the negotiating team. The calculations of my colleagues now indicate that, if we make certain optimistic assumptions, the government's program is indeed feasible with a structural adjustment facility from the Fund. I would therefore like to review a draft letter we have prepared to Your Excellency . . ."

Gonzalo went right on, no drama in his voice; but I was out of my chair, unable to contain a smile as big as the Equatoguinean budget deficit. I looked at Don Bonifacio. He hadn't smiled, but he had looked at Don Fausto, the Guinean head of our technical committee, and at Don Diego; and Bonifacio seemed now relaxed. A moment later I caught his eye. He nodded his head and pursed his lips in acknowledgment.

The rest was easy. It lasted till past midnight, but we had done it. We had an agreement. Finally the meeting concluded. Hands were shaken all around. The Fund team left first. I walked to the conference room door with Gonzalo.

"This will be very hard to sell in Washington," he said. "We stretched a long way to make this happen. I hope you know that."

I told him he wouldn't be sorry.

Then I returned to the conference table, where Bonifacio and Diego and the technical committee who had worked so hard on the program were standing and talking. Tired as they were, their relief and satisfaction were palpable. We felt like a team, a team that had won. We had developed a good strategy, and finally the IMF had accepted it. Don Bonifacio was thanking Don Fausto for his diligence. Fausto beamed. We gathered our papers and walked out together into the humid tropical night. After two years of frustration, after three months of careful preparations, we had done it. I thought it made all the pains and problems worthwhile.

8

Dissolution

THOUGH Equatorial Guinea needed the IMF's money urgently, the agreement was more important for what it represented. The IMF's approval of the government's economic strategy would ease the way for other lenders and aid donors and encourage foreign investors. It would also enable the long-delayed United Nations "round table" meeting with all the country's aid donors to move forward.

The next step was to get an agreement with the World Bank: a full-fledged structural adjustment program. Having succeeded with the IMF, we now had to detail not just what the government planned to do but how.

I agreed to stay till the end of October to help out. With Don Bonifacio of Finance and other Guinean officials, I would attend the annual meetings of the World Bank and the IMF in Berlin in late September. Then I would leave the country at the end of October, an agreement with the Bank (we hoped) in hand.

In August 1988, the technical committee that had worked so well on the IMF agreement began to meet again. The committee added two new members: the wise and able Saturnino, one of eight local professionals working on our economic rehabilitation project; and my assistant, Raúl. We began by dividing up the tasks that needed doing, and we met three times a week to move things along.

DISSOLUTION

Attempted Coup

Meanwhile, President Obiang began an August tour of the country. His idea was to discuss with the people the idea of a presidential election—one party only and probably only one candidate, but a national election nonetheless. The President had told diplomats that he wanted to get a sense of his own support in the countryside. If he perceived a lack of enthusiasm, he said he would consider retiring. Some people whispered that the *jefe* was growing weary of the burdens of the office. Others talked of opposition to the President. The pro-democracy Guineans living in Spain were active as usual, but the talk concerned regional opposition—and opposition within the ruling clan of the President's home town of Mongomo.

The chief of state's tour mobilized the ministers. Some accompanied him, others were advance men. The rest might suddenly have to go to Bata for consultations. With so many ministers away from Malabo, employees would come to work late and wander off early. The energy of the tiny capital city seemed to dissipate.

Then on Thursday, 9 August, an alarming rumor swept Malabo. On the mainland there had been an attempt on the President's life.

Details, versions seeped out. One story had a coup plot based in Mongomo itself. The President was to have been assassinated when he and his entourage arrived in his home town. The chief of police of Mongomo, plus locally based soldiers, were said to have stashed an armory for this purpose; but their designs had been uncovered. "Many" had been arrested. No official news on the matter—only rumor.

In Malabo all was calm. Business went on as usual on Friday, the weekend seemed normal, and on Monday our technical committee met. Everyone came but Saturnino. This was unlike him. After the meeting, I motorcycled over to the Ministry of Transportation to his office.

No sign of him. I asked one of the secretaries.

"Saturnino has not come today," she said softly, her eyes averted. "He will not come." Her voice and manner told me that something was wrong.

"Why?" I asked.

She wouldn't say. "Ask the secretary general."

I went to the secretary general's office. He looked grim. I had the feeling he knew why I was there. I explained that Saturnino had not appeared at this morning's meeting.

"I do not know, Roberto. Things have been said, but I do not know. Perhaps you should go to his house and find out."

I drove to public housing near the marketplace. The area was ugly and utilitarian, a bunch of blocklike concrete dwellings diagonally situated one after another on a large lot of packed dirt. I asked someone where Saturnino's place was. She took me there, past chickens and children and lines of tattered clothes. I knocked at the door. A shirtless teenage boy opened it and led me to the main room. It was barren and dark. Stark wooden chairs and tables, dull walls without decoration, a television. Two children were roaming on the floor. At a table against the far wall sat a woman. I introduced myself and asked about Saturnino.

"They came for him on Saturday," she said. "The police took him away. We do not know where he is or his condition."

She and Saturnino's teenage son related some details, which were few and uninformative. They did not know why Saturnino had been arrested. But over the weekend, others, too, had been picked up around Malabo.

"It has to do with the attempt to kill the President," the woman said.

Rumors roared through town. An ambush had been thwarted. The cause was an intra-clan battle, some said. Others cited the President's economic policies, the closing of the banks, the battening down of extrabudgetary spending. It could have been all of the above. In Malabo a Spanish-based opposition politician, who had been granted a visa subject to the promise not to stir up trouble, had been arrested. So had a number of middle-level government officials.

My assistant, Raúl, told me something he had not shared with me before.

"You know, Bob, two years ago when there was supposedly a coup attempt against the President? Well, I was locked up and interrogated. No reason at all. But you know, Bob, they tortured me."

Raúl quietly described having his elbows tied together behind his back for days. He had been blindfolded and immersed in drums of water until he felt as though he were drowning. He had been beaten.

"At the end they released me," Raúl said. "No charges were ever made. But it, well, it ruined me for a long time. I could not move my arms right for months afterward. It took months before I was ready to work again."

Searching for Saturnino

I had to find out where Saturnino was, make sure he was okay.

Don Camilo knew nothing. He told me not to worry.

"This is not the time of Macías, Roberto. He will be taken care of. His situation will be investigated and fairly judged."

Don Bonifacio also professed ignorance. He advised caution.

"Roberto, you will not be able to know anything. You cannot help Saturnino."

But we had to make sure he was all right, that his rights were respected. He worked for us, for our project. He was our colleague.

"I understand what you mean, Roberto. But you as an outsider cannot help him. This is a matter of national security. It has its own process."

I protested that it was precisely as an outsider that I might be able to help. Maybe push things that, say, a minister could not.

Bonifacio nodded, but still advised me to do nothing.

"Bonifacio, suppose it was me that was jailed. Would you do nothing?"

He paused, looked down, then looked back at me.

"No. I would try to help you." Another pause. "Be careful, Roberto."

I went to police headquarters, a rundown building at the edge of the sea. The corner office on the ground floor belonged to the chief of police, Don Armengol. He was the President's brother.

In the waiting room I gave my card to his secretary and wrote on the back, "This matter will take only five minutes." In a little while I was ushered into Don Armengol's office.

We had never met. He was lean and looked to be about forty. His feet were up on the corner of his desk, and he was doing something with his fingernails. He looked at me, said good afternoon, and motioned me to a chair by his desk.

"What can I do for you, Señor Klitgaard?"

I explained that I worked on a World Bank–funded project. He knew that. I told him that one of our project's employees had been taken from his home by the police on Saturday night. It was my obligation to find out what charges had been made and whether Saturnino was being treated fairly.

"I do not know where Saturnino is," the chief of police said. He picked at his nails.

I asked him how I might find out.

"There is no way to find out. This matter goes beyond the police. It is a matter of the security of the state."

I reiterated my questions. I was not judging anyone's guilt or innocence. I was interested only in ensuring human rights. This case was important to me, and would no doubt be also to the World Bank.

Armengol talked about national security for a while. He rambled. This was good. A little eye contact, a little tongue loosening.

241

I finally asked, "Do you think you could somehow get Saturnino a note from me?"

Armengol thought about it. "Yes," he said finally, "I could do that." Then he said that he thought Saturnino had been taken to the continent by boat, along with other prisoners from Malabo.

I spoke again of the importance of human rights and again dropped the World Bank's name. Would Armengol please do what he could to help me see Saturnino?

He said he would.

I returned two days later, then two days after that, then again the following week. Each time Armengol refused to receive me. His secretary said, "The chief of police tells me that he has nothing new for you. He says the matter is beyond his purview."

The inability to find out, to do something, was making me frantic. The World Bank, notified in Washington, cabled back in careful language. The legal department said that the Bank could do nothing. I phoned Esteban, the Bank's economist for Equatorial Guinea, to protest. He said there had been a battle within the Bank about it, but since Saturnino did not work for the Bank but only on a Bank-funded project, the institution could do nothing.

"What if it were me that was in jail?" I said. "Would you do nothing?" Esteban was anguished. But nothing was the answer.

And it was the answer around Malabo. The United Nations would soon celebrate an assembly dedicated to human rights. Equatorial Guinea had recently signed a U.N. convention on human rights. I asked the local U.N. representative if she could help on this matter.

"I'm very busy because I'm leaving for the assembly," she answered. "Anyway, affairs like this one do not fall within my terms of reference."

Futility and frustration everywhere. Then a new rumor. Saturnino's son heard that he had been tortured in Bata, that he was in "bad shape."

I tried to go to Bata to find Saturnino, perhaps to try to see the President himself. But in the wake of "the disturbances," as the news now termed them, flights to the continent had been canceled. Then, when the flights were resumed, the few seats on the tiny prop planes were overbooked. I was stuck in Malabo.

I was at the edge of exasperation. One Sunday morning, I went to Musto and Teodora's house. On their street I took some video pictures of the colonial dwellings. A young, belligerent Fang man emerged from his house. He was shirtless, and his shoulders and chest rippled.

"Let me see your permit for taking these pictures," he barked.

"It is back in the car," I said. The car was parked a hundred yards down the street.

"Well, get yourself down there and bring it to me."

I lost my cool.

"Who are you to ask for it? Are you a policeman?"

He screamed back, "Don't you worry who I am, you just get me that permit."

"You show me your authority," I said, "and I'll show you the permit."

"I'll take that camera away from you," he yelled.

"Come on and try," I said, placing the camera on the ground and squaring off to fight.

Our yelling brought people out of their houses. We pushed each other and snarled. But there was no fight. Musto and others pulled us apart, and we let them. My antagonist went to his house, and I got the camera and walked away. Later I was ashamed. I had acted like some kind of gangster.

Early September arrived: two weeks had passed, no news about Saturnino. My Guinean friends told me what they could. Yes, an inside job. Yes, over power and jealousy and maybe policy. Yes, everything was now under control. Why Saturnino? Speculation was that the Minister of Territorial Administration had something to do with it. Saturnino had audited him and found corruption. Now Saturnino was hauled off as some kind of subversive.

I departed in early September for two weeks of errands and vacation in the States before heading to Berlin. On the morning of my departure, Harry came by with another rumor. Saturnino's father in Bata had been able to see him. Saturnino was okay, was the story. No torture. It made the flight home much less anxious.

Four days later, back in the States, I spoke with people at the World Bank in Washington.

"Have you heard the news, Bob?"

"You mean about the coup attempt?"

"No, about the Minister of Finance."

"What?"

"We have just received a cable from the government. They tell us that there will be a new Minister of Finance attending the annual meetings in Berlin. The day after you left, Don Bonifacio was fired."

In Berlin, I stayed with Cord, the cocoa expert, and I met the new Finance Minister at a cocktail party the opening night. Don Fernando was extremely cordial and deferential. The next day we had a long talk. He did not know why Bonifacio had been replaced. He asked me about the economy—he had just returned from some time abroad. He wanted to talk about exports and corruption. He was intelligent, concerned.

Over the days of the meetings, we worked closely together. Equatorial Guinea would not get far with the Bank on this occasion. With the inaction occasioned by the President's trip and the disturbances, our work on a structural adjustment program had stalled.

But the IMF did inform Don Fernando that the agreement negotiated in July had been approved in Washington. So the new Minister of Finance could go home with that success in hand.

Saturnino's Story

After the Berlin meetings I flew to Malabo. The trip was less arduous than usual. Malabo's time was only an hour different from Berlin's, so no jet lag. The journey began at eight in the morning in Berlin, proceeded through Frankfurt with a three-and-a-half-hour layover, then to Madrid with an eight-hour layover. Finally after an all-night flight with a stop in Lagos we arrived in Malabo at eight in the morning.

It was pouring rain. We had to walk a couple of hundred yards across the runway. No umbrella. Just before entering the large shed that was called the terminal, we had to wade through a small river. I was soaked from crown to sole. Inside, while participating in the two-hour scrimmage of immigration, health control, baggage claim, and customs, I thought of a consolation. It was cool.

At last we were driving in from the airport, past the dense greens of the reeds and the ferns, the cocoa plantations, and the rain forest. The peak was packed in clouds as dark and rugged as steel wool. My mood, too, was gloomy. In three weeks I would be leaving again, this time for good. During those weeks I would be busier than an army of ants tying up the economic rehabilitation project and arranging personal matters. We had to help a Cameroonian accounting firm complete an audit of the economic rehabilitation project. But my anxiety had other causes. Was Saturnino out of jail? Was he all right? What had happened to Don Bonifacio? What did the coup attempt itself mean?

In the rain Malabo looked devastated. Dislodged by the monsoons of past weeks, stones and gravel and pieces of sidewalk littered the streets. In the downpour's dimness, the old buildings presented a pallid and jaundiced countenance, as if afflicted with some new strain of malaria. Because of the weather few people were out. I had the eerie feeling of being in a ghost town.

But, as always, arriving home at the Casa Verde was uplifting. The children who milled about under the covered sidewalks on both sides of the streets shouted my name. They ran to me and hugged me and danced around my suitcase. Hearing the noise, Chispa rushed to her observation point overlooking the street and began to bark in joy. Celestina and Consuelo, the maids, rushed down the stairs and hugged me, beaming. Even Alfredo the parrot, hearing my voice in the commotion, began to whistle his usual greeting whenever I would come home: "Ho-laa!" Soon there was a hot shower and a hot breakfast, then a welcome bed.

The afternoon cleared up as I unpacked, worked at odds and ends, assembled documents, and made a long list of things to do. At about six in the evening, I took a break and walked to the corner of the house overlooking Malabo. In the gorgeous light of late afternoon, the dilapidated wooden houses of colonial times looked like proud exhibits in a living museum. In the distance, the volcano was in full regalia, its verdant slopes satiny against the sunset, crowned by a pink and mother-of-pearl cloud that crested westward like a giant plume. This natural exultation contrasted with my own ominous forebodings, which I couldn't shake. Later I drove aimlessly around the darkened town. I didn't feel like seeing friends, only somehow reabsorbing my surroundings. It was Saturday night at the end of the world. Beneath the town's available sources of illumination, clumps of men played cards and checkers, little girls squealed as they hopscotched, boys kicked around small, dirty, half-inflated soccer balls. On the streets slow-moving old cars skirted potholes as if performing an elaborate minuet. The palm trees waved wearily in the tropical wind.

On Sunday we had electricity, and I spent the day working at home. By evening I had finished and, after reading some football magazines from the States, I dropped into a deep sleep. But I awoke at four o'clock, not from jet lag but in a pattern usual these past months and never before in my life: worrying about what to do. It seemed that even in sleep the problems would not leave me, and I would often awaken with a new insight or a new feeling of depression. I would turn on the short-wave for company. After an hour or so of mulling, I would sleep again.

Monday breakfast—glorious sunshine, Chispa begging for affection, the two kittens climbing my lap, Alfredo going through his entire repertoire to attract my attention. I suited up and went to the office. For my secretary there were new eyeglasses from the States, and for Raúl an economics book in Spanish.

Raúl and I went into my office, and he whispered disturbing news. Saturnino was out of prison, but his collarbone had been broken. He had been exonerated of all charges, but he had been tortured.

Suddenly, in walked Saturnino and Harry. Seeing Saturnino released a rush of relief and affection, and we embraced for a long time. I had to be careful, because his right arm and shoulder were swathed in bandages.

We all sat at the conference table. Saturnino produced an X ray of his collarbone showing a complicated fracture, which had not yet been set. He then handed over a remarkable document whose English translation was this:

MINISTRY OF NATIONAL DEFENSE
Military Jurisdiction

Final Military Court Credential

By means of the present document, it is certified that the Equatoguinean Don SATURNINO X., functionary of the Civil Administration of the State, with actual assignment to the World Bank (Project . . . Public Works), located in Malabo, arbitrarily detained during the practice of preliminary diligences in the Highest Cause inscribed in this Court for the offense of ATTEMPT AGAINST THE SECURITY OF THE STATE and, having proven to be IN- NOCENT of participation in the acts and the attributions of this same, was ABSOLVED at the beginning; being able therefore to exercise freely all the functions that he undertook before his detention; in proof of which, he is being granted this document of justification in Bata, the twentieth of Sep- tember of one thousand nine hundred eighty-eight.

FOR A BETTER GUINEA
THE COMMANDING INSTRUCTOR JUDGE
By Order of His Honor,

The Secretary

We remarked the words "arbitrarily detained" and "absolved at the beginning."

After some further exclamations of past worry, present relief, and future commitment, I asked Saturnino to explain what had happened.

He was at home working on Saturday evening, 12 August. At six thirty Rigoberto and a man from the presidential security force stopped by his house. Rigoberto was the director general in charge of the external debt in the Ministry of Finance, having assumed that position that summer. His office was two doors down my hall. Rigoberto was a member of the technical committee that prepared for the IMF negotiations. He had impressed me as quiet and, if not overly competent, at least attentive and hard-working. It now developed that he was simultaneously a captain in the police.

On that 12 August, Rigoberto said, "Saturnino, come along, I want to invite you for a drink." Rigoberto and Saturnino hailed from the same district on the continent. Saturnino agreed and went to change his clothes. As he dressed, his sister-in-law came into his room and said, "Saturnino, this is not normal. Rigoberto has never invited you before." But the three men departed, entered Rigoberto's car with the security man driving, Saturnino in the middle, and Rigoberto on the outside. They drove across town to a bar a block away from police headquarters. They went inside. Rigoberto and the security man ordered whiskey; Saturnino asked for a cola. As they drank they engaged in small talk.

After ten minutes Armengol, the chief of police and the President's brother, entered the bar. He called Rigoberto over and apparently gave him some orders. Rigoberto told Saturnino to finish his drink and asked him to come to the car. Saturnino now began to worry. They drove to one of the encampments of the Moroccan guards, an old building across from the cathedral on Malabo's main plaza, catty-corner to the Palace of the People.

They got out of the car. Rigoberto asked Saturnino, "Do you know Juaquín Mo?" Saturnino said he didn't.

Rigoberto, turning to one of the Moroccans, then said, "Detain him." Saturnino asked him why.

"You'll find out," Rigoberto said. Then he turned and walked away.

Saturnino was blindfolded with a mask like the ones airlines give for sleeping, topped off with tight rubber cords. He showed me a scar at the corner of his left eye from one of the cords. His blindfold was not removed for seventeen days.

He was taken to a cell, was pushed through the door, and found himself alone. He was told not to talk. He waited. Sometime in the middle of the night, men came, bound his arms, and took him out to a car, where he was pushed to the floor out of sight. The car drove round in circles for a while, apparently to confuse him; and then he was taken to the Point of African Unity on the east side of Malabo harbor. This was inside the presidential compound; the President's house was less than four hundred yards away.

Though Saturnino was not able to see, he discerned from their accents that both Moroccan and Equatoguinean personnel were present. And there was another prisoner: later Saturnino could hear a man's screams some distance away. Saturnino knew the two men who talked to him: Lorenzo, the Equatoguinean who directed his interrogation, sometimes in the Fang language; and Abdul, a Moroccan officer. Once Abdul had invited Saturnino out for a beer.

Without asking Saturnino a single question, his tormenters began their abuse. His arms were pulled behind his back so that his elbows almost touched, and bound there and at the wrists. He was pushed to the ground on his stomach, and his legs were bent so his heels touched his butt. Then his ankles were tied to his wrists. A pole was inserted under the ropes perpendicular to his body, and he was lifted off the ground. The poles were then supported on some sort of device designed for that purpose, perhaps like a weight-room rack. Saturnino hung there in acute pain. Large stones were placed on his back to increase the torment.

I learned later from other sources that in Equatorial Guinea this procedure is called the "Ethiopia." It was adopted during Macías's time via dedicated instructors provided by the fraternal revolutionary Marxist government of Ethiopia.

As Saturnino was hanging in this crippling position, the interrogation began. Lorenzo did the talking.

"Juan Bicomo is the head of a subversive organization, and you are the secretary. Teodoro Buñé and Alejandro Sudopo are also members." Juan was an important official in the Presidency, and Teodoro was a government official whose competence and dedication I respected. Lorenzo continued, "Tell me about this organization."

There was no such organization, Saturnino said. He was whipped. Lorenzo asked him about a meeting. He knew of no meeting, Saturnino responded. Lorenzo repeated the same questions again and again. Some of the people he was asked about were known to Saturnino, but he knew nothing about opposition or conspiracy. He said so.

The torturers kept feeling Saturnino's fingers. Finally, when the fingers were cold and he could no longer feel pain with them, he was lowered to the ground and untied. Abdul, the Moroccan, came close to Saturnino's ear and said, "Saturnino, tell the truth, you are suffering. We know each other." Saturnino was then bound up in a different position. He was placed in a crouch, and his wrists were tied together beneath his knees and again to his ankles. The pole was inserted, and he was hung upside-down.

The same questions. The same answers. After a while, new tortures. In between ordeals Abdul again spoke. "Saturnino, answer him. Answer in Spanish even if he asks you questions in Fang. We want to hear your answers." Saturnino was then tied up sitting down, his hands behind his back and his head pulled back so he was facing the sky. A cloth was placed over his mouth and nose so it was difficult to breathe. Whenever he gasped for air, his tormenters poured soapy water onto the cloth, forcing it to enter his mouth and nose, inducing choking and nausea. Lorenzo repeated the questions.

Later Saturnino was suspended by his ankles with his hands tied behind his back, like a marlin at the weigh scale. Below his head was placed a barrel of soapy water. He was lowered into the barrel and kept there until he choked. Then he was pulled up, questioned, and submerged again. Saturnino could say nothing to appease his interrogator, for there was nothing to the questions.

That first night Saturnino's ordeal lasted several hours—maybe four, he thought. But time must have lost meaning after a while.

Eventually Saturnino was led away from the tortures of the Point of African Unity. He was driven back to his place of confinement and taken to his cell. Before departing, one of his victimizers said, "Saturnino, it was rough tonight on you, wasn't it? Wait until tomorrow night."

He passed the next day alone in his small cell. He was told to ask when he wanted to relieve himself, and when he asked, his fly was pulled down and his penis extracted by a guard and he was allowed to urinate on the cell floor. Graciously, the guard would lead him to a toilet in order to defecate. A couple of times he was asked whether he wanted bread and water. When he said yes, he was told to open his mouth and then bread or water were placed inside. Saturnino was still not told anything about the reasons for his captivity.

Late that night—about midnight, he thought—the torturers returned for him. The same procedure: into the car clad only in undershorts, pushed to the floor, driven around, and taken to the point. The same questions were asked, in the same order so far as he could remember. And the same tortures began again, the same brutal tortures in the same order, only now even worse—now, as he was hanging, they whipped him on the back and feet with metal cables. But, again, there was nothing Saturnino could say to the questions.

Finally, after a long time, his tormentors made good on their threat of the night before.

"Saturnino, you won't talk to us. You won't tell us what you know. So now we are going to make you impotent for the rest of your life."

They pulled down Saturnino's undershorts and threw him to the ground. They spreadeagled him. They stuck a metal prod against his scrotum. Saturnino felt them press something on the prod, and then the prod blasted a long and powerful bolt of electricity into his testicles. Saturnino almost fainted. The torturers did it again. And after a minute, they administered a third electric shock.

Saturnino was taken back to his cell. He was to spend the next week there, but there was no more torture.

After four days a Moroccan guard came into his cell. He lifted Saturnino's blindfold and asked in a low voice, "Do you know me?"

Saturnino said he didn't.

"No? Well, listen to me. They have found you are innocent. They will take you to Bata, but you will be all right."

Over the next three days this guard surreptitiously shared his meals with Saturnino—sandwiches of sardines and meat.

On 21 August, Saturnino was taken to Bata on the patrol boat recently donated to Equatorial Guinea by the United States of America. Along with eight other prisoners, he was taken down to the old port in Malabo by a contingent of Equatoguineans, with a Moroccan on one side of him and a Guinean on the other. Some of the soldiers taunted him and the others. "These are the people who wanted to kill the President. They deserve the death sentence." When they reached the dock, the Guinean at his side pushed Saturnino into the sea.

His hands bound and in shock, Saturnino first sank like a stone. Then he kicked to the surface only to hit his head on the hull. Almost out of air, he went down again and came up successfully to the water's surface. As he gasped, two sailors jumped into the water and saved him. Eventually they wrapped a cable around him, and a kind of small crane on the boat began to lift him out of the water. He was raised way above the boat's deck. Then, maliciously, the cable was released and Saturnino made a free fall. How far he did not know: perhaps ten feet. He crashed on his side on a metal rail. This was how his collarbone was broken. He thought he had also fractured his ribs, but they turned out to be only painfully bruised. During all of this, Saturnino said nothing.

He was kept bound all the way to Bata. His arm and shoulder swelled ominously. When they arrived at Bata, the Moroccan officer in charge there saw Saturnino's condition and mercifully ordered the guards to untie him. Thereafter he was never bound again—the only one of the prisoners to have his hands free. In the days that followed, Saturnino dared occasionally to lift his blindfold. Once he was caught and lashed as punishment. But he was spared further torture. He was luckier than most of the other prisoners.

At the Bata port, the captives were put in the back of a refrigerated truck for carrying fish. It was a disgusting trip: the compartment contained a couple of feet of water dirty from the remains of rotten fish, in which the prisoners were forced to sit. They gagged from the foulness of the smell.

They were taken to the cells of the police station in Bata. The nine from Malabo were placed together in a compartment five feet wide and eight feet long. For the next three and a half days, the men were kept in this room, and they were starved. No food. No water. They had no alternative but to urinate and defecate in place. By the third day Saturnino's urine was red. He could peek out and see a microphone above the cell door—just in case anyone spoke. The prisoners identified themselves to each other. Saturnino whispered to them about the microphone so the conversations were minimal. He did learn that only two had been tortured in Malabo. Six of the rest would be tortured here in Bata.

Midnight was again the appointed hour. They took Saturnino out to the torturing site once, but only to listen. They wanted to scare him into talking. The supervisor of the torturing was a high official in the Ministry of Foreign Relations.

Saturnino did not know all the tortures that were used here. One prisoner nearly lost an eye. Among the tactics was a fake firing squad. "You will talk, or you will be shot." Ready, aim, fire. But the firing squad would shoot into the air.

Also present at some of the torturing sessions was one of the highest women officials in government. I couldn't believe it; I knew her. "Yeess!" assured Saturnino. "She is an insider, Roberto. Understand." Anyone could recognize this woman's distinctive speech. She was there with several other women; as the tortures took place, Saturnino could hear them laughing and joking.

On the fourth day a high-ranking police official came to their filthy cell. He gave them water. He asked them for the names of family members in Bata who might bring them food. Thereafter the prisoners received food twice a day—bread in the morning and a meal in the afternoon. The next day a doctor came and examined Saturnino's arm, which was disfigured and blue. The doctor did not set the arm but put a makeshift protective covering on it.

The prisoners spent a total of seven days in their tiny hovel. Then they were taken to the "model jail" in Bata, and their blindfolds removed. The conditions were better: toilets—and clean ones at that; water to bathe twice a day; meals twice a day from relatives. Because of his injury Saturnino was given a mattress upon which to sleep. After about three days, on 1 or

2 September, the *comisario adjunto* of presidential security came to take a written statement from Saturnino. In putting his questions, the *comisario* was a model of courtesy.

The *comisario* took Saturnino's answers to the military tribunal. On 5 September, someone came to Saturnino and read him a copy of his statement. "Do you ratify this or rectify it?" he was asked.

On 9 September, Saturnino was freed. But he was not allowed to leave Bata until the judgment of the other supposed conspirators was completed. In fact, Saturnino was compelled to attend the trial, which lasted from 13 to 16 September.

Now he was back in Malabo. Back at work, soon to go to Douala with Harry for medical treatment.

A Talk with Don Bonifacio

Later that day I tracked down Don Bonifacio at his mother-in-law's new restaurant.

"How are you, Roberto?" he asked, getting up to shake my hand.

I felt an unexpected rush of relief at seeing him. He looked healthy, in fact fitter than when I had last seen him a month before.

"Bonifacio! I'm fine, thanks. The question is, how are you?"

"Fine, now," Bonifacio said.

"What are you doing now?"

"I'm getting the new house set up. We had to move out of the house by the port, that's officially for the minister of finance. So we have an apartment over here where my mother-in-law has been living."

We left the restaurant and walked toward his apartment. Bonifacio kept talking as we traversed an eroded stretch of sidewalk as narrow as a path through the jungle.

At the apartment we sat in a small room crowded with oversized leather chairs and a couch. I told him how I had learned in the States about his dismissal. What had happened?

Bonifacio shrugged. "The President found someone else in whom he had more confidence."

Why now?

"This person was out of the country till a month ago," Bonifacio said, referring to Fernando, the new Finance Minister.

How did it happen?

"The President called me to Bata the day before you left, Roberto. In Bata the *jefe* called me to a meeting. He said I looked tired, burned out. He said he knew that I had been working hard. It was time for a rest. The *jefe* thanked me for being an invaluable member of the team."

The meeting had been cordial, Bonifacio said, but the letter of cessation was there. He said that at the next cabinet meeting—he was not present—the President had praised his many contributions, his hard work, and so forth.

Had these events had anything to do with the business with the Minister of Territorial Administration?

"No," Bonifacio said. But a few minutes later, he admitted, "They have been looking for an excuse for quite a few months, as you know. I didn't fit into their group, I caused them some problems."

We sipped our drinks. I ventured to tell him what the word was on the street about his dismissal: that it was because of corruption. I said I thought this was a rumor started by his opponents. He asked me if I had heard this from Guineans or whites. I said from three whites, but presumably they had heard it from Guineans.

Bonifacio shook his head silently. He looked gravely disappointed. *"Bien . . ."* he finally said, meaning literally "well" or "all right," but with overtones of resignation before the inevitable.

I had wanted to see Bonifacio, to console him somehow; but I also needed his advice. What could be done about the torturing of Saturnino? When I mentioned the episode obliquely, Bonifacio professed ignorance. So I related Saturnino's ordeal. Bonifacio was obviously deeply disturbed by each disgusting detail. Then we talked about what to do.

We talked about mobilizing the ambassadors, and I asked who inside the ruling group, besides the President, might be appropriate to talk to. On whom might international leverage be effective? Who would understand the importance of stopping such practices?

Bonifacio looked down, and his face darkened.

"No one, Roberto, absolutely no one."

Not even the President himself?

"I don't know, Roberto." Bonifacio paused. "When you talk with the President, be very tactful."

A Common Interest

I talked with the ministers of our coordinating committee. Camilo and Diego were frightened and quiet. The new Minister of Finance and I finally got together at four thirty on a Wednesday afternoon—an unusual hour, but we had not been able to meet all week. Fernando had abandoned his necktie and was smoking a cigar as we walked together up the back stairs of the ministry and entered his office. He turned on the air-conditioners but left the lights off. I sat on the couch, and he plopped down catty-corner on a chair of slick, light-green Naugahyde. From where I sat, Fernando was framed by the tall trapezoid of window behind him. The glare rendered the features of his face invisible. I could see only his silhouette, black against white. Eventually, halfway through our hour-and-a-half discussion, I rose and turned on the lights. It's hard to concentrate or have appropriate reactions when you're talking to a shadow.

I needed to talk with Fernando about preparing the structural adjustment program and completing our project, also about Saturnino. Fernando had the files on structural adjustment and our project, but wanted to talk about the political situation.

"You know, in Africa there are certain differences from the West and here even more so. People are suspicious, people are jealous. I am close with the President, and I talk to him so candidly you would not believe it. I'm not from his locality [meaning "clan"—though I had heard that Fernando was the cousin of the President's wife], but I did go to school with him, along with Bonifacio, Camilo, and the Minister of Education. The President was our monitor, he was older than us and watched over us. But all of us can talk to him. This leads some of the others here to be jealous of us. I know that some people close to the President were upset when I was named Minister of Finance.

"People here tend to cause trouble. If you have a car and someone else does not, he starts saying bad things about you. He wants the car, you see, and is envious. Then you find out he has been saying bad things and you try to get him. I will tell you the truth, these recent problems are a lot like that. There is a disturbance so they round up other people and go after them. The disturbance is within one little group, but they get people from other groups so that people say, 'Oh, they were involved, too? Well, that justifies big actions, it's a general problem, a general threat.'"

I asked whether this meant that the real disturbance had been within the clan and the non-clan arrests had been diversions. Fernando said, "Exactly," and then repeated his words about envy. "In such a situation, what can anyone do here?" he concluded rhetorically.

Fernando knew I was trying to meet with the President. I said I wanted to tell the President that all of us backed his ideals, his signing of the human rights agreement—praised, I informed Fernando, in the recently released annual report of Amnesty International—and the Democratic Party's promise to defend individual rights. I wanted to tell the President, too, that there were negative thinkers among the foreigners, who would say that torture had occurred and the President must have known about it. This would, in turn, harm the climate for investment and foreign aid. The President had to show that he repudiated torture, and could do so by launching an open investigation of the allegations.

"In Africa you have to understand that people do not have a common interest," Fernando replied. "Without a common interest, there are fights. Social conflict. In Africa, first comes the family, then the clan, then the province, then the region, and finally the country. But the country is the last thing. You vote for someone and you say, 'I'll vote for him because he's my uncle.' You have noticed how we all refer to each other—'He's my cousin, she's my aunt.' If no one is a member of your family broadly speaking, then you vote for someone from your clan. Or your district. Or Río Muni versus Bioko. And if it's a Nigerian involved, you always choose the Guinean, no matter how bad. That's the way it is in Africa, and that's the way it is here."

Fernando told a story about last year's preparations for the UDEAC conference in Bata. People had been commandeered to work on a runway extension and the refurbishing of the soccer stadium. Fernando said colonels worked side by side with privates and with people brought in from the countryside.

"Boom, boom, boom, boom—they worked and worked till late at night. And, you know, when the stadium was done—my God, compared to what was there before—it was something, and the people were so proud. And when the big jets came into the airport where before the runways were too short, when people saw them land, the people were proud of themselves. Later I saw the *jefe* and said, 'Did you notice the same detail as I?' 'What's that?' asked the *jefe*. 'The fact that though the people had to work without pay till late hours, when they finished they were proud.' This work created a common interest, and the people were proud.

"That is what we have to do when everyone is poor. When there is hunger, there is no common interest. And everyone thinks of families and clans. So to create a common interest, we need strong leadership. We need to launch works like hospitals, roads, and schools with the people working, where they can see the results and feel proud.

"There is no equilibrium in our societies," Fernando went on, and launched into a description of the current government. Then he said, "The problem of the President is that most of the people in government are incompetent and uncultured, they have no exposure to the outside world. These people are jealous of the few with outside training. But there are too few trained people for the President to have any choice. He needs the Guineans who left to come back from Spain, all the lawyers and engineers. They won't come because they talk about democracy and rights. But we won't have that until we have more trained people. The President faces a balancing act—he has to keep the uneducated top people happy, the jealous ones, because they have the ear of the people in the villages. If the President goes only with the educated few, that three or five percent, then he would be out of office in a week. It is a dangerous situation—he has no choice but to humor the backward, the reactionaries."

I talked about a similar problem in Mexico where, though the ruling party was corrupt top to bottom, and the new president could not attack everyone, he had nonetheless knocked out some of the worst offenders and defined a strategy to reduce corruption. So, too, we had to move toward a new solution. But Fernando would not let me finish. He repeated his account, with lots of enthusiasm and examples and "I don't know if you understand's."

"Africa is characterized by poverty and tribalism, which render the common interest as conceived in middle-class countries nonexistent. Thus, without a dictator who serves the interests of the masses, the powerful will exploit them. Or else the masses will rise up and exploit the advantaged. Some people see this and commit an error: they figure the more repressive they are, the more stability. In Africa we suffer from this error. We do need a dictator, however. When I say dictator, I mean one that does not permit either the privileged or the oppressed to dominate. There are people who are born to correct these disequilibria.

"The typical African is poor and hungry. What does he want? He wants three wives and eight, nine, ten children. Then he is happy. If someone has a car, he is bad—it creates jealousy and then instability. This is our reality. There is no common interest to defend. And there is so little education. Only a few percent. So if you allow complete freedom of speech and democracy as in England, you end up with conspiracies and nonsense.

"What has recently occurred must be seen in this light. Something happened within the group; everyone gets excited and casts aspersions on many others, innocent people. Then things happen, a person gets beaten or gets a broken collarbone like Saturnino. I am by no means defending torture or anything else. We can and we should do better. But we cannot have a democracy like England's."

I said I appreciated his description but had doubts about his prescription. Could the minister name any dictators who were serving the masses and "correcting disequilibria"?

Fernando thought. "Franco," he finally said.

I let that be, and asked, "In Africa?"

Fernando could think of none. I had a chance to say that Yes, there disequilibria and a leader has to maintain certain balances, even if tl means compromising with bad people. I agreed that one has to begin wi things as they are—but also has to have a strategy for moving forward. Or can begin by cutting out the worst excesses, especially if this is relativel easy to do. For example, torture: no excuse, it has to go, it is easy to halt. On issues clear orders, one eliminates the apparatus of torture. In the case of corruption, one has to have a strategy, a vision of where one wants to be five years hence and of the sequence of steps that will lead there.

Fernando responded dramatically. There is no way, he said, to appreciate this country without having known it under Macías. Then he said it twice more.

"I was away for sixteen years, but I know. Without this understanding, the parameters of comparison are not objective." These were his words. "You have to compare with the subject itself, not its neighbor. If we were under Macías, there would be sixty people dead now—including Bonifacio and Saturnino. If you had come to my office like this after hours under Macías, then I would be in jail. Now these people are on the streets with their rights."

I reminded him of Saturnino's broken collarbone, the torture.

"We started at a level of minus ten. You can't just look at our current situation and say 'plus five' or 'zero' or 'minus five.' "

Fernando went on for a long time in this vein, making a good point at too great length. I tried to acknowledge it several times and respond, but no dice. He was an excellent talker but on this subject not a listener.

Finally I said, "Torture is not acceptable wherever you start. Equatorial Guinea acknowledges this, so does the rest of the world."

"But before, they'd have been shot," Fernando replied. " 'What, somebody said something bad about me?' someone would ask. Boom, he'd be dead. Now they are not killed."

I agreed that we should not look to present-day England for comparison. But neither should we think of the problem as a choice between two extremes, or we would have a Macías by default. And, yes, we should look at how far we have come, and many people do not do this. But to avoid being simple-minded like such people, we should go beyond that perspective and look also at where we are and ask, How easy will it be to make improvements? What should we do next? I repeated that systematic torture is easy to stop. There is no excuse for it.

Fernando said, "There is something else you must know by now about this place—the psychosis of crime. The people have seen so much suffering and so much death that they are shocked, they startle themselves, they invent things. In their subconscious they think of what was then, and they transform that into what exists now."

I agreed that stories here were unreliable. All the more reason to investigate.

"Few countries have suffered as we have," Fernando said. "You cannot help but think like an American."

I shook my head, but Fernando went on.

"No, listen to me, if you had seen Equatorial Guinea under Macías, you would see that we have come the furthest of any country. That, comparatively, it's a paradise."

The President's Ear

I consulted some of the important ambassadors—Spain, France, European Community, United States, and China. We shared information about the stories of torture. An idea hatched. The ambassadors should combine forces and urge the President to denounce torture publicly and launch an open investigation of the allegations.

The ambassadors agreed to do this.

The Chinese ambassador had become a friend. During my girlfriend's visits he had doted on her, offering elegant dinners for us and the Chinese first secretary and his wife. These were my first Chinese friends, and I cherished their good will.

On the day we discussed the "Equatoguinean disturbances," I told the ambassador and the first secretary in detail about Saturnino's torture and, briefly, about other stories of torture I had heard.

"This is indeed serious business," the ambassador said slowly when I had finished. "I had not heard this information before. There had been some rumors, but nothing this concrete. I will have to study the matter and will do so carefully."

I suggested that he gather more information from the other ambassadors. The Spaniards in particular had good sources. I told him how I was trying to see the President—an appointment for yesterday had been canceled suddenly—and what I planned to say. The ambassador listened, nodded.

"I agree with your ideas." He paused for a moment. "The official you mentioned in the Ministry of Foreign Affairs, who supervised the Bata

tortures, is very close to the President. The President must have known."

I said I hoped not, that we should act with the President as if he had not known.

"The person in charge of such a task would have to be someone of confidence," he reflected.

I agreed.

Then his eyes narrowed, and he spoke in more of a whisper.

"China will give no new aid to this country. Spain and France will not increase their aid either, I am told. 'Stop,' they say." The ambassador used the English word.

I had nothing to add to that. We said goodbye.

The first secretary drove me back to the city.

"Frankly, Roberto, I think your initiative will not have concrete results. The President may be informed of the problems, but nothing concrete will happen, I am afraid." Then he stopped and said, "But torture like this, that is unacceptable everywhere."

I underlined that point.

"You know, Roberto, ambassadors are all alike. Unless something affects the interests of their country directly, they will move very slowly. In the two weeks you have remaining here, there will not be enough time for your deliberate approach to have effect. You may have to threaten action now to get their attention."

I said that didn't seem like a good idea.

But he turned out to be right. Yes, the key ambassadors expressed support for the idea of a common appeal to the chief of state. He should both publicly condemn torture and take steps to abolish its instruments, and launch an open investigation of the torturing. This much was agreed. But the ambassadors moved slowly—except the U.S. ambassador, who talked with his peers and then with President Obiang. Nothing happened before I left.

Indeed, before I departed two weeks later, I did not get to see the President. He remained on the continent, and no appointment could be arranged. Since I needed to talk with him about my final report about the economy, and about torture, I decided to return after I had fulfilled a long-standing commitment to visit three liberal universities in South Africa.

"Hi, Bob, since you left all hell has broken loose," Harry greeted me upon my return a week and a half later, in mid-October. The audit of our project was all right, he went on. But Raúl had been jailed yesterday. Something to do with the old, preposterous charge of corruption in our project's spending on the city of Malabo.

"Last night I was with the Minister of Planning and the Minister of Industry and Commerce," Harry said. "I've never seen them so down. You know how they usually have an aura of being ministers, or at least Camilo does—you know, a toughness? Well, last night, they were just guys on the street. They had been in a meeting with the President all day. Camilo said last night that the charges about the city of Malabo have a deeper political motivation."

The clouds of mystery and intrigue were as thick and mysterious as those that enveloped the volcano.

"The new Minister of Finance had not signed the things you left for him," Harry said. "He's standing back from it all till the dust clears. I wouldn't be surprised if both our ministers are in jail by this afternoon. I tell you, Bob, I told my wife that we might have to leave the country this Saturday. You and I don't know what's happening here, Bob. We can't know."

I went to the police station to try to see Raúl. To my surprise, he was sitting on a bench in a back room at the station, along with two policemen and six visitors. The room's door was open, and it was like a hospital visit. Last night, Raúl said, he was let out to have a drink.

I asked him what had happened.

He was picked up at two in the afternoon. Later he saw the Minister of Territorial Administration, who said Raúl had been detained in regard to the supposed theft of 90,000,000 *cefas* (over $300,000) in the course of our project's work with Malabo.

"Why didn't they jail me or the ministers instead of you?" I asked.

Raúl laughed. "I've thought the same thing myself."

I told him I'd see what I could do.

I went to Aurelio for help and advice. He had been trying to arrange my meeting with the President. I asked if he could also arrange an appointment with the Minister of Territorial Administration. He did not answer directly. Instead, he recounted a long story about his conversations and letters to President. Unusually, Aurelio did not look me in the eyes.

"I will see the President tomorrow at eight forty-five in the morning, and report to you at nine. Also, I will try to arrange something with the Minister of Territorial Administration."

Aurelio had read my final report. I asked him if it was too blunt.

"No, it is not too tough," he said. "We need to hear it."

The next morning the sun broke through the clouds early and the city heated up. I began the final packing for my Saturday departure. I went to my office at eight thirty to meet briefly with the auditors. Then I returned home to wait for word from Aurelio. Nothing by nine twenty. I had to leave to run errands. All day long, I kept returning to the house to see if Aurelio had left word. Nothing.

At six I went to his house. He had bad news.

"The President's uncle has died, Roberto," he said. "There was no way to arrange an appointment today." Aurelio explained that in Fang culture the uncle is often a more important figure in a boy's life than the father. This had been the President's special uncle.

I was starting to fear that this return trip would accomplish nothing. I had talked to the Minister of Planning, Don Diego, who had promised to arrange a meeting of the coordinating committee for today. Nothing happened. Now this with the President.

"I'll try again tomorrow," Aurelio said.

Friday was my last full day in Equatorial Guinea. I went to the office to meet with the accountants. Everything looked fine, they said. Just then, in walked Aurelio.

"What, no tie and jacket?" he joked. "Come on, it's time for your appointment with the *jefe.*"

Aurelio drove me to my house, where I donned a suit, and took me through the main gate to the presidential ghetto. The sky was white, and the air heavy. No breeze moved the palm trees, whose fronds looked old and frail. Aurelio and I entered the downstairs waiting area of the presidential offices. The head of protocol was summoned.

Aurelio explained to him in Fang the reason for my presence. A bad sign, I thought. The President must not have me on his schedule, or this guy would already know. He said to wait. Aurelio departed. I sat on a couch. The leather of the arms was cracked like the skin of old reptiles.

I waited. Various people drifted through the room. A slim Moroccan plainclothesman, dressed in a double-breasted beige jacket, baggy trousers in brown plaid, an unbuttoned white shirt with rounded collars, a plum-colored tie. A Guinean trooper in camouflage fatigues, red beret, pistol on belt, trousers tucked into combat boots. He cordially shook my hand. Two more Moroccan plainclothesmen, who sat near me. A very young Guinean, who wore a mod suit of light gray material with oversized shoulder pads and the sleeves rolled up.

I waited some more. The air-conditioner looked normal but produced a heavy blowing noise and a roar that reminded me of a large industrial freezing plant. The windows were covered with open venetian blinds, which played with the lines of the palm branches' spikes. Looking out the east windows, I could see the President's lovely house across the street—the lustrous greens of the garden's plants and trees, the green shutters and metal bars above the white walls, the brown balconies, the orange tile roof. The day was without shadows, without wind. The sky was bleached and vacant.

Wait and wait. I talked a bit with the two Moroccans. Their Spanish was limited. One had been here for four months. The other, during his eight months in country, had contracted malaria five times.

The waiting reached the two-hour mark. In flashed an apparently adolescent Guinean, wearing a bold pink striped shirt, a kind of white hospital jacket with the sleeves rolled up, and baggy gray pants. As he sat down I noticed that, like one of the Moroccans, he carried a walkie-talkie. Juvenile security? I wondered.

The two Moroccans silently smoked. Every now and again a suit-clad official or pistol-packing soldier would traverse the sitting room. I moved to the corner of the couch, put my elbow up on the high leather arm, and covered my eyes with my hand. The past weeks I had been on some long plane trips, and with my eyes shut I felt I was on another. The air-conditioner's combination of expiration and moaning could have been a jet engine on the wing, and thanks to the Moroccans' smoke the air had an airliner impurity to it that made my throat constrict.

At three o'clock—the time everyone went home for lunch—I was called upstairs. In the small, second-floor waiting room, which was the temperature of a meat locker, waited a Guinean official. He told me he had been here yesterday for four hours waiting unsuccessfully for an audience with the President, and today so far three: but he was up next. Ten minutes later he was beckoned.

I talked with the chief of protocol. He said, "It is so late. I hope you'll make it brief." I explained that I had returned especially to talk with the President about the economy and would need at least a half-hour. Could we meet later today, after lunch, or this evening?

He shook his head, "Very difficult. What time are you leaving tomorrow?"

The early morning flight to Madrid.

More head shaking. "Well, I can ask him."

Three forty-five. Protocol returned. The President said Yes. Tonight at eight thirty. I went downstairs. I had to wait a few minutes while the President, flanked by a bevy of Moroccan plainclothesmen and Guinean combat troops and accompanied by an unusual trumpet solo military style, crossed the street to his home. Finally I was allowed to leave and was taken home.

I had a hurried lunch. At four thirty we were to have the final meeting of our project's coordinating committee.

At about five Don Fernando arrived. "The other ministers couldn't make the meeting," he said. "Diego says he is too tired, and Camilo was not at home. What I need is a summary of the state of the current situation on the project. I don't care what went before, what was decided in the past. Just what was spent, what is left, and what is budgeted."

That was contained in my final report, I said, along with ideas about the economy and how to fix it. Fernando said he had not received the report.

I suggested we review four initiatives for the future. Reorienting cocoa, promoting indigenous enterprise, promoting nontraditional exports, and reforming the public sector.

Fernando said he agreed about cocoa: we should be replanting rather than rehabilitating old trees. But my point was diversification. Fernando liked the ideas regarding small business and made some notes. Then he launched into an explanation. Guineans were unable to work hard, he said, because they had no needs. Their families, the jungle, would provide. He held forth.

We never got to the other topics.

I went back to my office. Later I saw Bonifacio briefly to tell him I was meeting the President and what I was going to cover—the final report, human rights, and now the imprisonment of Raúl. Bonifacio said to talk about the charges of corruption involving Malabo and our project.

I went home. At eight thirty a horn sounded outside. It was the protocol chief.

"We're here to get you," he shouted.

I followed in the Land Cruiser, through the harborside gate to the presidential ghetto. We parked, and the protocol chief went into the President's house. Out front four Moroccans in a suitclad cluster were kicking playfully at the parallelograms of metal prongs that unfolded to cover the street and prevent vehicles from passing. The protocol chief emerged and signaled me to come over. When I reached the front door, he left, and the President was before me.

"Good evening, Señor Klitgaard! How are you! Please excuse me for making you wait so long today and yesterday."

The chief of state pumped my hand. His face was rounder than I remembered, and without his glasses he looked friendlier. He wore a bush suit in pure white. On the shirt embroidered decoration proceeded in parallel lines down both breasts. He led me into the house past an almost life-size oil painting of himself in full gear. All the way he praised my report, which—as we turned into the living room with the TV on and sat down on old-fashioned couches—I saw lying open on the coffee table.

"Your report is invaluable," the President was saying. He went on to talk about my appreciation of the realities of his country. "I want to study it in detail. Tomorrow I will form a commission to consider it."

"The report was not too brusque?" I asked.

"No, it is frank and realistic," he replied earnestly. "We need to find exactly the ways to concretize these ideas. What a pity you are leaving."

He guided me to a chair and sat across from me on the edge of the couch. No one else was present. I had not been searched, X rayed, or accompanied.

I thanked the President for his kind words. I was grateful for this opportunity to say goodbye and present my suggestions for future priorities. I, too, wished that we might have worked together more closely, but I had always felt a barrier was placed between us. I reminded him of the idea of the workshops for the cabinet.

"Yes, that was a pity," the President said as earnestly as before. "I wanted it—but when it came to the ministers, certain of them felt that it would somehow lower them to participate in conferences with an outsider. As ministers, some of them erroneously think they have nothing to learn. This is, of course, wrong, as I know. We have much to learn."

"And so do we who visit your country," I replied. "You are the experts on the distinctive realities of Equatorial Guinea. All that we from outside can offer is the benefit of experience from other countries. Your Excellency is a student of many things. I believe you are learning French?"

"Yes, I have been studying French for some time, every day. I decided I wanted to be able to speak at our meetings of African leaders. So, two years ago, I stopped using interpreters. It is important always to keep learning."

An attendant appeared. The President asked him whether there were refreshments, perhaps champagne. The attendant disappeared. The President got up to turn off the television. The attendant returned with two crystal flutes and poured us both champagne.

After we toasted one another, the President waited as if for me to begin.

I thought I might as well start at the top. I said that, apart from economic strategy, I wanted to bring up another matter to His Excellency. I reminded him that many outsiders had a terrible impression of Equatorial Guinea, and in the country itself many people had negative attitudes. When I had first come to his country, some World Bank people had asked me why I wanted to go to such a piece of shit—the Spanish word *mierda*, forceful, though lacking the impact of its English equivalent. Some people had said that Equatorial Guinea would not have a structural adjustment program till 1992 or 1993. But we had all been trying to convince the negative thinkers that they were wrong. I told the President how much I admired his economic reform program. Thanks to these steps by His Excellency and now to the excellent work of the ministers involved in the economic rehabilitation project—in particular, the ex-Minister of Finance Don Bonifacio— even the World Bank was rectifying its impression of Equatorial Guinea. All of these positive steps were now paying off. For example, the country had an IMF agreement, and now there were hopes that the World Bank would provide a structural adjustment loan early next year.

But, I went on, several happenings endangered the progress effected by His Excellency's reforms. First, the disturbances in August: though I did not know what had happened, there were many reports of systematic torture. Then, in the middle of the negotiations with the World Bank, the Minister of Finance was sacked—a man who had earned the trust of the international community. Now this week when I returned with the senior World Bank official whom His Excellency today had met, we found that one of the people working on the economic rehabilitation project had been jailed, without charges.

I explained what a bad image this gave to the outside world. The country's detractors would say, "Why do we want to get involved in a country like this?" I said that I admired the President's signing of the United Nations human rights agreement. If nothing were done about torture and arbitrary imprisonments, people would assume the President knew and would believe the worst.

For these reasons I recommended, with all humility and respect, that the President launch an investigation into the tortures. An open and transparent investigation.

The President had listened carefully. Now he responded without hostility and without missing a beat.

"When the incidents of August occurred, I was on my tour of the continent, and then I was in Libreville. Only later did I learn of what had happened in Bata, the abuses. There was torture. This is against my wishes and my policy. I am now investigating these events.

"It is no excuse, but the mentality sometimes is from the former regime." The President screwed his forefinger into the side of his head. "You would not believe how many military men and how many police I have sanctioned in the last ten years for abuses of various kinds."

I agreed that much progress had been made. But systematic torture of the kind alleged was inexcusable. It was relatively easy to control. It had to be stopped.

The President nodded and said that he was investigating. I said something about Malabo, but he said he was sure nothing had happened here. I said I had two stories that I believed, and the names of people involved. The President said that there were many stories. People sometimes exaggerated. I agreed that this was a feature of this environment—but was this not all the more reason for an open investigation, without which people would believe the worst if they were disposed to do so?

The President did not answer directly. Later he talked about the situation behind Bonifacio's firing.

"There was Javier, who studied in Spain. There were reports even then of indiscretions. When he returned, I made this person a sergeant, since he was well trained, in the presidential police. But he was dissatisfied. He wanted to be my adviser, he said. I talked with him several times. He was very young, and I told him, 'Look, your father was my teacher and I have great respect for him, but you are inexperienced and too ambitious right now.' "

The President then described events that remained unclear to me. The person he was talking about had talked to other people about advising the President, then had begun to deal with other people—opposition folks, I inferred.

"To find out what was up, we asked this person to provide a list of the cabinet who would be in the new government. Foolishly, he provided it. Bonifacio's name was on this list. I said, 'Nonsense! Bonifacio wasn't involved.' I told Bonifacio this as well."

I inferred that the person the President was talking about had been implicated in the August coup attempt.

"But then in inquiries after the August incident, someone else mentioned Bonifacio's name. He said that Bonifacio had told some students or young opposition people not to talk when inquiries were made. Then I called Bonifacio in and told him. This story had cast doubts, so I removed him.

"But it is not like before. I do not want it to be like other countries or here in the past, where a minister is jumped on when he is out of office and his property is taken from him. Bonifacio is a free man and can do what he wishes, he is not in disgrace. He was a valued member of the cabinet, and he is still a valued person who can sit down at our table. He is the best finance minister we have had here."

I agreed and remarked how diligent Bonifacio had been.

"Yes, I know he worked day and night."

I said Bonifacio had worked unselfishly.

The President went on about the importance of the cabinet, his team, presenting an absolutely solid front. He told stories of removing ministers in the past. He had fired a former agricultural minister for messing up an agricultural deal. Where the President had wanted a five-million-dollar poultry project, the minister had obtained twelve-million dollars of useless machinery. But, the President noted, the fired minister had not been punished. He was now working in the European Community.

The President recounted the dismissal of a former educational minister, who had had a dream about the former dictator Macías and had told a bunch of people about it. In the dream Macías had said, "The President is letting down our people." This meant the Fang, the President explained. The Prime Minister was what the President called a minority; at that time the supreme court chief was also a minority, as was the head of the assembly. In the dream Macías had said that the only one left with power was the President himself, that he had taken everything and left his people out.

"I heard about this," the President went on, "and called the minister in. I asked him why he had not told the dream to me, but to others. All such a dream could do would be to get people upset. So I had to remove him."

The President recounted this story as if its circumstances were the most normal and reasonable in the world. I didn't have anything to offer. The President returned to his point.

"We in the government have to present an absolutely united front to the people." Then he went back to the fired finance minister. "Bonifacio is a good economist but as a politician he is very young."

I praised Bonifacio again. I told the President that the job of finance minister was difficult everywhere in the world. Most finance ministers burn out in a couple of years, because the outside world beats them up for defending the government and yet within a cabinet they are often beaten up for seeming to be defending the outside world, like the IMF. The President's observation about lacking experience was a good one, I went on, and perhaps Don Bonifacio should go abroad to work or study for a year or so. The President said this was fine.

Then we talked about the current disturbance over the city of Malabo.

I said that all the materials our project had ordered were things the city had asked for, although we had not ordered everything they had asked for. I told him of the international audit just completed, which had verified once again that everything purchased had arrived and been warehoused in good shape. Anyone, including His Excellency, could verify this in two hours. I didn't know what obscure motivations had raised the charges of corruption.

"I first heard of these charges a long time ago, before my tour of the mainland," he said. "So I ordered a report, and a couple of weeks ago this report was submitted. It questioned the cleaning up of the *chatarra* [old vehicles and fallen trees and so forth] around the city streets. It criticized the clean-up for saying it had done more than it had, also for being a one-shot affair instead of a system to clean up the city."

I agreed with the latter distinction but wished to separate two things: routine garbage collection and the removal of *chatarra*. The latter had emerged as a need because of our road maintenance program. The President nodded, he knew of that program. Our expert had told us that we could not redo Malabo's streets without getting rid of the *chatarra* on the streets. We carried competitive bidding for this work. It was true that in the meantime the former mayor had cleaned up some of this *chatarra*. But we had a map of where each piece had been, we had monitored each week's work, and all of the removed *chatarra* was sitting in a cemetery outside town. This, too, could be verified.

There had been no fraud, I went on. One could say that money could have been spent more wisely, and this sort of criticism was good criticism. But there was no reason to imprison Raúl. If they had wanted to imprison someone, they should have imprisoned me or one of the ministers, not the equivalent of a lieutenant.

"I don't know anything about imprisonment," the President said. "This must be related to an investigation since the report came in."

"Mr. President, no one has asked me about what happened, and I was the administrator of the project."

"You were out of the country."

"Not for two months while the report was being written."

The President said he would take the case personally at hand. I thanked him.

Then he brought up some of the things in my final report. Incentives. Then, corruption.

"This is our biggest problem," he said with feeling. "People are diverting funds. In taxes, for permits. We are asked to raise pay, but we simply can't afford it."

I mentioned an example from Bolivia where customs officials are given financial incentives based on customs revenues. A pause. He thought, nodded. "This is an excellent idea." But then he frowned.

"One year as a kind of experiment, at the beginning of the year I gave each ministry a budget for expenses—for their offices, travel, and so forth. By the middle of the year, all the funds had been spent. These ministers just do not understand budgeting."

"Could one imagine incentives or even prizes for ministers who do better?" I asked. The minister or ministry that does the best job of reducing corruption or raising revenues or controlling expenditures could get a prize. Or just presidential praise. I told him how important his praise was to people here, how since I first arrived, people had told me that the President knew everything that was going on. Perhaps this knowledge could be translated into praise, or rewards.

He talked about his information sources, how he received many reports about what the ministers were doing, what the officials were doing. He did not mention the foreign experts.

"I do this not for bad reasons but for good ones, to control illegal transfers and flight of money."

It was almost ten. But, though the President looked tired, I wanted to touch several key points in my report.

In cocoa, the big idea was not to rely on it. The President had championed agricultural diversification in a speech in 1986. Now the cocoa project's several components—credit, agronomic assistance, the role of the Chamber—needed to be aimed at other crops besides cocoa. The President might discuss this with the World Bank agricultural mission that had just arrived.

The President talked for a while about the need to diversify agricultural exports. He described Río Muni's agricultural problems and potential. We discussed the prospects for exporting food to Gabon, and the obstacles: bureaucracy, transport, and the Gabonese customs officials. The President said the Gabonese people were different.

"The border people are really savages. They beat people. Some time back they killed someone for not paying a fee at the border. Transport is also a problem. We recently lost fourteen Equatoguineans in a canoe accident. Each year scores of people die at sea in the unsafe boats that go from Río Muni to Gabon. I am looking into a ferry that would ply the coast— Gabon, Cogo, Mbini, Bata, Río Campo."

Then we talked about small business. I told him that his courageous economic program might eventually have success in terms of GNP but other countries had had problems making the benefits arrive at the little guy. We had studied small business in Equatorial Guinea. The principal problem was credit, and the country needed a credit project focused on microenterprise and small-scale agriculture.

The President mused for a while about the country's lack of entrepreneurial spirit. We talked about promoting small business. I said that the Ministry of Industry, Commerce, and Enterprise Promotion was in fact a brake on all three. This was not unusual in poor countries, I explained. Such ministries had defined their objectives during times of overvalued currency, food shortages, and monopolistic foreigners. Now, however, Equatorial Guinea had a good currency, there was food in the market, and there was lots of competition. So this ministry should redefine its mission: not to control and regulate, but to promote and assist. The President nodded, "No, not to control but to promote." For example, its employees could be paid in part depending on how small businesses were doing, how well they promoted nontraditional exports. And the country required too many permits.

"Our officials spend their time enforcing permits and not doing their jobs," the President responded. "That is very interesting about redefining the role of the ministry."

We talked about similar changes in the Chamber of Agriculture, how it shouldn't be a monopoly marketing board but rather a promoter of the private sector.

But now I saw the President's gaze was beginning to wander. So I thanked him for receiving me, after such a long and busy day. I had enjoyed it very much.

"I, too," he said. "Your report is very important, and we will work on it, my advisers and I, beginning tomorrow. What a shame that you are leaving now."

I told him that I often returned to countries where I had worked before, and could here if he wished. "But Mr. President, permit me one more word on the problem of torture. If there is an open investigation of these unfortunate events, I as well as all of your friends and well-wishers will only be too happy to help. If not, well, then I . . . would wait."

He took this as unblinkingly as he had the whole discussion. "I will investigate," he said.

Besosso's Song

Later I told Harry the parts about Saturnino and Raúl. Then Aurelio and I met at the restaurant of Bonifacio's mother-in-law. I told Aurelio how much I'd enjoyed the presidential interview—its frankness and openness. He beamed.

"I knew that if they gave you two the chance you would get along so well," he said.

I also saw Bonifacio that evening. I told him that the President had called him the best finance minister in the country's history. Also, that when I had gone through the Malabo question in detail, the President had listened and seemed to absorb what I said. This made Bonifacio very happy. I didn't tell him the bad parts.

At dawn on Saturday the birds were singing. I looked out at the volcano. Above the peak the sun had created a vertical aura, diaphanous and eerie. The town was bathed in a kind of glowing vapor. I hadn't seen a morning like it.

Harry's driver took me to the airport. Consuelo and Celestina came along. As we arrived and got out of the car, the rear tire started hissing—a flat. But we'd made it.

The American ambassador showed up to hear about the presidential meeting. He was happy it had gone well. He talked about his sessions with the President, how frank they had been.

"I think I know people well, and I believe this guy wants to do what's right. Oh, he's involved in lots of things, but deep down I think he wants to set this place right.

"You know, Bob, at some level we'll never understand these people. We've had two hundred years of independence, they've only had twenty. It's like going back hundreds of years here. When you talk to them, they may not understand you, or me. You know, up to twenty years ago they didn't run things or administer things or even work at things—the Nigerians did the work, the Spaniards gave the orders, and they were inbetween. They still deal with white people that way, they're leery of taking orders or seeming to, but at the same time they watch us and want to be like us. The President last night was submissive to you."

I said I wouldn't have used that word.

But the ambassador went on, "He was submissive in the sense that he put himself open to your advice. No one else there? No. Not with me either.

"There's a point beyond which you can't expect to understand them or meet their needs. The story he told you about the Macías dream—it's just different, and we have to recognize that."

He walked me to the plane, carrying my laptop computer. We said goodbye. I waved to friends at the edge of the tarmac. On board I had a window seat and looked out at the jungle. The plane taxied and then took off. There was Malabo in a white haze, the jungle, the harbor—and then it was gone.

Jean, the young French financial adviser, was aboard and came to sit by me. He wanted to hear about the presidential interview. I told him about some of it.

Jean asked me how I felt leaving. Had we had accomplished what I had hoped?

I had not really thought about it.

"No," I heard myself saying. "I was happy when we got the IMF agreement, but then things began to unravel in August. I don't know what will happen now."

"I first came to Equatorial Guinea in 1985," Jean said, "and I thought things looked ready for a boom. You know, the entry into the UDEAC, the conversion to the *cefa*. And a lot has happened, you can see it. But somehow they could have done so much more. Five times more. It could have been a real turnaround."

"Maybe it still will be," I said. "I think the ministers I was working with figured out a lot of what this country needs to develop, beyond the macroeconomic reforms. And I thought I saw real movement by the government, a sense of understanding and commitment. But the process of reform seems to have provoked a political reaction, one I still don't understand."

Then I told Jean about a recent visit to my house by the rock star Besosso. He came with two musicians and their girls.

"Hi, Bob! Hey, you have to hear it. Hot off the presses. My new record."

Besosso had just returned to the country after making the recording in France. A pile of cassettes would be coming soon; he had brought the master tape with him.

"You will love it, Bob. It is going to be very big all over central Africa."

I brought out refreshments, and we sat in the living room. We put on the tape. Besosso and the band bashed their way through a successful series of songs mixing African rhythms and Latin American melodies. This was Besosso's trademark.

I was struck by one song in particular.

"You know, the President helped me make this recording," Besosso said. "He wanted a special song for independence day in October. Listen to what we did."

On came a song praising independent Equatorial Guinea. Suddenly in the middle, as the instrumentalists did their thing in the background, President Obiang's husky voice could be heard.

"I promise that the Democratic Party of Equatorial Guinea will uphold and protect absolutely the human rights of the people."

Besosso explained. "We had the tape of the President, and we had to design the song around it. That's why it has such a slow beat. You see how the drums in the background are perfectly in time with what the *jefe* says?"

NOTES

PREFACE

1. James Clifford, *The Predicament of Culture: Twentieth-Century Ethnography, Literature, and Art* (Cambridge, Mass.: Harvard University Press, 1988), p. 65.

CHAPTER 1.

1. The data in the following paragraphs are drawn from various publications in the *Africa Update* series, 1988/89, presented by the World Bank at the Bank–IMF annual meeting in West Berlin, 26–28 September 1988; and from *Sub-Saharan Africa: From Crisis to Sustainable Growth: A Long-Term Perspective Study* (Washington, D.C.: World Bank, November 1989).

2. Teodoro Obiang Nguema Mbasogo, *Guinea Ecuatorial, País Jóven: Testimonios Políticos* (Malabo: Ediciones Guinea, 1985), p. 118. Official references to President Obiang no longer use the name Teodoro.

3. Country Economics Department, *Adjustment Lending: An Evaluation of Ten Years of Experience,* Policy and Research Series No. 1 (Washington, D.C.: World Bank, December 1988), p. 56.

4. John Steinbeck, *The Log from the Sea of Cortez* (New York: Viking, 1951), pp. lxiv–lxv.

NOTES

CHAPTER 3.

1. Cited in John R. Baker, *Race* (New York and London: Oxford University Press, 1974), p. 391.

2. Cited in John Keay, *Explorers Extraordinary* (Los Angeles: Jeremy R. Tarcher, 1986), p. 118.

3. José Manuel Novoa Ruíz, *Guinea Ecuatorial: Historia, Costumbres y Tradiciones* (Madrid: Expedición, 1984), pp. 157, 159. Novoa Ruíz, who spent considerable time in Fang villages, provides unique descriptions and photographs of Fang rites.

CHAPTER 5.

1. Geoffrey Lamb, "Managing Economic Policy Change: Institutional Dimensions," *World Bank Discussion Papers* No. 14, June 1987, p. 18. The country was not identified.

2. Mohsin S. Khan, "Macroeconomic Adjustment in Developing Countries: A Policy Perspective," *World Bank Research Observer* 2 (1 [January 1987]): 37–38.

INDEX

277

INDEX